D0208124

Newswriting for the Electronic Media

WADSWORTH SERIES IN MASS COMMUNICATION

Rebecca Hayden, Senior Editor

General

MEDIAMERICA: Form, Content, and Consequence of Mass Communication, 2d edition, by Edward Jay Whetmore

MASS COMMUNICATION AND EVERYDAY LIFE: A Perspective on Theory and Effects by Dennis K. Davis and Stanley J. Baran

THE INTERNSHIP EXPERIENCE by Lynne Schafer Gross

Journalism

REPORTING PROCESSES AND PRACTICES: Newswriting for Today's Readers by Everette E. Dennis and Arnold H. Ismach

THE NEWSPAPER: An Introduction to Newswriting and Reporting by Ronald P. Lovell

FREE-LANCER AND STAFF WRITER: Newspaper Features and Magazine Articles, 3d edition, by William L. Rivers and Shelley Smolkin

NEWSWRITING FOR THE ELECTRONIC MEDIA: Principles, Examples, Applications by Daniel E. Garvey and William L. Rivers

THIS IS PR: The Realities of Public Relations, 2d edition, by Doug Newsom and Alan Scott

WRITING IN PUBLIC RELATIONS PRACTICE: Form and Style by Doug Newsom and Tom Siegfried

CREATIVE STRATEGY IN ADVERTISING by A. Jerome Jewler

PICTURES ON A PAGE: Photojournalism and Picture Editing by Harold Evans

Telecommunications

BROADCASTING AND THE PUBLIC, 2d edition, by Harrison B. Summers, Robert E. Summers, and John H. Pennybacker

STAY TUNED: A Concise History of American Broadcasting by Christopher H. Sterling and John M. Kittross

BROADCAST PROGRAMMING: Strategies for Winning Television and Radio Audiences by Susan Tyler Eastman, Sydney W. Head, and Lewis Klein

MODERN RADIO STATION PRACTICES, 2d edition, by Joseph S. Johnson and Kenneth K. Jones

THE MAGIC MEDIUM: An Introduction to Radio in America by Edward Jay Whetmore

TELEVISION PRODUCTION HANDBOOK, 3d edition, by Herbert Zettl

TELEVISION PRODUCTION WORKBOOK, 3d edition, by Herbert Zettl

AUDIO IN MEDIA by Stanley R. Alten

SIGHT-SOUND-MOTION: Applied Media Aesthetics by Herbert Zettl

ADVERTISING IN THE BROADCAST MEDIA by Elizabeth J. Heighton and Don R. Cunningham

EDUCATIONAL TELECOMMUNICATIONS by Donald N. Wood and Donald G. Wylie

NEWSWRITING
For the Electronic Media
PRINCIPLES, EXAMPLES, APPLICATIONS

DANIEL E. GARVEY
CALIFORNIA STATE UNIVERSITY AT LONG BEACH

WILLIAM L. RIVERS
STANFORD UNIVERSITY

25

Wadsworth Publishing Company
Belmont, California
A Division of Wadsworth, Inc.

82 9358

Senior Editor: Rebecca Hayden
Production Editor: Judith McKibben
Designer: Janet Wood
Managing Designer: Cynthia Bassett

Printed in the United States of America

1　2　3　4　5　6　7　8　9　10 — 86　85　84　83　82

Library of Congress Cataloging in Publication Data

Garvey, Daniel E.
Newswriting for the electronic media.

(Wadsworth series in mass communication)
Includes index.
1. Broadcast journalism—Authorship.　I. Rivers,
William L.　II. Title.　III. Series.
PN4784.B75G3　　808'.06607021　　81-11543
ISBN 0-534-01069-5　　　　　　　　　　AACR2

Preface

This book is meant to teach you the basics of newswriting for the electronic media. There are about ten thousand broadcasting stations in the United States today, and most of them have news departments. There are also some 4,300 cable systems, with more and more of them producing their own local news programs. Satellites now beam news programming to cable systems twenty-four hours a day. Soon satellites will beam programs directly into the home. New technology is creating new media with additional jobs for electronic journalists. Teletext systems are already in use in some American cities, permitting viewers to call up the news and information of their choice. Newswriting for the electronic media is a field in which someone who is willing to start off at a small station or cable system can almost always find a job.

Most books about the electronic news media try to cover all aspects of the field. We think the field is too big to be covered successfully in a single book. In this book, we have chosen to concentrate on the writing and reporting of news for the electronic media. Thus, we have organized the book to take you step-by-step through the various elements of writing news for the rapidly growing constellation of electronic media.

In Chapter 1, we help you understand the basic elements that make up news stories for the electronic media. Chapter 2 deals with the most crucial part of the story—the lead. In Chapters 3, 4, and 5, we discuss the actual writing of the story—first explaining the elements that are common to newswriting for all electronic media, then discussing the special requirements for radio, television, and field reporting.

Chapter 6 explains how to edit news copy for the electronic media. Chapters 7, 8, and 9 examine the job of the reporter, giving special emphasis to the techniques of interviewing. The last two chapters discuss some of the major types of stories with which the newswriter for the electronic media deals, including the documentary.

In the Appendices, you will find a complete stylebook that summarizes the basic rules of newswriting for electronic media. You can turn to this for a quick reference when you need help on some particular point.

We have also included a glossary of the terms you will encounter in the field.

Many of the examples in the book are stories actually broadcast by stations. We have also provided pictures with some of the television examples so you can see how the stories looked on the air and match the words of the script to the pictures that accompanied them.

Each chapter ends with a series of exercises to help you develop the skills discussed in that chapter. By completing these exercises, you will soon find yourself writing real news stories for the electronic media.

Practice is important. Writing skills only grow as you write. You need to write and to have your writing critiqued by experienced news-writers. You also need to become seriously interested in news. You must keep your knowledge of news events current, and you must learn to watch and to listen to news as a critic, always thinking of better ways that the stories could have been presented.

It is not possible in a book like this one to cover the wide variety of ways in which news is prepared at different stations. No two stations handle news in exactly the same fashion. We have been warned by some readers of this book that what we have written may create too many expectations in the minds of students. Most students will start their careers at small stations or cable systems where facilities are limited, staffs are small, and standards are sometimes not as stringent as those of larger organizations. Small stations are great places to learn about broadcasting and about news. However, they may also require you to do some *un*learn-ing. Such matters as line counting and correct margin setting may be ignored. The same may be true of providing fill copy or using specific formats.

What we have written in this book is as 'standard' for electronic news as it is possible to be in a business where virtually every station or cable operation sets its own standards. There is no doubt that you are more likely to encounter the particular rules and formats about which we have written in medium-sized and larger-market stations. We believe this book will give you a good idea of how broadcast news is written—though it will not necessarily describe the way news is written at any particular station.

Your ultimate teachers will be at the station where you work. They will teach you what has been found to work in that setting. Perhaps, from what you learn from this book and in your class, you may be able to make suggestions that will improve the way your station handles news. On the other hand, too many suggestions from a new staff member may not be looked upon kindly—however useful you think your suggestions are. Don't reject the way things are done at a particular station simply because they are different. Learn what is expected of you. In time, when you have earned both the respect of your fellow workers and a solid understanding of the strengths and weaknesses of the system in which you are working, you may be able to suggest some useful changes. Or quite possibly, you may be able to suggest to us what we should put in the next edition of this book.

The authors would like to thank at least a few of the many people who helped make this book possible. In particular, we want to express our sincere thanks to the reviewers—those patient people who read through the original manuscript and whose helpful comments aided us in shaping the book into its present form. Our heartfelt thanks to Marsha Della-Giustina of Emerson College, Jack W. Deskin of Central State University, Kenneth L. Eich of South Dakota State University, Jerry Jacobs of California State University, Northridge, William B. Steis of Georgia State University, and Ed J. Zuchelli of California Polytechnic University of San Luis Obispo. And an extra vote of thanks to Jules Dundes of Stanford and Elmer Lower of the University of Missouri for their helpful critiques.

It would be impossible to list all the other people who contributed in one way or another to this book, but we will name just a few. Sincere thanks to Bill Banks of KNAC, Long Beach, Michael Hinton, William and Marylyn Montapert, Tom DeLloyd of CBS, and David Perkin. Thanks to the Associated Press, United Press International, the *Los Angeles Times,* the *Long Beach Press-Telegram,* ABC News, CBS News, KABC, KNXT, and KNAC for their help and the use of their news copy.

An extra vote of thanks to Rebecca Hayden and Judith McKibben for their helpful editing. Also thanks to Sarah Rivers and Jane Garvey for the care and feeding of the authors, with an extra vote of thanks to Jane Garvey for proofreading and editing the authors' copy.

Contents

1

The Electronic News Program

Often the most obvious things are the hardest to define. We live surrounded by electronic news. We get up in the morning, turn on the radio, and there's news. Turn on the television at breakfast, more news. Turn on the radio while driving, news again. There's television news at dinner time and at bedtime. In many cities there are radio stations that broadcast nothing but news twenty-four hours a day, and satellites are now being used to provide twenty-four-hour television news for cable television. With all this electronic news around us, we certainly should be able to say precisely what electronic news is, and yet, it defies a simple definition with which everyone would agree. The trees are so thick that it is indeed impossible to see the forest.

Perhaps the most succinct definition of electronic news was given by a well-known television journalist who said, "News is what we put on the air." Perhaps you can come up with your own definition of electronic news by carefully watching television news programs and listening to radio news programs. However, that really isn't enough. You will also have to study newspapers, news magazines, and other news media so you can understand what is unique about electronic news.

UNDERSTANDING NEWS PROGRAMS

To begin with, let's look at some of the characteristics that apply to all news, regardless of medium. First, news is factual. That means, to the best of the knowledge and abilities of those who prepare it, news is true. Some "New Journalists" of the 1970s argued that the "inner truth" of a story was more important than strict adherence to facts. We won't get into arguing the pros and cons of that position here. It suffices to say that the traditional approach to news is that it is inherently factual.

However, there are many kinds of facts. There are simple facts: "The time is 7:35, and the temperature is sixty-five degrees." There are events:

"The president is asking Congress to lift the ceiling on federal spending." And there are opinions: "Iowa's Senator Milo Maize says the president is trying to spend himself into a second term with the taxpayers' money." Such statements themselves need not be factual (Senator Maize may be wrong), but it is a fact that the senator made the statement. In effect, the reporting of an opinion can be considered another form of reporting events, the events being the expression of opinions. It may seem a little confusing at first. Obviously, opinions are not facts. Even events may be something other than they are purported to be, and they may be what Daniel Boorstin, our Librarian of Congress, has called "pseudo-events"—events that are staged for news coverage and might never occur if the news media were not there to report them. The "factual" element in the reporting of events and opinions is that the events occurred and the opinions were expressed. The reporter does not vouch for the validity of the opinions reported nor is the reporter necessarily obligated to explain why an event occurred—although more and more reporters are recognizing the importance of helping the public to distinguish between real events and pseudo-events. But there must be a fact to report. Ascribing an opinion to someone who did not express it or describing an event that did not happen is not news.

Second, news is timely. Students sometimes find otherwise well-written news stories returned by their instructors with this note: "Where's the news peg?" The instructor is telling the student that there must be a reason for broadcasting this story *today*. We always deal with today's news. An event reported need not have occurred today, but it must somehow be linked to today's events or it is not news. Even feature stories normally begin with some link to the news of the day. For example: "Roller skating is fast becoming one of the most popular sports in America. KWLR's Bob Fenton has been looking into that phenomenon and has this report." The lead sentence establishes that the story has something to do with today's news. Just saying, "Bob Fenton has been looking into roller skating," won't do. We ask why Fenton is doing a story on roller skating. The answer is that something new—something timely—is happening. The popularity of the sport is growing at great speed—now.

The third characteristic of news is that it is of interest to a significant number of people—although "significant number" is a very unspecific quantity. If you have your tonsils out, that's probably not news. If Robert Redford has his tonsils out, it probably is news. If the president of the United States or the head of the Soviet Union has his tonsils out, it is definitely news. Millions of people are interested in what happens to these persons. Alas, too few care about you and your tonsils to make your tonsilectomy news.

We have, then, a definition of what constitutes news in general: news is the timely report of events, facts, and opinions that interest a significant number of people.

Communication researchers, those crusty academics who want to treat our understanding of media as a science (while all those in the media are quite sure it is an art), sometimes talk about news in terms of rewards. The viewers, listeners, or readers of news get an immediate reward from some stories and a delayed reward from others. What the researchers mean by "reward" is often a far cry from our usual understanding of that word. We can get an immediate reward from stories about sports, accidents, crimes, and corruption. Human interest stories and stories about social events or celebrities can also give an immediate reward. In essence, these stories amuse or interest us. They involve us psychologically for the moment, but they have little or no implied effect on our own lives in the future. Some, such as stories about crime and corruption, may affect us in the future, but in general, we are concerned with them only for the instant. Then, for the most part, they are over and done with.

Delayed reward stories are work for us. They require that we absorb information now primarily because it will be of use to us later. The future they suggest is often not a pleasant one. Today's cost of living figures may warn that it is going to be harder to make ends meet in the coming months. Today's battles in the Middle East could threaten a world war in the future.

Which stories a person selects says much about that person's frame of mind. Immediate reward stories are often like good novels or short stories. They absorb our interest, but they rarely threaten us and seldom demand any action on our part. Delayed reward stories are like textbooks—full of new facts to be mastered and often not very interesting. We presume that the information we get from them may be useful in the future, but not necessarily today.

It's wise to note here that the means by which an individual selects the type of story to be read, seen, or heard differs with the medium. The first step in the selection process is, of course, the selection of the media "package." We are free to buy a newspaper or ignore it, to watch a program or change channels. The package we select says much about the "mix" of delayed- and immediate-reward stories we prefer. If I buy the *Wall Street Journal,* I am looking for delayed (and, I hope, lucrative) rewards. If I buy the *National Enquirer,* I am looking mainly for immediate rewards.

Once we have selected a media package, our selection of the stories in it depends on the medium. We can skim a newspaper or magazine, pausing when we see an item that we want to read. We do not have that luxury with broadcast news. We must sit through the entire program or turn it off. But all of us have the ability to "turn off" a program mentally— and usually that's exactly what we do. We do not listen or watch with full attention. Our minds wander elsewhere. Only when a story interests us do we give it our full attention. There are important implications in this phenomenon for broadcast writers, and we will have a great deal to say about it in later chapters. Here we simply note the peculiar contradiction of news selection: the audience has a far greater need of delayed-reward stories, but it would much rather select immediate-reward stories.

UNDERSTANDING NEWS STORY SELECTION

Certain characteristics make some news stories more likely to be used than others. Here are some of the most important ones:

Proximity

An automobile accident in Salem, Oregon, is of little interest to people in Salem, Massachusetts—except when the people involved are famous or are from Salem, Massachusetts. Students often tend to downplay local news. They forget that while national and international events do affect our lives, they rarely do so as swiftly or personally as events happening in our own hometown. It is true that a United Nations vote today might lead to a war in six months or that a speech by the president might mean a tax cut next year. But when your hometown garbage collectors go on strike, that affects you right now. And it affects you in a more personal way than lower taxes and perhaps even a war might. Of course, we need to know what Congress is doing, but we also need to know that the inbound lanes of the downtown freeway will be closed tomorrow for repairs. You can get by if you miss the national news for a day or two, but you will be very unhappy if you miss an important appointment because you did not know the freeway would be closed. Things close to home almost always have more interest to the audience than things happening elsewhere.

Consequence

Of course, we still need to know the important news, even when it happens elsewhere. Usually that means news that will, or could, have important effects on us or on others in whom we take an interest. When OPEC meets to force oil prices higher, the world shudders. We are all affected. When we make our choices among candidates for public office, we are making choices that will affect everyone whose life is somehow touched by the decisions of those officials.

Prominence

Who does something (or to whom something is done) makes a difference. We noted earlier that your tonsils have no news value, but Robert Redford's do. Perhaps there is something a little illogical about that, but it is a fact of life. And the reason is not purely whimsy. Important people touch more lives with the things they do. Reporters have been known to make foolish mistakes by assuming that the great and famous have the same right to privacy as ordinary citizens. It sounds logical. But when Wilbur Mills, one of the most powerful men in the United States Congress, wound up in the Washington Tidal Basin in a car with a nightclub stripper, reporters had to admit that the congressman's drinking habits and personal life were something more than a private matter. The congressman's drinking and nightclubbing should have been reported routinely right along. The voters had a right to know.

What if a political candidate engages in extramarital dalliances? Isn't a person's sex life irrelevant to the political issues? Perhaps, but if a man habitually cheats on his wife (or a woman on her husband), how faithful is that person likely to be to vows made to voters he or she hasn't even seen? It's not a question of sexual morality. It is a question of character evaluation. The voters have a right to know.

Not only political figures matter. Some people pattern their lives on the great or the near great. We all have a right to know what kind of a model such a person really is.

It is impossible to deny that some curiosity about the famous is pointless. But much of our interest in famous people has reasonable enough bases. And, justifiable or not, the prominence of the persons involved is one of the things that makes people pay attention to a story.

Unusualness

Novelty is always something in which people are interested. The old journalism chestnut says that "Dog bites man" is not news, but "Man bites dog" is. News is full of "firsts"—the first person to fly the English Channel in a human-powered plane, the first "test-tube baby," the first man to set foot on the moon. It is also full of record-setters—the person who holds the Olympic record for speed-skating, the first person to pole vault over twenty feet (which may happen before this book is published), or the first person to live to be two hundred years old (which probably won't happen before this book is published or very soon after).

But you don't have to hold an Olympic record to be newsworthy. Simply doing something out of the ordinary can be newsworthy. Plenty of people have swum the English Channel, but each new attempt draws interest because it is still an unusual happening.

A line must be drawn somewhere, of course. Some things can be unusual and still not be very interesting. Suppose someone in your town has one of the largest collections of shoestrings in the world. A good reporter could make an interesting little feature story out of it, but face it, a shoestring collection really isn't a very interesting subject. The reporter also has to decide where to draw the line on pseudo-events. A group announces that its members will walk naked to the city hall to protest the closing of a nudist beach. The event is unusual enough that you would have to cover it. However, it's really just a publicity stunt. The marchers could make their protest just as well with their clothes on, but they wouldn't get the media coverage. Newspersons are growing weary of this kind of story. One hopes the public is, too. Then assignment editors will be able to respond politely to a call announcing a nude march with the suggestion, "Take plenty of suntan oil," and go back to covering real news.

Conflict

Any struggle between people, groups, or nations can be interesting. We like to assume that the natural condition of life is tranquility. The assumption is probably wrong. We see conflict as a threat to the status quo, but given world history, conflict probably is the status quo. Still, it is conflict that holds our attention. Conflict can lead to change, and change can affect our lives. It is also possible that animal instincts buried not too far below the veneer of civilization lead us to like a good fight. The popularity of sports testifies to this, since most sports are essentially ritualized conflicts.

Human Interest

Communication theorist Daniel Lerner has suggested that a major distinction between primitive and advanced societies is the ability of the members of the society to empathize—essentially, to put themselves in other people's shoes. In traditional societies, the role of each individual is so rigidly defined that the individual finds it virtually impossible to conceive of any other role. In more advanced societies, it is possible for the individual to think, "I don't have to be a baker, I might make a very good candlestick maker," or "If I were the president, I'd show OPEC a thing or two!" Such notions may be impossible dreams, but they are dreams possible to dream. Lerner notes that as this ability to empathize grows in a society, so do literacy and the mass media.

All this is a somewhat roundabout way of saying that we always take an interest in other people, especially if we can envision ourselves in the same fix as the people about whom we are hearing or reading. People who suffer, people who overcome adversity, people whose hopes are dashed by cruel fate—they are all good material for a news story, if they are people with whom the audience can empathize. People like news about people. It's as simple as that.

Sex

We had to get to it sooner or later. In a couple of decades, we've gone from being a society that rarely mentioned sex to one that rarely seems to mention anything else. Of course, it has never been a secret to journalists that the public is interested in sex. Newspapers and magazines have known for years that sex sells. Radio and television have been somewhat timid about using sex-oriented news. One obvious reason is that the U.S. Supreme Court has ruled that broadcasters may be subjected to certain types of censorship. The Federal Communications Commission (FCC) may take action against a station that broadcasts material deemed to be obscene. Although relatively little of the material appearing in a news program is likely to be obscene, it might be defamatory or might invade someone's privacy. So broadcast newspeople are cautious about stories involving sex.

Stories involving sex may also be trivial, and with very little time to devote to even major stories, broadcast newswriters correctly relegate most sexually oriented stories to the lowest priority for use in a show. Nevertheless, in a listing of types of material that interest an audience, it would be amiss to leave out sex. Moreover, there are legitimate stories involving sex that serve purposes more important than giving the audience a cheap thrill. It is just as bad to omit a story because it includes sex as it is to use it for the same reason.

The great difficulty that stories involving sex present is that sexual activity, by its nature, is hard to verify. The rumors about the sex lives of various famous people could fill (and, in some cases, already have filled) stacks of books. But proving even the most persistent rumors of this sort is virtually impossible. So if you do use sex as a means of getting the audience interested, remember that news should always be factual.

DEFINING ELECTRONIC NEWS

What are the unique characteristics of electronic news? We've already hinted at some of them. There are obvious limitations on what the broadcast newsperson can say. However, most of these limitations are not imposed by law but by the time and by the ability of the audience to absorb electronic information.

Let's take a few comparisons. A morning newspaper, a dinner-hour television news program, and a five-minute radio news summary all have the same news of the day to cover. The *Washington Post* carries about 125,000 words in a weekday edition. That's the equivalent of a 500-page book. A half-hour television news program contains about twenty-four minutes of news. The speed at which newscasters read varies somewhat. The figure usually given is 150 words per minute. However, that is an average, and 180 words per minute is fairly common for networks and large stations. At 180 words per minute, a twenty-four-minute newscast contains 4,320 words. That's about the same as a seventeen-page chapter in a book. A five-minute radio newscast contains about three and one-half minutes of news. At about 180 words per minute, the newscast contains about 630 words. That's roughly two and one-half typed, double-spaced pages. At an average reading speed of 150 words per minute, a radio newscast contains only 525 words. Yet the newspaper, the television newscast, and the radio newscast all have the same news to deal with. Do you begin to get the picture?

Time limitations force two important restrictions on electronic news. First, electronic news is more selective. It uses fewer of the day's news stories than does a newspaper. Second, electronic news stories are less detailed than newspaper stories. They must be shorter than newspaper stories, and this brevity is accomplished primarily by eliminating details.

It might be argued that more detail could be provided in electronic news by using "tighter" writing, paring down the number of words rather than the number of details. There is no doubt that most broadcast writing is tight, but so is good newspaper writing. Therefore, the savings that could be realized through tighter writing are relatively small.

But there is a more important reason that savings are hard to achieve through tighter writing: the audience cannot absorb as much information from a broadcast story as it can from a printed story of similar length. Written material can be gone over at leisure. It can be reread as desired. Uncertainties about what was said can be resolved by examining the text. None of these luxuries is available to the broadcast audience. Everything must be understood at the time it is heard and seen. This means that added details are likely to be lost on the audience and that extra material must sometimes be written into a story to help the audience absorb the details more easily. There are also situations in television newswriting in which extra information must be provided to accompany material being shown on videotape or film.

So the basic approach to an electronic news story is to keep the number of facts and details to the bare minimum. You must delete unnecessary words, of course, as you would in any good writing. However, your first job is to learn to see each story in its essential details.

Let's take a few brief examples. Newspapers usually give the ages of people in stories. But do you really care if a man charged with robbing a bank is twenty-seven or fifty-one? If he is twelve or ninety-five his age is newsworthy and relevant; otherwise, age is an unnecessary detail. Newspapers often give addresses of people in stories. Yet, unless there is some important reason for specifying where the person lives, such information is just excess baggage in an electronic news report. Even names are frequently unnecessary. Do you really need the names of people involved in a highway accident if those people have no local ties?

The argument is often made that keeping more details in electronic news stories helps police to catch criminals. In a few cases, this may be true, especially if the news medium is television and you have a good picture of the suspect. However, most descriptions of suspects are too general to be of use, and some may do more harm than good. The description, "a black male, about six feet tall, around twenty years old, and weighing about 170 pounds," with no other data, could apply to thousands of people in most American cities. Such a description not only wastes space in the newscast, it casts suspicion on innocent people and feeds bigotry. Many good journalists may disagree, but we think most details of this sort simply waste precious time in a newscast.

The most important difference between print and broadcast news is in the handling of the opening sentence or *lead* of a story. This difference stems from the dissimilar ways in which people scan newspapers and broadcast news reports. The newspaper reader looks at the heading on the story and the first sentence or so to decide whether the rest of the story is worth reading. So the traditional newspaper lead tries to capsulize the key elements of the story. But when a broadcast writer has capsulized the key elements of a story, that usually is the *entire* broadcast news story.

More importantly, a viewer's or listener's tendency to scan by mentally "turning off" the news program when a story is not of interest means that when the next story begins, the viewer or listener has usually not mentally "turned on" the program again. Thus, if an important detail appears in the broadcast lead, it may be missed. Instead, the broadcast lead has to contain material that helps the members of the audience decide whether to "tune back in" for the story. To oversimplify, what the lead says by implication (although certainly not in these words) is, "Hey! Here's a story about food prices. Do you want to hear it?" The important details must come after the audience has been told what's coming.

So how can we define electronic news? Perhaps it is the timely report of events, facts, and opinions that interest a significant number of people, written to conform to the time limitations of the medium and the ability of the audience to absorb spoken information. That's a long-winded definition. You may be able to come up with a better one on your own. But if you examine our definition, you should begin to understand what we will be discussing throughout the rest of this book.

BECOMING A BROADCAST WRITER

Writing broadcast news is not something mysterious. It is a simple process that almost anyone can learn. However, like any skill, it takes patience and practice to develop. It is important that you have relatively good verbal skills to start with. Our purpose here is to teach you to write broadcast news, not how to write good English. And you also must have some interest in news. Trying to write news without paying attention to the day's events is like trying to cook without ever tasting food.

Being a good broadcast writer carries a great responsibility. Study after study has shown that the American people rate television as the "most reliable" medium. More than half the American people get most of their news from television. Taking into consideration what we have said above, that is not a comforting thought. We know that broadcast news must present news in skeleton form. NBC Newsman David Brinkley has said, "When it comes to covering news in any thorough and detailed way, we are just not in the ball game and we know it."

Furthermore, according to communication researchers Serena Wade and Wilbur Schramm: "Broadcast news is more likely to be the major source of public information for people with little education, for females, nonwhites, and farm and blue-collar workers than for others; whereas the print media are more likely to be the major source for the highly educated groups, whites, males, professional, managerial and white-collar workers, and high-income groups than for others." The broadcast newsperson can do little to change the makeup of the broadcast news audience. So it becomes all the more important to see that those who depend upon broadcast news get the most comprehensive news possible within the limitations of the medium.

SELECTING STORIES FOR BROADCAST NEWS

You cannot use every news story of the day in your newscast any more than a newspaper can use every story to which it has access. You have a very limited amount of time, and you must pick the most important stories of the day to use. That means the most important stories for your audience. The stories of importance in Coos, New Hampshire, are not necessarily the important stories in Coos Bay, Oregon. Nor are the stories of importance to the audience of a classical music station identical to those of interest to the audience of a country-and-western station.

Also, while we have stressed the importance of local news, there are major political and economic stories that must be covered. They may originate in Washington or Moscow, but they are important to your local audience. Emphasizing local news is not an excuse for overlooking important national and international stories. Use the definitions we have provided of news to determine which stories are potential material for your program—then try to analyze the needs of your specific audience to assign priorities to your stories.

You can categorize stories by asking yourself the following questions. If you answer "yes" to the first question, the story is very important. If you answer "yes" to question 2, the story is a little less important, and so on.

1. Is this a story my audience *must* know about immediately to protect their health and safety? (If so, the story probably should be presented as a bulletin and repeated in regular newscasts.)

2. Must my audience know the information in this story to perform their normal daily activities or to function as citizens in a democratic society? (If so, the story should be included in your regular daily newscasts.)

3. Is this a story that my audience *must* know, but need not be told

immediately? (Stories about planned future events that will affect your audience should be reported, but may be omitted from individual newscasts if the available time is being given to higher priority stories and if there are later newscasts that can be used to tell the story. The planned closing of a major road or the annual change to Daylight Saving Time are examples.)

4. Is this story of importance to a substantial portion of my audience? (News about farm parity support levels would be important in a farming community, but of less interest in nonagricultural communities. Defense allocations would be of more interest in areas with many aerospace workers than in rural areas. You must know your audience and the subgroups within it.)

5. Is this story important to a substantial portion of my audience, but of such a nature that it can be delayed? (Most stories that are important to substantial portions of your audience cannot be delayed because they cease to be timely. No newsperson likes to run the risk of leaving out an important story that a competitor may be using. However, on occasion you may find a story of this nature that can be postponed to a later newscast if there is insufficient time for it on the program you are preparing. The awarding of a big contract to an important local employer is one type of story that might be delayed.)

6. Is this story not essential, but still of interest to a large portion of my audience? (The marriage of the Prince of Wales has no direct impact on Muncie, Indiana, but it is still of interest to many people there. In a very strict sense, the outcome of the World Series has no direct effect on most people, but millions of people are interested in it.)

7. Is this story entertaining? (Although broadcast news is tight, there is still time, occasionally, for stories that serve no real purpose except entertainment.)

This set of priorities is only a rough guideline. News judgment is learned through experience—by working with good teachers and experienced co-workers. Most professional newspersons make their news selections intuitively, based on their long experience working with news. Our set of priorities is suggested only to help you as you begin to learn about broadcast news. Later you will develop your own set of priorities. Certainly, no checklist can cover all the questions of selection you will face in day-to-day work in the field.

Guidelines can also be set out for determining the sequence of stories in your newscast. Again, the advice we give here will be modified by your own experience in the field and by the particular preferences of the news department in which you work.

Our first general rule is to try to lead (open your program) with the most important stories of the hour. This is the news your audience will want to hear. Many audience members will already have heard something about these stories from other sources. They tune in expecting to learn the important details of these stories. If they do not get these details fairly quickly, they will switch around from station to station until they find a program that is giving them.

The second general rule is to arrange your stories so that each one logically leads to the next in an easy-to-follow pattern. Some newscasts stick to a rigid *format* of international news, national news, local news, sports, stocks, and weather. However, the modern trend is to proceed from the top stories of the day in a pattern that groups similar stories and flows logically from one topic to the next. For example, a story about war in the Middle East might logically be followed by a story about increasing fuel prices caused by the disruption of the Middle Eastern fuel supply, which might lead to a story about the cost of living, which might lead to a story about a local strike, and so on. Beyond these basics, the rules differ slightly for radio and for television.

For television:

1.   Get into a *videotape* (or film) story as quickly as you can.

2.   Balance the stories read on-camera by the newscaster with those on film or videotape so that there are no long stretches of one or the other to bore the viewer.

3.   Make the last videotape or film story one that can be dropped from the program with no great loss if the show is running overtime.

4.   Be sure you have several minutes of on-camera *pad* stories—short, nonessential stories that can be used to fill in where needed to make the timing come out correctly.

For radio:

1.   Try to get a story with audio in it as early in your script as possible. (Since these stories are generally recorded on tape cartridges—or *carts*— we will usually refer to this type of material as a "cart story.") Try to distribute other cart stories through the script so that there are no long dull periods of just the newscaster reading.

2.   Do not place a cart story within the last minute of the show. If the engineer starts the cart running too late, she or he may be forced to cut off the story in the middle in order to end the program on time. There may be exceptions to this rule if the cart story is very short and not placed too close to the end of the script.

3.   Do not place a long story at the end of the program. It may make it difficult to end the program at the correct time.

4.   The final cart story should be one that can be cut from the show for timing purposes.

5.   Provide at least one minute of pad.

Exercises
MMMMMMMMM

Exercise 1

Use the following wire service "News in Brief" stories to prepare a one-minute radio news broadcast with no commercials. Assume that the line lengths of the wire copy are correct for radio. A one-minute broadcast would require about fifteen such lines. Put the stories in the order you think they should be presented over the air. Your selection should cover a variety of topics of interest to the local audience. Be prepared to defend your selections in class.

AN ANTI-NUCLEAR ENVIRONMENTALIST PARTY HAS FAILED TO DO
WELL IN ELECTIONS IN WEST GERMANY. THE PARTY, CALLED THE
GREEN PARTY, DREW ONLY TWO POINT FOUR PERCENT OF THE VOTE.
—0—

CANADIAN OFFICIALS REPORT TWO TORONTO NUCLEAR PLANT
WORKERS RECEIVED MORE THAN A YEAR'S NORMAL RADIATION IN ONE
DAY WHILE CARRYING OUT REPAIRS RECENTLY.
—0—

FIVE HAPPY SOVIET DISSIDENTS HELD A NEWS CONFERENCE IN
NEW YORK TODAY . . . AND THANKED THE UNITED STATES FOR
WINNING THEIR FREEDOM IN A PRISONER SWAP WITH THE SOVIET
UNION.
—0—

TWO NUCLEAR POWER PLANTS—ONE IN CALIFORNIA, THE OTHER
IN SOUTH CAROLINA—STARTED SHUTTING DOWN TODAY—AS
ORDERED BY THE NUCLEAR REGULATORY COMMISSION. OPERATORS
WILL HAVE TO MAKE SAFETY IMPROVEMENTS BEFORE THE PLANTS
WILL BE ALLOWED TO REOPEN.
—0—

NO NEW TALKS ARE SET IN DENVER NEGOTIATIONS BETWEEN
UNITED AIR LINES AND STRIKING GROUND PERSONNEL. LATEST
EFFORTS TO WORK OUT A SETTLEMENT IN THE NEARLY MONTH-LONG
STRIKE BROKE OFF YESTERDAY.
—0—

RETURNS IN ECUADOR'S FIRST MAJOR ELECTIONS AFTER NINE
YEARS OF MILITARY RULE INDICATE THAT MODERATE LEFTIST
CANDIDATE JAIME ROLDOS (HIGH'MAY ROW' DOHZ) HAS WON A
LANDSLIDE VICTORY IN THE PRESIDENTIAL RACE.
—0—

UNITED RUBBER WORKERS UNION REPRESENTATIVES WILL MEET IN
OHIO MONDAY TO DECIDE THEIR NEXT COURSE OF ACTION . . .
EITHER TO STRIKE UNIROYAL OR TO AIM THEIR CONTRACT EFFORTS AT
THE OTHER THREE MAJOR TIRE MAKERS.
—0—

JAPANESE PRIME MINISTER MASAYOSHI OHIRA
(MAH-SAH-YOH'-SHEE OH-HEE'-RAH) IS FLYING TO WASHINGTON FOR
TALKS WITH PRESIDENT REAGAN THAT GET UNDER WAY WEDNESDAY.
A TOP ITEM FOR DISCUSSION WILL BE AMERICA'S ADVERSE BALANCE
OF TRADE WITH JAPAN.
—0—
SENATE MAJORITY LEADER HOWARD BAKER INCHES A STEP CLOSER
TODAY TO AN EXPECTED ANNOUNCEMENT LATER THAT HE WILL SEEK
THE G-O-P PRESIDENTIAL NOMINATION. THE TENNESSEE LAWMAKER
HAS SCHEDULED A NEWS CONFERENCE THIS MORNING TO INTRODUCE
TWO 1984 CAMPAIGN AIDES.

###

Exercise 2

The news story that follows was written for a radio audience and
distributed to stations throughout the country. Consider this story and its
parts to determine how well it fulfills the function of a broadcast news
story. Write a critique (about two typed, double-spaced pages) of the story
and try to answer these questions:

1. Is the topic of the story a good one? Is there widespread interest in
    the Equal Rights Amendment (E.R.A.)?

2. Does the story explain what the E.R.A. is? Is it important that it do so?

3. Would the story be of interest to an audience in New York City? To
    an audience in Lost Springs, Wyoming?

4. After reading the story, do you understand the legal processes
    described? Would you understand them just as well if you had only
    heard the story on the radio and not read it?

5. Does the story tell you what "rescission" is? Did you know anyway?

6. How does the story make use of quotations? Are all of the quotations
    necessary?

7. Does the story make clear what "bipartisan support" is?

8. Was the story interesting?

E.R.A.

*Idaho Attorney General David LeRoy says he will file what he is
calling a "landmark suit of monumental consequences" in U.S.
District Court in Boise within the next two weeks to rescind
Idaho's ratification of the Equal Rights Amendment (E.R.A.).*

*The suit will be the first challenge to the E.R.A. in federal court.
Several states have previously filed suits against the E.R.A. in state
courts.*

*The federal government has refused to recognize resolutions that
rescind ratification of the E.R.A., including such resolutions from
Idaho, South Dakota, Tennessee, Kentucky, and Nebraska.*

*LeRoy is claiming that the Idaho suit—which has bipartisan sup-
port from Idaho Governor John Evans as well as that state's representatives and senators—could doom the E.R.A. and reshape
the constitutional amendment process.*

*LeRoy says the suit will also challenge Congress's right to extend
the ratification time for the E.R.A. from the original cutoff date of
March 1979 to 1982.*

*Says LeRoy—in his words—"Our objective is to better define the
rights, authorities, and processes for state legislatures concerning
processes of amending the constitution. This will be a landmark
suit of monumental consequences."*

*Congress has never in the past accepted an amendment rescis-
sion. This is the first time, however, that process will be tested in
court.*

Exercise 3

Broadcast sentences are usually brief. Check each sentence in the
E.R.A. story. Rewrite any sentence that seems too long or uses difficult
words.

Exercise 4

Read the E.R.A. story again and decide whether it is an immediate-
reward story or a delayed-reward story. Use your decision as the basis for
class discussion.

Exercise 5

For each of the following stories, identify the characteristic that makes
the story interesting to an audience—whether conflict, proximity, prominence, unusualness, human interest, consequence, or sex. Some of these
stories may contain a combination of these elements. If so, and if they are
applicable, list them. (Consider proximity in terms of your local community.)

1. Dr. Peter Brown, Michigan State University scientist, has perfected a radiation treatment that gives relief to arthritis victims. Tests of 82 patients have produced very encouraging results.

_____

2. Secretary of State Jerry Stevens plans to marry Betty Schwartz, a movie star, next week in the state executive offices. Stevens is 54. Schwartz is 26.

_____

3. A hurricane has caused an estimated 800-thousand dollars in damage. Two lives were lost, and more than 100 persons were injured.

_____

4. Thieves broke into the home of Mayor Steve Brocato and stole clothing and jewelry valued at 28-hundred dollars. At the time of the robbery, the mayor and his family were attending a City Museum art show.

_____

5. Seven-year-old Mary Schonert wore a wide smile after she rescued her 3-year-old brother this morning from the fire that was destroying their Chicago home. Their parents were at work when the fire broke out at 8:30 this morning.

_____

6. You have only one more day to register to vote. According to City Clerk John Durham, registration is far ahead of last year's election turnout, but he warns that many citizens will lose their right to vote if they fail to register by 5 P.M. tomorrow.

_____

7. Governor Joseph Christenson has signed the Rodriguez–Diamond bill, giving taxpayers a 7 percent cut in their state income taxes.

_____

8. Mayor Steve Brocato has fired a city detective for allegedly taking graft.

_____

9. Ron Walsh, assistant basketball coach at the University of the North-

east, was promoted this morning. Walsh became head coach, taking over for Don Hartman, who has moved on to the Wayne Indiana professionals.

---

10. A local college woman has charged that one of her professors tried to fondle instead of punish her for skipping classes.

Exercise 6

For television:

List A lists all the stories you have that might be used on your 6 o'clock evening news program. List B lists the stories that you have on videotape. After you deduct the time required for the standard opening and the commercial and closing credits, you have twenty-two minutes to fill with news. Stories from List A that do not appear in List B will have to be treated as *readers* or *on-camera* stories to be read on camera by the studio newscasters without film or videotape. (In a regular news program, many of these on-camera stories would be read with slides or some other artwork to illustrate them.)

Using a form similar to the sample provided at the end of this exercise, make a list of the on-camera and videotape stories you would use, in the order in which you would use them. Assume that all videotape stories must run for the full length of time given. After each on-camera story, note your estimated reading time for the story. These should be reasonable estimates. Total time for all on-camera and videotaped stories should be twenty-two minutes. Keep in mind the rules outlined in Chapter 1 for the selection and arrangement of news items.

Newscasts are often measured in lines of copy instead of seconds. Estimate two seconds per line for television stories. Enter the line count for each story in the space provided on the chart.

List at the bottom of the chart the stories you would include in the pad for the program. Assume each pad story runs about fifteen seconds.

List A

Environmental Protection Agency announces recall of 400,000 Apache automobiles for defective exhaust systems.

Consumer prices take biggest monthly jump in four years.

State Department of Motor Vehicles recommends tax to penalize cars that get less than seventeen miles a gallon.

The sheriff's office has arrested sixty-four persons and is looking for forty-five more in the biggest heroin trafficking investigation in county history.

Police critically wound man in suburban bank holdup this morning. They say he may be responsible for twelve recent bank holdups.

Famous actor Henry Wunda is doing well after a prostate operation in a local hospital this morning.

A tear-gas cannister was thrown into a sewing factory in the downtown area this morning. Nine persons, including a sixteen-month-old baby, were taken to Our Lady of Lourdes Hospital for treatment. No one seriously hurt. Motive unknown. No clues to person who threw the tear gas.

Law goes into effect Monday requiring state inspections of cars for smog emissions before they can be sold. Cost will be 11 dollars.

Local professional baseball team wins seventh straight game in out-of-town contest.

Mexican-American community celebrates Cinco de Mayo.

President visits two nearby states.

School board hears antibusing spokesmen.

Kentucky Derby to be run tomorrow.

Sand castle contest at local beach.

TV star marries in New York.

Tomorrow is Mother's Day.

Garbage collectors' strike in major suburb.

Dental convention meets.

Police continue investigation of "Southside Slasher" murders.

Local professional basketball loses in out-of-town game.

Councilman John Kemper seeks to avoid election for his recall.

Local ice-skater running third in Women's World Figure-skating championships in Vienna.

Weather.

Latest Dow-Jones averages.

List B

Star of top TV series gets married in New York.   :31

Mexican-American community celebrates Cinco de Mayo.	1:59
Review of new film about rock music.	1:27
Mother's Day at local zoo. Newborn animals.	1:10
Report on garbage collectors' strike in major suburb.	2:01
Speaker at dental convention urges checkups for mouth cancer.	1:37
President visits two nearby states.	:34
Police continue investigation of string of local murders thought to be work of "Southside Slasher."	1:14
Local professional basketball team losing to Philadelphia in Philadelphia last night.	:15
City Councilman John Kemper seeks to avoid recall election.	2:19
Preparations for tomorrow's Kentucky Derby.	2:08
School board hears antibusing witnesses.	:45
Sand castle building contest at local beach.	:50
New office building opens downtown.	:45
Manufacturer shows new low-cost contact lenses.	:53

STORY	RUNNING TIME	LINE COUNT
TOTAL		
PAD		

Exercise 7

For radio:

List C gives the stories for which you have recorded audio to use on your morning news program. After deducting time for the program's standard opening, closing, and commercials, you have three minutes and twenty seconds for your newscast.

Use List A from Exercise 6 as a list of stories you might want to use. Use stories not on List C only as *readers*—stories your newscaster reads without any cart audio. Using the same type of form you used in Exercise 6, list each of the stories you would use and give the sequence in which you would use them. Cart stories must run at the lengths specified. Estimate the reading time required for each noncart story and write your own estimate after each story selected. Total time for all material should be 3:20. For radio, you may estimate reading time at four seconds per line, so the program should run fifty lines. Note reading times for all material in your script first in seconds, then in lines. For cart stories, you will have to convert the running time to a line count. At the bottom of the chart, list the stories you would put into the pad. They should be unimportant stories that can be reduced to the briefest form and used to make the program come out on time. Estimate reading time for pad stories at about ten seconds each.

List C

Antibusing speaker at school board.	:30
Interview with contestant at sand castle contest.	:45
Man-on-the-street interviews on meaning of Cinco de Mayo.	1:00
City Councilman John Kemper argues against recall election to remove him from office.	:50
Interview with leaders of garbage strike.	:45
Interview with police spokesman on "Southside Slasher" case.	:58
Phone interview with basketball player on last night's loss to Philadelphia team in that city.	1:02
Dental convention speaker urges checkups to prevent mouth cancer.	:40
Trainer discusses chances of favorite horse in tomorrow's Kentucky Derby.	:30

2

The Electronic News Lead

From what you have read in the previous chapter, you may already have some idea of the way to write an electronic news lead. Remember that the lead is a signal to the audience to start listening, so it should not carry any important details. It is never the "Who?–What?–Why?–Where?–When?–and–How?" newspaper lead. One or two of those six traditional questions may be answered, but never all of them. The lead should contain few, perhaps none, of the important details of the story. Any details you do put in an electronic news lead should be placed near the end. You should assume that the audience will pay no attention to the first few words of the lead. These beginning words should not be counted on to convey any important information.

GIVING THE INFORMATION

Think of the lead as initiating a conversation between the newscaster and the audience. Pretend it is a telephone call to your Uncle John in Duluth. You don't say, "Uncle John, a four-alarm blaze swept downtown Lotusville this morning, gutting three stores and causing an estimated $200,000 in damage." You say, "Uncle John, did you hear about the fire we had here today?" Now, if you turn that around, you can convert the question into a statement something like, "There has been a major fire in downtown Lotusville." And that's your broadcast lead.

Telling "Where?"

Of the six traditional newspaper lead questions, the two questions you are most likely to answer in your broadcast lead are "What?" and "Where?" A broadcast lead usually gives us a general idea of what happened (there was a fire), and quite frequently it says where it happened (in downtown Lotusville). There is a good reason for this. The programs of most broadcasting stations are likely to reach several communities. The listener always needs to be told where the action took place. Putting this information in the lead—preferably near the end—helps the listener to decide whether to "tune in" mentally to the story or to ignore it. The logical presumption, if no location is specified, is that the action took place "right here," that is, in the community in which the listener lives or in a larger community nearby where most of the local media are located. Inexperienced writers sometimes overlook this assumption and come up with leads like this:

An escaped mental patient, armed with a gun, ran amok today. The man killed three persons and wounded six others before he was subdued. Italian police cornered the man on a downtown street in Milan, and. . . .

The audience has to wait almost ten seconds to discover the crime took place in Milan, Italy, not Lotusville, U.S.A. The "where" of the story needed to be in the lead.

In newspaper and wire-service stories, the "where" is taken care of by the *dateline*. The story above might come off a wire-service teletype reading:

(MILAN, ITALY) AN ESCAPED MENTAL PATIENT, ARMED WITH. . . .

Newspaper copy might read:

MILAN, ITALY—An escaped mental patient, armed with. . . .

Very few radio and television stations use datelines in their stories. For those that do, it is strictly a matter of style. Most stations omit the dateline. This means that the lead often has to be rewritten, even though it was taken from the radio or television wire of the wire service. Here's a typical example of the kind of story that often traps inexperienced writers:

(NEW YORK) SECRETARY OF STATE ERNEST SELDEN TOLD A GROUP OF NEWSPAPER EDITORS MEETING HERE TODAY. . . .

If you blithely cross out the dateline and read the story as written, your audience will be justified in assuming that the secretary of state made his address right here in Lotusville because that's what "here" means in an electronic news story. You need to recast the lead so it reads something like this:

In New York, today, Secretary of State Ernest Selden told a group. . . .

As we will later explain, this is still not a good lead. We offer it here only to show the minimum change you would have to make in the wire-copy to make it intelligible to a broadcast audience.

A problem can also arise in references to persons or places following a dateline. For example:

(DUBUQUE, IOWA) SENATOR MILO MAIZE SPOKE HERE TODAY AT THE GROUND BREAKING FOR THE WORLD'S LARGEST HOG FARM.

If you simply delete the dateline, the audience is justified in assuming that Senator Maize is from their state and that the world's largest hog farm is going to be constructed in their own town. Listeners won't like it. Senator Maize won't like it. The hogs won't like it. So, instead, you have to lead the story with something like this:

Iowa's Senator Milo Maize says he wants to set the record straight about that much-maligned creature, the hog. The Senator was speaking in Dubuque, Iowa. . . .

Parochialism is the downfall of many inexperienced writers. Remember that the signal from your station can carry for hundreds of miles. When you must state locations, state them specifically. Don't assume "everyone knows where that is." They don't. Your audience is not made up exclusively of people from one community. Moreover, not everyone within your community is likely to understand imprecise references. After all, statistics tell us that about one-third of the families in America move every year. There are certain to be people in your audience who are newcomers.

Students who write news for college radio stations are among the worst offenders. Don't write: "A homecoming rally will be held tonight in the Benson Quad." There are certain to be people on the campus who will not understand the reference. Moreover, there will be listeners off-campus who won't even know what university you are talking about. You should write it: "There will be a homecoming rally for the Flakey State football team. The rally is scheduled for eight tonight in the Benson Quad. That's just south of the gymnasium on the Flakey State campus."

Don't let parochialism and imprecision trap you in giving place names. Do you have any idea of how many Glendales there are in the United States—or Peorias—or Pittsburghs? Probably no one would assume that you meant Paris, Kentucky, if you said something happened in Paris, but if your station was near Paris, Kentucky, you'd have to give some thought to references to either Paris. And when you mention something happening in Frankfurt, Germany, which one do you mean? There's more than one, you know. There are countries named Mexico and Cuba and a state named Louisiana—but all those are names of towns, too. Adding a couple of extra words can help you avoid all this ambiguity.

Telling "What?"

The "what" of a lead can be many things. Often it is a simple statement of the main point of the story:

The cost of living keeps going up.

A plane crash has taken the life of a star of the silent screen.

There's going to be an investigation of the State Legislature.

Another type of "what" lead—and a good one—is one that focuses on the effect the event reported will have on members of the audience. This approach involves the viewers or listeners in the story and is much more likely to attract the attention of the audience. For example, "Gasoline prices are going up" is a perfectly good lead, but, "You'll be paying more for gasoline next month" is better. And a possibly even better lead is one that includes the newscaster with the audience: "We'll be paying more for gasoline next month."

Here are a couple of typical "what" leads that emphasize effects of events on the audience:

Don't spend the money from that income tax cut yet. . . .

We can all sleep an hour later tomorrow morning.

Telling "Who?"

The "who" of a story should not be given in the lead, except when the "who" is someone famous. Unfamiliar names should not appear in a lead. While a famous name by itself can tell the listeners to "tune in" mentally to the story, any other kind of name will simply confuse them. However, we do not mean that the key people in a story should not be mentioned in the lead. You can identify them by what they do instead of by their names. Take these examples:

The Pope is coming to the United States. . . .

There's no problem with that lead. Most of the audience know who the Pope is. But what about this lead:

Gertrudl Schmuecker is coming to the United States. . . .

Your audience is bound to ask, "Who?"—until you add:

. . . The Swiss national yodeling champion will compete. . . .

It's clear that leading with an unfamiliar name only confuses an audience. Whether the name comes in the lead or later in the story, we need to know what a person does before we are told that person's name. Famous names are an exception because we already know what they do. The lead above should be rewritten:

> *Switzerland's champion yodeler is coming to the United States. That's right. Gertrudl Schmuecker topped a field of almost 500 men and women at the annual Swiss competition in that tonsil-twisting vocal form, and now she is challenging. . . .*

Young writers often overestimate the fame of important persons. There are really very few people in the world whose names can safely be used without some sort of indication of what they do. You can assume that people know the name of the president of the United States, probably the governor of the state in which they live, and possibly the names of their state's senators. Beyond that, there is little you can assume safely. The president of France, the mayor of a nearby suburb, a local congressman—these, unfortunately, are not names you can expect everyone to know. This goes for entertainment personalities as well as political figures. Always err on the side of caution.

In all cases, it is better to precede a name—well known or otherwise—with some identifying phrase:

Instead of: *Elton John is in town.*

Make it: *Rock-star Elton John is in town.*

In a great many cases, we can do without an unfamiliar name altogether. The description of what the person does may be sufficient. For example:

> *A British inventor has developed a self-washing dish. The inventor says. . . .*

The name of the inventor really adds nothing to the story. It is one more fact for the audience to remember, and we want to keep the number of facts to the minimum.

Giving news sources. "Who said it?" is a question that broadcast writers handle quite differently from newspaper journalists. Newspaper writers usually delay citing their sources until the end of the lead. In most cases, what happened is more important than who said it, so the rule makes good sense—for newspaper writing. But it will not work for broadcast newswriting. People need to know the source of a story to evaluate its importance. Because we cannot go back over material we get from electronic news, we need to know the source of the material first. Then we know how much importance to attach to it. If we do not hear the source before we get the information, we assume the source is the news department itself—and that is a source of very high credibility. If a newscaster reports that, "The dam has broken. Citizens of Lotusville are warned to seek high ground immediately," people will assume the report is correct. They may not even wait long enough to hear the rest of the story. That is why it is a serious error to write something like this:

> *"The dam has broken. Citizens of Lotusville are warned to seek high ground immediately." Those signs were posted all over Lotusville yesterday to publicize the new disaster movie,* Flood.

A newspaper reader can see the quotation marks around the material at the start of the story, but the broadcast listener or viewer cannot. The broadcast audience members can put this story in perspective only if the source of the quote comes first.

We can draw two rules from this. First, never lead with a quotation. In general, broadcasters try to avoid written quotes anywhere in a story—but it is particularly important to keep them out of leads. Second, always give the source of any information before you give the information. Again, this is a general rule of broadcast newswriting, but it is a particularly important one to observe in leads. It is one of the key differences between the newspaper lead and the broadcast lead.

Telling "How?" and "How Much?"

"How" is another element of the newspaper lead that rarely finds a place in the broadcast lead. Be particularly careful of "how much." Numbers are unwanted baggage in any electronic news story. They represent added details for your audience to remember. Particular effort should be made to keep them out of leads. The audience is not ready to listen to details in a lead, so any mention of numbers is almost certain to be misunderstood or missed. Where there seems no way to avoid using a number in the lead, follow these two rules: (1) Try to use no more than one number, and (2) delay that number to the end of the lead.

Furthermore, numbers should be rounded off. Consider this example:

> *Twenty-three persons were injured in a chain collision that involved 2 buses, 4 trucks, and 16 passenger cars on Highway 40 about 6 this morning in heavy fog.*

No one could be expected to remember all those numbers, and the "twenty-three" that is the first word is certain to be missed. Try it this way:

> *A chain collision of vehicles in this morning's dense fog has left 23 persons injured.*

By cutting out all but one number—the most important one—and delaying that number to the end of the lead, we have made the lead much easier to understand.[1]

Here are a couple of bad leads. Think how you might rewrite each one to get rid of the numbers:

Four of the 5 incumbents on the Worcester City Council have been re-elected.

May 6th is the last day to get your city on-street parking sticker.

Telling "When?"

The "when" of a story does not often appear in broadcast leads, and indeed, broadcast writers tend to leave it out of the rest of the story, too. Just as a broadcast audience will assume, unless told otherwise, that a story has taken place "here," so the audience will assume that the story took place "today."

Newspaper writers must deal with the inescapable time lag between the occurrence of an event and the time their audience reads about the event. It is essential, therefore, that specific times and dates be included in newspaper stories. What the newspaper loses in timeliness, it makes up for by providing details that often must be left out of electronic news. So broadcast newswriters emphasize what they are best able to provide— today's news.

References to time are often omitted from electronic news stories, or at least kept out of the leads. Broadcast newswriters do not overburden their stories by mentioning that each event occurred "today." In fact, to avoid excessive detail they usually ignore exact times as well. Instead of writing, "The fire broke out at 3:58 A.M.," the broadcast writer will say, "The fire broke out early this morning." Although not all broadcast news-writers agree on this point, many newsrooms ban all references to A.M. and P.M. because listeners may not hear them correctly or may transpose them in their minds.

Some broadcast news editors have made their aversion to the word "today" a crusade. The word is not that sinister. There are times when it is needed. But try to use it only when it is needed. Frequently, it can be postponed and kept out of the lead.

---

[1] Some broadcast writers would object to the use of "persons" and "injured," preferring the more conversational "people" and "hurt." Conversational style is discussed later, but we mention it here because there are some battles in the field of broadcast journalism that never end. "Persons" versus "people" is one. For every news director who insists that "people" is more conversational, you will find another who demands that "persons" be used with any specific number—"many people," but "12 persons." We side with the "persons" school simply because news directors who insist on "persons" are the crusty type who are likely to fire you for saying "people." News directors who prefer the conversational "people" may give you a chance to learn their style instead of throwing you out on your ear.

Instead of: *The mayor announced an antismoking campaign today.*

Write: *The mayor is launching an antismoking campaign. At kick-off ceremonies at City Hall. . . .*

If there were some reason that members of the audience might assume the action did not take place today, you could insert "today" after "City Hall" in the second sentence. But notice that the story reads all right without any reference to a specific time.

Earlier we gave an example of rewriting a wire-service lead to provide the "where" information from the dateline. The example we gave is acceptable if the writer's goal is to get the material on the air as quickly as possible, to do a minimum of rewriting, and to leave the rest of the wire copy as it was received:

In New York today, Secretary of State Ernest Selden told. . . .

However, a better lead would concentrate on the topic of the speech and present the "today" at a later point in the story:

The United States is apparently changing its policy toward Cuba. Speaking to a group of newspaper editors in New York today, Secretary of State. . . .

One of the main techniques used by broadcast writers to keep time references out of their leads is to write each lead in the present or present progressive tense. Instead of writing "Governor Larry Fern told reporters today that he will take a two-week vacation in Brazil," the broadcast newswriter would make the lead, "Governor Fern is going to Brazil." The present progressive tense eliminates any need to specify "today."

Sometimes it is possible to speak of a past event in the present progressive tense. The present progressive tense implies that the action is still going on. However, in many cases the reported event is part of a continuing activity. For example, many writers would reject our use of "is launching" in the lead, "The mayor is launching an antismoking campaign." Technically, the campaign has already been launched, and the launching does not continue. Yet, in the broader sense of getting the campaign under way, it can be argued that the launching process is still going on. Most imprecise writing is the result of fuzzy thinking, and we wish neither to condone fuzzy thinking nor to be accused of it. On the other hand, there are times when strict grammatical logic can be stretched a bit to get more use from the present progressive tense.

When a lead cannot be written in the present or present progressive tense, the broadcast newswriter will try to put it in the present perfect tense. If the dam broke hours ago, it would not do to write:

The Tinker Dam is breaking. . . .

However, while it is not wrong, this lead unnecessarily uses "this morning":

The Tinker Dam broke early this morning. . . .

A better broadcast lead would be:

The Tinker Dam has broken. . . .

There are times, of course, when the past tense is needed. In the example just given, if half of your listeners are sitting in two feet of water, there isn't much point in coyly using the present perfect tense. They know the dam has broken, and you might just as well say when. When an event is obviously over and done with, there is not much point in avoiding a specific mention of time.

Let's review the priority of verb tenses to use for leads:

1. When possible, lead in the present tense or present progressive tense.

2. When present tense or present progressive won't work, use the present perfect tense.

3. Past tense should be your last choice, but be realistic. Don't try to force events clearly past and done with into the present or present perfect tense.

Telling "Why?"

"Why?" is a question almost never answered in a broadcast lead. The reason is fairly simple. Before you get to "why," you must usually tell the audience "what," and once you have told the audience "what," you have usually completed your lead. You want to keep your lead as simple and uncluttered as possible, and the "why" can almost always be delayed in the story. For example, this lead is all right:

Governor Fern has fired State Highway Chief Magnus Terkel because Terkel disagreed with the governor's master plan for state highways.

However, while tolerable, this lead is far too long and overburdened with details. It would be much better to present the "why" in a later sentence:

Governor Fern has fired the state's top highway official. Magnus Terkel was appointed State Highway Chief only last March. The governor reportedly fired Terkel because Terkel disagreed with the governor's master plan for state highways.

Summary: Some Things to Avoid in Leads

Always check leads for:

Numbers. Keep them out of the lead. Omit them from the story entirely, if possible. If you must use a number in the lead, delay it to the end of the lead.

Unfamiliar names. Keep them out of the lead. Always tell what a person does (or why the name appears in the story) before you give the name. Even with a famous name, it is safest to give some reference to what the person does before using the name. Ask yourself if the name really needs to be used at all in the story.

Times. Proper selection of verb tense helps. Minimize use of "today." Phrases such as "early this morning," "about an hour ago," or "just a few minutes ago," are preferable. Use specific times (for example, "3:17 this morning") *only* when the exact time is essential to the story. If a time must be used in a lead, delay it to the latter part of the lead. Check for the approved style in your newsroom before using "A.M." and "P.M."

MAINTAINING THE ACTIVE VOICE

It is a good rule to use the active voice and to avoid the passive voice in any type of writing. Pay special attention to that rule when writing leads.

Compare: *A bill has been passed by the city council. . . .*

With: *The city council has passed a bill. . . .*

The second lead is shorter, stronger, and easier to understand. Any time you can get rid of the passive voice in your writing, it is likely to improve what you have written. This is noticeably true in leads.

One tip-off to problems in your leads—or other writing—is the presence of too many prepositions. The passive voice in the first example forces the use of the prepositional phrase, "by the city council." Not every preposition or prepositional phrase weakens your writing, but it is good practice to see how many of them you can eliminate.

USING NONSPECIFIC AND QUESTION LEADS

It is possible to write a lead that includes no specific information about a story, but this approach should be done sparingly and with careful attention to the type of story. These leads attract the attention of the audience by sparking its curiosity. For example:

There's a sadder but wiser tomcat in Newport tonight.

> *The Port Washington Chamber of Commerce may have to take swimming lessons.*

In almost all cases, this type of lead is best reserved for light stories.

A lead to avoid is the question lead. For some reason, inexperienced writers like to write leads that sound like riddles:

> *Who's the happiest man in Boston tonight?*

> *Why are they painting City Hall pink?*

In the hands of the right writer (and, more particularly, when read by the right reader), leads like this can work. They often crop up in sports stories. But most of them do little to draw the attention of the audience, and they always waste precious time. Perhaps it would be wrong to say categorically, "Never lead with a question," but we do strongly recommend avoiding question leads.

IMPROVING YOUR LEADS

There are many rules to learn about writing broadcast leads. The lead is the most important part of a story. If it is weak, the listener won't bother with the rest of the story. It takes time and practice to become a good writer of broadcast leads, but that time and practice are well spent. If you have a good lead, writing the rest of the story is usually easy.

Here are some examples of leads that contain errors. They were written by students in broadcast journalism courses. The first set of leads was written for a story about the purported plans of the People's Republic of China to join the International Monetary Fund and borrow money for development projects:

> *China seems to be going capitalist these days. . . .*

This lead fails to give the reader an appropriate clue to the content of the story. The listener would know that the upcoming story was about China, but not that it concerned the I.M.F. or that borrowing money was involved.

> *According to a Japanese newspaper, China needs money.*

The lead again does not suggest the I.M.F. angle.

> *In an effort to gain the more than 15 (B) billion dollars it needs to complete its modernization plan, China reportedly plans to join the International Monetary Fund and seek loans from the World Bank.*

This lead goes to the opposite extreme from the others. It contains too much information. It is too long for a broadcast lead. Probably the lead for this story should read something like this:

China reportedly wants to borrow money for development projects and may ask to join the International Monetary Fund.

Here are some weak leads for another story.

A train that derailed in central Los Angeles at 9:45 this morning is still blocking traffic in the immediate area.

The precise time is not needed here. The phrase "immediate area" has no meaning because all we know is that the derailment took place somewhere in the city of Los Angeles.

Commuters in central Los Angeles were sidetracked today when 8 cars of a Southern Pacific freight train derailed.

This is not too bad, but it may be confusing. The "commuters" referred to were motorists who could not get through the intersection blocked by the derailment. However, the audience might think that the story was going to be about problems getting rail traffic through. Also, the specific name of the railroad involved is not really needed in the lead.

Several cars of a Southern Pacific freight train have derailed in central Los Angeles today.

This lead contains a too-common error for student writers. The use of the present perfect verb, "have derailed," makes it incorrect to state the specific time, "today." If you give a specific time, use the past tense. If you use the present perfect tense, then do not specify a time. The story might be written better this way:

There was a train derailment in downtown Los Angeles this morning, and some streets are still blocked.

Here is another poorly written lead for a different story:

It is believed that arsonists have started a fire in the San Bernardino National Forest which has flared from 600 acres to 16-hundred overnight.

This lead contains too many details. The use of the present perfect "have started" is wrong here. The act of starting the fire was a single event that is over and done with. It should, therefore, be treated in the past tense. Used with "it is believed," the present perfect tense suggests that the authorities do not know if there really is a fire burning. Furthermore, to begin the lead with "it is believed" is weak because it puts emphasis on the wrong element in the story. The key element here is that the fire has spread dramatically. The "it is believed" opening would be all right if the rapid spread of the fire had already been emphasized in earlier stories. However, in that case, more emphasis should be placed on the cause aspect of the story: "It is now believed. . . ." or " Authorities say that fire in the San Bernardino Forest may have been caused by arson." The phrase, "National Forest which has flared," could be rewritten to avoid the separation of "fire" from "which has flared." As written, it sounds as if the forest had flared, not the fire. Actually, the writer left out the main point, which was that the fire was almost under control.

A 16-hundred acre fire burning in the San Bernardino National Forest is nearly under control according to fire officials.

That is strictly a newspaper lead. The attribution of source, "according to fire officials," must come before the material in the lead. One way to write the lead would be this:

Fire officials say they have that fire in the San Bernardino Forest almost under control.

Here, for one last story, is another lead that needed more work:

In San Francisco today, cable car service is still being affected by damage reportedly suffered in an earthquake.

The lead makes it sound as if the earthquake had just occurred. In this case, the earthquake had happened several weeks earlier. The "today" in the lead is not needed. The verb "affected" lacks precision. In fact, the cable cars had not been running at all, while "affected" suggests reduced service. And, to be precise, service is not being affected "by damage," it is being affected *because of* damage. The "reportedly" casts too much doubt on the cause. The student used it because the original story said that officials of the cable car system said they believed the damage had been caused by an earthquake. All that information could have been left out of the lead and reported in a subsequent sentence. A simple enough lead would have been:

In San Francisco, the cable cars are still not running.

You should see from these examples that every word in a lead must count. Each word must be the right word, and each word must be there for a purpose.

DEALING WITH TELEVISION LEADS

In general, the rules for radio and television leads are the same. However, there are some differences to be considered. In the first place, the rule about keeping verbs in the present, present progressive, or present perfect tense is not observed as strictly in television. There is a stronger sense that television newscasters are telling the audience about events that happened earlier, and therefore, there is a far greater use of past tense in television leads. This is particularly true when the story contains film or videotape segments because these were clearly recorded at an earlier time. (And, in fact, it is a violation of FCC regulations to try to pass off recorded material as live material.) The television lead may begin in the past tense, or it may be written in present tense (or present perfect or present progressive) with the story switching to the past tense in subsequent sentences. A lead might read:

> There was a confrontation between police and striking city workers this morning at City Hall.

Or the story could begin with this lead:

> There has been another confrontation between police and those city workers who are on strike. WDEG's Paul Pry was on the scene when the trouble started.

The story could then switch to the report prepared by the station reporter.

Television provides a greater variety of ways to begin a story, so it is worthwhile to examine the most commonly used ones.

For either radio or television, a story may be a *reader,* one read from start to finish by the newscaster. In such stories, the present, present progressive, or present perfect tense lead is usually best for radio and will also work most of the time for television.

In either medium, the lead may simply introduce a story to be presented by a reporter. This is sometimes called a *reporter package.* Again, present, present progressive, or present perfect tense will work for both media, but there is a stronger probability that you will use past tense in television. The examples given earlier indicate the different approaches that might be taken.

It is never a good policy for the studio newscaster to open a story by reading over film or videotape. Almost every story needs an on-camera introduction or *lead-in* by the newscaster. However, if the story that follows is a reporter package, the way the reporter begins her or his segment of the story may vary greatly. There could be a new lead-in by the reporter in the studio. It might begin in the past tense like this:

PAUL ON CAMERA
Yes, Rod, there was a lot of pushing and shoving, and several times it flared into real violence.

SIVT/VO (:27)
It started when police tried to move the pickets away from. . . .

However, the reporter could begin in the present perfect tense and then switch to the past tense:

PAUL ON CAMERA
Yes, Rod, the hostility between the police and the strikers has been simmering for some time now, and today it broke into real violence.

SIVT/VO (:27)
It started when. . . .

Even though the story began in the present perfect, it was necessary to switch to the past tense ("broke") before starting the filmed section of the story. It is also worth noting here that, while the reporter begins by responding to the anchorperson, the story is really told to the viewers, and the reporter must take pains to keep that goal in mind.

The reporter package could begin with a *stand-up* opening of the reporter filmed or videotaped at the scene of the story. Stand-ups are usually begun in the present tense. Then they usually switch to the past tense.

It's quiet here at City Hall now, but earlier this morning, it was anything but peaceful.

Or the videotaped or filmed portion of the story could begin with the reporter's voice over the visual material. In this case, the lead is usually in the past tense:

The trouble at City Hall began when the strikers tried. . . .

If there is no *voice-over* material in the story to be read in the studio, then the actual program script will simply show the on-camera lead-in and the cues for the videotaped or filmed story, something like this:

> (ROD ON CAMERA)
>
> There has been another confrontation between police and those city workers who are on strike. WDEG's Paul Pry was on the scene when the trouble started.

> (SOVT (:32))
>
> OC: " . . . be worse tomorrow."
>
> FILL: Pry says that violence broke out when police tried to push pickets away from the main entrance and out onto the sidewalk. Two policemen were slightly injured. One striker was hospitalized with a minor foot injury. The union says the strikers will be back at the main entrance tomorrow. That probably means more violence.

The script indicates where the videotape is to run, how long it will run (thirty-two seconds), and what the *out cue* (*OC*) is. The out cue is the last three or four words heard at the end of the videotape story. The script also includes *fill*. (Some stations use *fill* to describe what we have already called pad in this book, and they use the term *back-up script* or *back-up copy* for the material we call fill.) The fill is material provided for the anchorperson to read in case the tape fails to run properly after the lead-in has been given.

The script that the reporter used to prepare her or his package would probably be in the form of notes instead of a completed script. However, for purposes of studying the lead, we'll assume the reporter completely scripted that portion of the story. Here's how such a script might look if the story began with a stand-up:

> (PAUL STAND-UP)
>
> It's quiet here at City Hall now, but earlier this afternoon it was anything but quiet.

> (SOVT/VO (:28)
>
> Nat. Sound Under)
>
> The pickets have been walking their line here before the main entrance of City Hall ever since they went on strike 2 weeks ago. Then about 2 this afternoon, the word came from the mayor's office to. . . .

In this treatment, the verb tenses were chosen to match the visuals. The reporter, on camera, began in the present tense. Leading into the videotape portion, he prepared the audience by switching to the past tense. Then, because he wished to tell the story in a chronological sequence, and because he had reason to believe that the picketing in front of the main entrance would resume, he began the videotaped segment in the present perfect tense. Finally, he switched to the past tense to tell the story.

COORDINATING VERB TENSES AND VISUALS

Coordinating verb tenses and visuals may seem complicated, but it is not. The present tense and present progressive tense are used to stress what is happening as the reporter speaks—even though what he says will not be heard on the air until later. The present perfect tense serves when we are looking at scenes of things that happened earlier than the time at which the reporter is speaking—but which have not necessarily ended. The past tense is used to tell us we are looking at things that are over and done with. These rules apply to television newswriting in general, but they are particularly important to observe when writing leads because the leads prepare the audience for what is to follow. In the previous example, the phrase "have been walking" clearly warned the audience to expect to be told later that the picketing at that location may continue. If the reporter had chosen to say "had been walking"—the verb tense the audience would normally expect at the start of videotape or film—then the audience would expect to hear that the pickets were no longer at that location.

Without the stand-up opening, the story would most likely begin in the past tense:

| SOVT/VO (:38) | Things were quiet at City Hall until about 2 |
| Nat. Sound Under | this afternoon. Then. . . . |

Either radio or television might have a lead into a *live remote* report during the course of a program. Because television news programs are generally longer than radio news programs, there is more likelihood of such live inserts in television news. The lead-in by the studio announcer would almost always be in the present, present progressive, or present perfect tense:

ROD ON CAMERA	For 2 weeks now, the School Board has been
	trying to reach a unified position on the
	busing issue. Reporter Mary Mintz has been
	following those deliberations, and she's at
	the School Board right now. Mary, I
	understand the board still has not reached a
	decision.

Mary's response, certainly unscripted but probably read from notes, would also begin in present, present progressive, or present perfect tense.

> MINTZ LIVE REMOTE | That's right, Rod, they still cannot reach an agreement. One faction wants to. . . .

GIVING VISUAL INFORMATION

Beyond the matter of verb tenses, the major differences to be found between television and radio leads lie in the nature of the two media. In radio, the lead must sometimes provide more information than in television because the television lead conveys some information visually. The television lead should make use of visual elements whenever possible.

For example, a story about snow and ski resorts might begin this way for radio:

> *Heavy snows last night brought sighs of relief to anxious skiers and ski resort owners alike.*

For television, the lead for the same story might read like this and be followed by a voice-over story with videotape of snow and skiing:

> SELMA ON CAMERA | Well, skiers and ski lodge owners finally got what they've been waiting for. . . .
>
> KEY Slide A-73: Snow |
>
> SIVT/VO (:20) | The snow started falling late last night, and by 10 this morning. . . .

There is no point in overemphasizing the differences between radio and television leads. The same basic rules apply to both. But it is wise for the student to keep in mind that each medium has techniques that are uniquely suited to it. You can best learn these techniques by listening carefully to the leads used on good radio and television news programs.

Take some time to reread this chapter. Audiotape some news stories from radio and television so that you can listen to and analyze the leads. Look at the leads on several stories in your daily newspaper and try rewriting them as broadcast leads. You'll soon find it comes almost without effort. It may seem strange at first, but broadcast newswriting really is as easy as talking on the telephone to your Uncle John.

Exercises
~~~~~~~~~~~~

Exercise 1

Rewrite these newspaper leads from the *Los Angeles Times* so they make good broadcast leads:

> Environmentalists won a hard-fought showdown with developers Wednesday when the House overwhelmingly approved legislation to set aside one-third of Alaska in protected parks, wildlife refuges, forests and wilderness areas.
>
> President Carter, saying he hoped the worst of the gasoline shortage is nearly over, Wednesday announced a series of measures specifically aimed at relieving problems in California.
>
> NEW YORK (AP)—A. Philip Randolph, labor leader and grand old man of the modern civil rights movement died here Wednesday night, civil rights leader Bayard Rustin said.
>
> BEIRUT, Lebanon—Premier Salim Hoss, frustrated in efforts to restore peace amid Palestinian guerilla attacks and repeated Israeli reprisals, resigned Wednesday to end Lebanon's longest-running government since World War II.
>
> BRUSSELS, Belgium—Defense ministers of the Atlantic Alliance gave their endorsement to the new strategic arms limitation treaty here Wednesday with the declaration that "it will improve the Security of NATO."

Exercise 2

Create a good broadcast lead for each of the following stories:

1. A girl from the neighboring city of Clarkdale has received an appointment to the U.S. Military Academy at West Point. She is the first woman from your state to receive an appointment to one of the national military academies. Her name is Mary Jean Silverman. She is eighteen. She lives at 2834 Dilman Road. She is an only child. Her father is a stockbroker. Her mother is a housewife. She attends North Clarkdale High School. She is a straight-A student. She intends to make the army her career. She says women should fight side-by-side with men in the front lines in time of war.

2. The president of Lotus State University, which is in your town, has been arrested for drunk driving and trying to outrun a patrol car. His name is Robert R. Belknap. He holds a doctorate in Physical Chem-

istry. He was appointed president in 1979. Before that, he had been Dean of Students at Upper Peabody Technological College in What Cheer, Iowa. He was once arrested in What Cheer for speeding. He is divorced. He lives in Apartment 7-A of the Toledo Apartments, 18 North Toledo Street, your city. He is fifty-two years old.

3. A local nursing home is holding a birthday party for its oldest resident. Her name is Agatha Lennox Crenshaw. She is 103 years old. She has lived all her life in your town, which is only 105 years old itself. Mrs. Crenshaw has been widowed four times. Her last husband died when she was eighty-two. She has been at the nursing home for the last fifteen years. Before that she lived alone. The nursing home is called Golden Years. It is located at 4928 South 5th Avenue. It was cited by state inspectors last year for having unsanitary conditions. Mrs. Crenshaw attributes her long life to prayer and drinking two ounces of 100 proof straight bourbon each night before going to bed.

4. A nine-year-old boy has died of brain cancer. His name was Robert Marquardt Simpson. He was known as "Bobby." His condition was diagnosed one year ago. Local newspapers and broadcasting stations held a drive to raise the $75,000 needed for an operation for Bobby. The money was raised, but the operation was not successful. Bobby received thousands of cards and letters from well-wishers. Bobby's idol, football star Rock Czeznievski (chehz-nee-EHV-skee) visited Bobby last week in the hospital and gave him a football autographed by all the members of the Lotus Leopards team of the NFL. Bobby lapsed into a coma two days ago. He died in St. Agnes Hospital at 10:48 this morning. His parents, the Robert J. Simpsons of 12 Leeward Drive, this city, ask that donations be sent to the American Cancer Society. The Simpsons have a younger child, Audrey, age three.

5. The docket of the local court reveals that Martin Harrison Caldicott is suing his estranged wife, Nora Quentin Rossburg Van Melling Caldicott, for alimony. Caldicott, age twenty-seven, says his wife, age fifty-three, can easily afford to help him financially because she inherited almost $10 million from her father, real estate tycoon Sanford (Sandy Acres) Quentin. He says she also received a large divorce settlement from her first husband, financier Hugo Rossburg. Caldicott says he gave up a promising career as an actor to marry Mrs. Caldicott four years ago. He says it will be difficult for him to resume his career. He is asking possession of Mrs. Caldicott's beach home in Malibu, California, and support payments of $1000 per week. Caldicott claims his wife deserted him six months ago and ran off with Lat Dorsey, an instructor at a health spa. Mrs. Caldicott and her attorneys are saying nothing. Dorsey says his relationship with Mrs. Caldicott is strictly business, and that she is planning to finance a chain of health spas for the former Mr. Universe runner-up.

Exercise 3

Do you think you could improve upon any of these leads from the Associated Press Radio Wire? Check those you think *cannot* be improved. Rewrite those you can improve. Be prepared to defend your decisions and revisions in class.

TRUSTEES OF THE SOCIAL SECURITY SYSTEM SAY A RECESSION COULD JEOPARDIZE THE SYSTEM'S ABILITY TO PAY RETIREMENT BENEFITS ON TIME BY 1983.

PRESIDENT REAGAN HAS PICKED NAVY ADMIRAL ROWLAND FREEMAN TO SUCCEED JAY SOLOMON, WHO RESIGNED THIS WEEK AS HEAD OF THE GENERAL SERVICES ADMINISTRATION.

THE CARNEGIE COUNCIL ON POLICY STUDIES IN HIGHER EDUCATION REPORTS CHEATING, THEFT AND OTHER FORMS OF DISHONESTY ARE RISING ON AMERICAN UNIVERSITY AND COLLEGE CAMPUSES.

A CONGRESSIONAL STUDY, RELEASED TODAY, SAYS THE LIFTING OF PRICE CONTROLS ON OIL—CALLED FOR BY PRESIDENT REAGAN—WILL CREATE MORE INFLATION.

THE CHAIRMAN OF THE PRESIDENT'S COUNCIL ON ENVIRONMENTAL QUALITY SAYS ABANDONMENT OF A PIPELINE PROJECT TO CARRY ALASKA OIL FROM CALIFORNIA TO TEXAS WAS NO GREAT LOSS TO THE NATION

SIXTY-FOUR PEOPLE HAVE BEEN ARRESTED AND 45 MORE ARE BEING SOUGHT BY SHERIFF'S DEPUTIES, COMPLETING ONE OF THE LARGEST HEROIN TRAFFICKING INVESTIGATIONS IN ORANGE COUNTY HISTORY.

POLICE SAY A MAN BELIEVED RESPONSIBLE FOR 12 BANK HOLDUPS IN THE BELLFLOWER AREA OF LOS ANGELES HAS BEEN SHOT AND CRITICALLY WOUNDED DURING A BANK ROBBERY.

A RESOLUTION ASKING CONGRESS TO LET STATES SET THEIR OWN SPEED LIMITS WITHOUT LOSS OF FEDERAL FUNDS WAS APPROVED BY A CALIFORNIA SENATE COMMITTEE TODAY.

A 16-MONTH-OLD BABY AND EIGHT OTHER PEOPLE WERE OVERCOME BY TEAR GAS TODAY AFTER A CANNISTER WAS THROWN AT A SEWING FACTORY IN DOWNTOWN LOS ANGELES.

ROD CAREW HAD FOUR HITS, DROVE IN TWO RUNS AND SCORED THREE TIMES TODAY AS CALIFORNIA BOMBED MINNESOTA ELEVEN-TO-SIX AND WON ITS SEVENTH STRAIGHT GAME.

Exercise 4

Rewrite these newspaper leads from the Associated Press as broadcast leads.

LADIERA DO PINHEIRA, Portugal (Reuters)—A forty-eight-year-old mechanic's wife who claims to have visited heaven, hell and purgatory frequently and who says the moon is inhabited is being hailed as a saint by thousands of Portuguese.

Gas-starved motorists who endured long lines and "Closed" signs at service stations in Southern California this past weekend should brace themselves for an even worse fuel crunch in May, auto experts warned Monday.

Actress Claudia Cardinale gave birth to a daughter Sunday in Rome, just a few weeks after she became a grandmother following the birth of her son Patrick's child.

Prince Philip, husband of Britain's Queen Elizabeth, crawled through brush in a driving rain to help save the noisy Australian scrub bird, according to an interview published Monday in the newsletter of the World Wildlife Fund.

QUITO, Ecuador—Ecuador's newest switch to democratic from military rule will be led by center-left President-elect Jaime Roldos (HAI-may ROLL-dohs), a thirty-eight-year-old political newcomer who polled more votes Sunday than any other candidate in the country's history.

WASHINGTON—States may commit a person to a mental hospital against his will by providing "clear and convincing" proof that he is dangerously insane, the Supreme Court ruled Monday.

SAN FRANCISCO (AP)—Defense attorneys for former Supervisor Dan White, accused of killing Mayor George Moscone and Supervisor Harvey Milk will challenge the constitutionality of part of a newly-passed state death penalty law as opening arguments start today.

DENVER (AP)—Saying most hazardous wastes are not disposed of with adequate safeguards, the Environmental Protection Agency announced Monday that it will seek legislation to create a $400 million annual fund to pay for emergency waste cleanups.

WASHINGTON—The raw meat and poultry you buy at the supermarket may be considerably more hazardous to your health than the government has reported, according to a new government study.

WASHINGTON (UPI)—The Fish and Wildlife Service plans to capture four California condors in January, the start of an extensive effort to breed the birds in captivity and save them from extinction, sources said yesterday.

Exercise 5

These are some leads from the United Press International Radio Wire. See if you can improve them by rewriting them.

TENNESSEE OFFICIALS SAY AN AGING, THREE-STORY HOTEL THAT WAS SWEPT BY FLAMES EARLY THIS MORNING HAD BEEN CITED FOR SAFETY VIOLATIONS IN THE LAST TWO MONTHS.

THE GOVERNMENT ROLLED OUT ANOTHER WEAPON TODAY IN ITS FIGHT TO STOP CONGRESS FROM TRYING TO ROLL BACK THE BIG SOCIAL SECURITY TAX INCREASE SET TO TAKE EFFECT NEXT YEAR.

(SACRAMENTO)—GOVERNOR BROWN TODAY APPOINTED BOREN CHERTOKOV, CHIEF COUNSEL TO THE HOUSE ETHICS COMMITTEE, AS THE NEW CHIEF ADMINISTRATOR OF THE STATE AGRICULTURAL LABOR RELATIONS BOARD.

THE RHODESIAN MILITARY COMMAND SAYS 50 BLACK CIVILIANS WERE KILLED SUNDAY NIGHT WHEN SECURITY FORCES SURPRISED GUERRILLAS ADDRESSING A CROWD OF TRIBESMEN AND THE GUERRILLAS FIRED THROUGH THE CROWD TO GET AT THE SECURITY MEN.

(LOS ANGELES)—FOURTEEN PERCENT OF THE MEMBERS OF THE LARGEST FIRE-FIGHTING UNION IN LOS ANGELES HAVE VOTED TO SUPPORT PROPOSITION 13 . . . DESPITE PREDICTIONS THAT PASSAGE OF THE TAX LIMITATION INITIATIVE WOULD RESULT IN MASSIVE LAYOFFS.

(SACRAMENTO)—DESPITE HIS OPPOSITION TO THE JARVIS-GANN PROPERTY TAX INITIATIVE . . . SENATOR ARLEN GREGORIO TODAY PROPOSED LEGISLATION AIMED AT FORTIFYING LOCAL GOVERNMENTS WITH WHATEVER STATE REVENUE IS AVAILABLE IF THE BALLOT MEASURE IS APPROVED BY VOTERS IN JUNE.

(SAN DIEGO)—A POSSIBLE CASE OF LUNG DAMAGE FROM SMOKING PARAQUAT-CONTAMINATED MARIJUANA IS BEING INVESTIGATED BY THE SAN DIEGO COUNTY HEALTH DEPARTMENT.

DANIEL CLIFFORD, JR., OF BOSTON, MASSACHUSETTS, WAS SENTENCED TO FOUR YEARS IN PRISON TODAY FOR ADMITTEDLY SMUGGLING AN ESTIMATED 4-POINT-2 MILLION DOLLARS WORTH OF COCAINE INTO LOS ANGELES.

(LOS ANGELES)—JOSEPH "PEGLEG" MORGAN, REPUTED FOUNDER OF THE MEXICAN MAFIA PRISON GANG, HAS BEEN SENTENCED TO FIVE YEARS IN PRISON FOR VIOLATING FEDERAL FIREARMS POSSESSION LAWS.

THE SANTA CRUZ COUNTY DISTRICT ATTORNEY HAS FILED FORMAL CHARGES IN CONNECTION WITH A BARROOM BRAWL AGAINST BLACK PANTHER LEADER HUEY NEWTON AND HIS BODYGUARD.

Exercise 6

News handouts by various public relations agencies are questionable sources of news. Many newsrooms forbid their use. Almost none are written in proper broadcast style. Here are some actual leads from public relations handouts. If, for some reason, you *were* going to use them, how would you rewrite these?

The Long Beach Water Department and the Long Beach Unified School District have completed a plan to introduce the "Captain Hydro" Water Education Program into every sixth-grade classroom throughout our community, it was announced today by Ida Frances Lowry, President of the Long Beach Board of Water Commissioners.

James C. Hankla, Director of the City of Long Beach's Community Development Department, has been elected Vice-President of the National Council for Urban Economic Development (NCUED) at its November annual meeting held in Washington, D.C.

The largest promotional schedule in the history of the Los Angeles Dodgers, starting on Opening Day—April 14th—was disclosed by Dodger Vice-President Fred Claire.

Supervisor James Hayes said today that after several months of "intensive negotiations" with the U.S. Department of Housing and Urban Development agreement has been reached that will clear the way for the county to rehabilitate 861 abandoned houses for resale to moderate- and low-income families.

Valuable objects impounded by the City Police as evidence, will be auctioned off on December 3 at 9:00 A.M., at 621 Golden Avenue, Long Beach.

Supervisor Kenneth Hahn reports the Board of Supervisors has approved his motion to instruct the Los Angeles County Fire Chief to review several complaints by citizens of the Topanga Canyon community who face the aftermath of that area's tragic fire.

Abandoned railroad lines could be converted for future transportation use, including bikeways, for the benefit of all county citizens, Supervisor Kenneth Hahn believes.

The traditional Annual Student Art Sale at California State University, Long Beach, will offer one-of-a-kind, handcrafted, practical and decorative gifts for sale to the campus and community on Thursday, December 1, from noon to 9 P.M. and on Friday, December 2, from noon to 4 P.M. in the Fine Arts Patio (located between buildings FA2 and FA3).

A variety of innovative energy conservation efforts undertaken by the City of Long Beach are highlighted this month in an article appearing in *Western City* magazine, today disclosed Robert O'Donnell, General Manager of the Long Beach City Gas Department.

SACRAMENTO—State General Fund cash receipts for the first quarter of the Fiscal Year were $2,942,271,701 while government cost expenditures totaled $2,943,315,001 for the same period, State Controller Kenneth Cory reported today.

3

Electronic News Stories

We said in Chapter 2 that you can pattern an entire news story after a telephone call to your Uncle John. We also told you that once you write the lead, the rest of the story will tend to fall into place. The reason is that you must think out the content of the entire story in order to write a good lead. You have to assign priorities to the facts in the story and decide which ones to use and where to place the ones you do use.

"That doesn't sound like a call to Uncle John," you say. Well, think about it for a minute.

TELLING UNCLE JOHN

Writers like to describe broadcast newswriting as "conversational." That description can be misleading. Conversations are wordy, rambling, and studded with redundancies, imprecise statements, and incomplete thoughts. Broadcast news must be tightly written, precise, and easy to understand.

By "conversational," we mean that your story will often follow the logical pattern of a conversation between two people. The introduction of a new item into a conversation usually begins with a phrase like, "Did you hear about . . . ?" and continues from there. Let's take a short newspaper story and see how you might tell it to your Uncle John.

> ST. CLAIR, Michigan (AP)—Two freighters collided in heavy fog early Wednesday on the St. Clair River, ripping open the bows of both vessels, the U.S. Coast Guard reported. No injuries were reported and authorities said neither vessel was in danger of sinking. (*Los Angeles Times*, June 26, 1980)

You might ask why you'd bother to relay such information to Uncle John—and that's a very good question. Unless your station was in the general area of the accident you'd probably want to ask yourself if you wanted to use the story at all. But, to provide an example here, let's assume that Uncle John lives in view of Lake Superior and just loves boat wrecks.

YOU:	Uncle John, did you hear about the boat collision?
JOHN:	Golly! Here in Duluth?
YOU:	No, over in Michigan. On the St. Clair River.
JOHN:	When'd it happen?
YOU:	Yesterday.
JOHN:	Anybody hurt?
YOU:	The Coast Guard says nobody was hurt.
JOHN:	Well, that was lucky. What happened?
YOU:	Two freighters ran into each other in the fog.
JOHN:	Do much damage?
YOU:	Ripped open the bows on both ships, but neither one is in any danger of sinking.
JOHN:	Well, that's a relief. Anything else?
YOU:	No, I just thought you'd like to know.
JOHN:	Well, thanks for calling, you know how I love a good boat wreck.

Okay. It's pretty clear that we can't go on the air with a verbatim copy of that conversation. But the way the conversation developed is the way your story should develop.

Compare the conversation with the newspaper story. We know the newspaper lead won't work in broadcasting. It begins with a number, and it packs too many details into the lead. We want to delay any details that we do use until the end of the lead.

But how did you tell your story to Uncle John? First, you told him there'd been a boat collision, and then you told him where it happened. That's enough for your lead:

There's been a boat collision on Michigan's St. Clair River.

Then you told him no one was hurt:

There were no serious injuries.

Then you gave details:

The two freighters collided in dense fog yesterday. The Coast Guard says neither vessel is in danger of sinking.

That's your story. We've left out some details of lesser importance. We could probably tighten the story a bit more by doing two things. First, because there were no serious injuries, that fact becomes less important. If there had been injuries, that fact would have to come early in the story, but as it stands, that fact could be delayed to the end of the story. Second, because there is no reason to doubt the information that the vessels are not in danger of sinking, it becomes less important to cite the source of that information, so we could delete the reference to the Coast Guard:

> There's been a boat collision on Michigan's St. Clair River. Two freighters collided in dense fog yesterday. Neither is reported to be in danger of sinking and there were no serious injuries.

Another change we might consider here is to put the story into the past tense. We always prefer to use the present tense or, as in this case, the present perfect tense—but this story is at least twenty-four hours old. It is unlikely that we would really use a story this old on the air, but for purposes of studying writing style, we'll pretend here that there was a valid reason for running such an old story. If it had already been reported elsewhere, it would be rather pointless to treat it as a new event. If it had not been widely reported, we might still opt for past tense here because the elapsed time is so great. We might write it this way:

> There was a boat collision yesterday on Michigan's St. Clair River. Two freighters rammed each other in heavy fog. There were no injuries, and neither ship is reported in danger of sinking.

There are those in broadcast writing who would argue that you should never use the word "yesterday" in a lead. We disagree. It is misleading and dishonest to try to pass off a day-old story as today's news. The fact that broadcast news is today's news makes it all the more important that we let the audience know when that is not the case. If you omit that fact, you are misleading your audience. If you delay letting them know, they will be confused or feel annoyed when you do reveal that the story is a day old because they will have assumed it is today's news.

We can cite an actual case. A California television station had sent a reporter to cover the governor's news conference in Sacramento. The reporter's return flight was delayed, and the videotape of the news conference arrived too late to be aired that day. Two other stations in the same market had better luck and got their stories of the news conference on the day it occurred. The following day, the news director at the unlucky station decided to run the videotape of the governor's news conference anyway and instructed the writers to omit any reference to the fact that the news conference had happened a day earlier. We think that decision was, at best, silly. Anyone who had caught the story on a competing station knew it was a day old. At worst, the news director's decision was dishonest. You will undoubtedly meet many sincere broadcast newswriters who think the news director did the right thing—but the authors of this book think otherwise.

To return to our discussion of the conversational element in broadcast newswriting, let us remind you that people in a conversation usually share a common frame of reference that does not exist between the newswriter and the audience. Uncle John might know the territory well enough that we didn't have to tell him that the St. Clair River was in Michigan. But you can't assume your audience will know that. Observe that we did not abandon our desire to keep the story brief in order to make it conversational. We simply used conversation as a framework on which to construct a very tight story. If one has to pick a single word to describe broadcast newswriting, "short" is almost certain to win over "conversational."

There are other characteristics of conversational broadcast newswriting. Each story must be both easy to read aloud and easy to understand. Often you will see a broadcast newsperson reading copy aloud while preparing it. This technique helps the writer to check the reading time for the copy and also make sure that the words are easy to speak and easy to understand. Let's take an example: "Bronkowski suffered a sprained ankle and twisted wrist." Read that sentence aloud. It's not too bad, but the phrase "twisted wrist" could be difficult to read aloud. You can make the statement easier to read by changing it to, "Bronkowski suffered minor injuries to his arm and leg."

Or how about this one: "Kirby said he was in favor of a tax on illegal aliens." Someone in the audience might hear that as, "Kirby said he was in favor of attacks on illegal aliens." You had better change it: "Kirby says illegal aliens should pay a special tax."

DECIDING WHAT TO CUT

But what happened to our decision to keep the story short? Remember what we said in Chapter 1: we try to shorten copy by cutting out words only after we have shortened it by cutting out facts. That is not a license to be wordy, but you should never cut words where they are needed to make a statement easier to understand. Years ago, Paul White, who wrote one of the first important books on broadcast newswriting, stressed the crucial difference: repetition is not bad newswriting, but redundancy is.

The distinction between repetition and redundancy shouldn't be hard to grasp. Repetition is saying something more than once to make sure it is understood. If you listen to people speaking, you will see that repeating words and phrases is, in fact, conversational. That is one reason why repetition is frequently used in broadcast newswriting. An old axiom states that if you want something to be understood by a radio audience, you must say it three times. We don't often go to that extreme in a story, but information is frequently given at least twice. Remember that, both in the psychological sense and in the actual sense, people often tune in to a story late. For that reason, repeated words and phrases are not as annoying to the ear as they are to the eye.

Redundancy is quite another thing. Redundancy is using more words than you need to say something. Although redundancy is conversational, too, we simply can't afford it in broadcast writing. It wastes too much time. Let's look at an example of repetition:

Cooper found a box on the shelf. The box was about the right size, and the box was the right color.

Obviously, we could substitute "it" for "the box" in the second sentence—but we would lose some precision by doing so. "It" could also refer to the shelf. Moreover, if you read the example aloud, you will see that the repetition of the word "box" sounds perfectly natural. A writer for print might search for other words to replace the word "box":

The cardboard container was about the right size. The label was the right color.

Here the new phrases add detail. However, unless that detail is needed, we don't want it added in a broadcast news story. The repetition in the original version is perfectly good broadcast newswriting. But what about this:

Cooper got up at 7 A.M. this morning.

We've already explained that "A.M." and "P.M." are not used at many stations, but even if they were, the "A.M." would be redundant here. To say "at 7 this morning" is sufficient.

Redundancies are always pointless. No one would say, "He threw the round baseball," or "She turned on the electric television." Nevertheless, redundancies do have a way of slipping into the language. News stories are forever noting that someone was "indicted by the grand jury." Since only a grand jury can indict someone, it's a waste of breath to say more than "He was indicted." "It was raining outside" is another silly redundancy. Just say, "It was raining."

BENDING THE RULES

"Conversational" also means that you can sometimes use a bit of slang and bend the formal rules of grammar a little. But don't overuse this privilege. Most rules of grammar exist to make writing more precise. You should never do anything that makes your copy less easy to understand or that makes it subject to ambiguity. Any time that what you have written can be understood in any way other than the one you intend, you have done a poor job of writing and should rewrite the material. Breaking rules of grammar can also simply stamp the writer as ignorant rather than conversational. This will destroy the credibility of your news program. So break the rules of grammar very sparingly, and be sure you know what you are doing whenever you do violate a rule.

Probably the most common way that broadcast newswriters deliberately violate grammatical rules is by using incomplete sentences. Usually these incomplete sentences are little interjections to personalize the delivery of a story.

> There's a new state hog-calling champion. Well . . . almost. Last night. . . .

Incomplete sentences can also serve as transitions from one set of news stories to another.

> . . . next month in Cairo.
> Turning to the local news . . . Salem schools will open. . . .

Incomplete sentences should be used only when they serve a purpose and do not detract from clarity. Usually the incomplete sentence is simply the mark of a careless or inexperienced writer. There is a place in broadcast writing for incomplete sentences, but that does not excuse failure to write complete sentences where they are needed.

Use slang as infrequently as you would violate the rules of grammar. Again, using slang without a definite purpose can stamp the writer as ignorant and the writer's copy as not worth listening to. A particular danger with slang is that it changes rapidly and its usage is usually limited to subgroups in society. You cannot be sure that the slang terms you use will be understood by all your listeners. Radio newswriters, whose audience is more differentiated by station than is that of television newswriters, can afford to be a bit freer with slang. But it is always a risky business. We are aware that many stations now encourage their news departments to use slang to match the "image" of the station. However, we think a little slang goes a long way. Remember that stations change formats faster than designers change hemlines. You may just have succeeded in getting your news script to match the Top-40 argot of your station and then discover the station is switching to a country-and-western format. If you stick mostly to plain, simple English, people will understand you, regardless of their preference in music.

On the other hand, it is to your advantage to learn as much of the various current types of slang as you can. Anything you write that is subject to more than one meaning is bad writing. So you must always be aware of possible double meanings of words. Since contemporary slang dialects tend to give new meanings to old words rather than creating new words, you must be aware of the slang meanings of ordinary words. And they change constantly. At this writing, "hash" and "coke" are not necessarily something to order at a lunch counter, and "When I was young and gay," is no longer a good beginning for a memoir. The words change over time, but the problem remains.

BEING AWARE OF LOCAL INTEREST

A final thought about being conversational and chatting with Uncle John. Remember that you called Uncle John because you knew shipwrecks interested him. You would also call Uncle John if you knew about something that might affect him.

YOU: Uncle John, you'd better make some changes in your vacation plans.

JOHN: What for? You know I drive to Yellowstone Park every summer.

YOU: Well, the park rangers are going to close the park to tourists for a while. There's been a drought there, and they say there's too great a fire danger.

It is always important to let your listeners know of things that may affect them. The story above would affect many people. Something close to home, like the closing of a main street for road work, the shutdown of power in sections of your city at certain hours, the approach of a dangerous storm—these are all events that affect people and must be reported. The more you can write your stories so that they emphasize the effect of the reported event on people in the audience, the more your audience is likely to pay attention. Your conversation with Uncle John would work nicely into a story like this:

If you've been planning a trip to Yellowstone Park this summer, you may be in for a disappointment. Park Service officials have closed the park to tourists. A searing, three-year drought has left the park tinder dry, and officials say the fire hazard is just too great to allow visitors this year.

THE NEWS SCRIPT

Let's take a look at a five-minute radio news script and see what we can learn from it.

The following is a five-minute "World in Brief" as it ran on the radio wire of United Press International.[1] The material is written to be read in approximately two-and-one-half minutes, leaving time in a five-minute news format for the latest stock market reports, local weather, commercials, and opening and closing statements:

120YR

ELEVENTH-WORLD IN BRIEF

—16—

REPORTS OF WIDESPREAD VIOLENCE IN AFRICA. U-P-I HAS THAT STORY . . . AND MORE . . . NEXT.

IN AFRICA TODAY . . . REPORTS OF FIERCE CONFLICT IN THREE NATIONS. . . .

THE RHODESIAN MILITARY COMMAND SAYS 50 BLACK CIVILIANS WERE KILLED SUNDAY NIGHT WHEN SECURITY FORCES SURPRISED GUERRILLAS ADDRESSING A CROWD OF TRIBESMEN AND THE GUERRILLAS FIRED THROUGH THE CROWD TO GET AT THE SECURITY MEN. IT WAS THE WORST CIVILIAN LOSS OF LIFE IN THE FIVE-YEAR-OLD WAR IN RHODESIA.

ETHIOPIA BEGAN A MASSIVE CAMPAIGN TO CRUSH THE 17-YEAR-OLD WAR OF INDEPENDENCE IN THE NORTHERN PROVINCE OF ERITREA. REBEL SPOKESMEN SAY THE ETHIOPIANS THREW MORE THAN 40-THOUSAND MEN AGAINST THEM WITH ARMOR, NAVAL AND AIR SUPPORT AND BROKE THROUGH THEIR FIRST DEFENSE LINE SOUTH OF ASMARA, THE PROVINCIAL CAPITAL.

THE GOVERNMENT OF ZAIRE DROPPED PARATROOPERS NEAR KOLWEZI TODAY TO REINFORCE GROUND TROOPS IN AN ATTEMPT TO RECAPTURE THE KEY MINING CENTER. THE REBELS WHO SEIZED THE CITY ARE REPORTED HOLDING SEVERAL THOUSAND FOREIGNERS WHO LIVE IN KOLWEZI.

—16—

THE ENERGY DEPARTMENT IS SHIFTING 163-MILLION DOLLARS IN ITS BUDGET TO SPEED THE DEVELOPMENT OF COAL CONVERSION TO GAS AND THE RESEARCH ON SOLAR POWER. A SPOKESMAN FOR THE ENERGY DEPARTMENT SAYS THE SHIFTS ARE PART-ONE OF PRESIDENT CARTER'S ENERGY POLICY . . . AND THAT PART-TWO WILL BE ANNOUNCED NEXT WINTER.

—16—

THE GOVERNMENT TOSSED OUT SOME STATISTICS TODAY INDICATING IMPROVEMENTS IN THE ECONOMY. GOVERNMENT REPORTS SHOWED NEW HOUSING STARTS AT A 1978 HIGH . . . A SECOND CONSECUTIVE MONTHLY GAIN IN INDUSTRIAL PRODUCTION . . . AND IMPROVEMENTS IN BUSINESS SALES AND INVENTORIES.

---

[1] Courtesy United Press International.

—16—

AUTHORITIES IN JELLICO, TENNESSEE, SAY THAT AT LEAST 11 PEOPLE WERE KILLED BY AN EARLY MORNING FIRE THAT APPARENTLY STARTED IN THE LOBBY OF A THREE-STORY HOTEL AND QUICKLY RAGED THROUGHOUT THE ANCIENT BUILDNG. SOME RESIDENTS WERE INJURED AS THEY JUMPED FROM WINDOWS.

—16—

TEAMSTERS PRESIDENT FRANK FITZSIMMONS WAS ORDERED TO APPEAR BEFORE A DISCIPLINARY HEARING TODAY TO ANSWER CHARGES THAT HE LED THE UNION INTO CORRUPTION. ISTEAD, FITSIMMONS STAYED AWAY AND SENT ANOTHER UNION OFFICIAL.

—16—

THE GOVERNMENT SAYS THERE WERE WILLFUL AND SERIOUS SAFETY VIOLATIONS AT THE WESTWEGO, LOUISIANA, GRAIN COMPLEX THAT BLEW UP LAST DECEMBER, KILLING 36 PEOPLE. THE OCCUPATIONAL SAFETY AND HEALTH ADMINISTRATION WANTS TO FINE THE CONTINENTAL GRAIN COMPANYS SOME 47-THOUSAND DOLLARS FOR THE ALLEGED VIOLATIONS.

—16—

THE VETERANS ADMINISTRATION HAS TOLD ALL OF ITS MEDICAL FACILITIES TO KEEP CHECK ON VIETNAM VETS FOR POSSIBLE AFTER-EFFECTS OF THE DEFOLIANT "AGENT ORANGE" WIDELY USED DURING THE VIETNAM WAR. SOME RESEARCHERS SUSPECT POSSIBLE LINKS BETWEEN AGENT ORANGE AND CANCER OR BIRTH DEFECTS ALTHOUGH LONG-TERM EFFECTS HAVE NEVER BEEN MEDICALLY PROVEN.

UPI 05—16 101:16 PPD

You can learn a great deal by studying this typical wire-service news script. It should be evident to you why there is a role for a news department at every station. Wire stories cover only national and international events. Regional material is provided periodically during the day, but if you want to have news of your own immediate area, you will probably have to write it yourself—and it is local news that people like to hear. You may be surprised to find a few errors in the wire copy. Don't be. Wire copy has to be produced under continuing deadline pressures. Errors are bound to creep in, and there is rarely much time to polish up and rewrite weak copy. From your standpoint that's good because it means that stations need a good news department to correct the errors and weaknesses of the wire copy.

Note, for example, the two typographical errors in the Teamsters story—"istead" for "instead," and the misspelling of Fitzsimmon's name in the second sentence. These are minor errors, but in another newscast script that moved on the wire just before this one, there was a more serious error. A sentence began: "BUT MANY OF STARTED TO HAVE SECOND THOUGHTS. . . ." Possibly the writer meant "many have," but was care-less in typing and transposed the word "have" into "of." Or perhaps a word or phrase was left out after the "of." Either way, the story must be corrected before it can be used on the air. It's the job of the news department to catch and correct such errors.

The UPI writer has clustered related stories together. This makes it easier for the listener to follow the material. If the listener has mentally tuned in to one story, he may stay tuned in for stories dealing with similar topics. Moreover, less information needs to be supplied in some stories if they follow other stories with the same locale or subject. For example, some listeners might not know where Zaire is. If the story about Zaire were used by itself, we might write the lead, "In the African nation of Zaire. . . ." But because it appears in a group of stories about Africa, we need not supply that extra information.

Observe here that the location of most stories is set out in the first sentence. Exceptions are stories dealing with the federal government, where the locale is presumed to be Washington, D. C., and the Teamsters story in which the locale is not likely to be presumed to be Lotusville, and is not particularly important to the story.

Note how short the stories are. A few lines must cover what might take columns in a newspaper. However, the length of the stories is varied. If all the stories were the same length it would give the program a monotonous pattern. The listeners might not quite perceive why, but they would become bored with the show.

Broadcast sentences, too, are normally very short—but again, there should be a variety of sentence lengths or the stories will have a sing-song quality when they are read. Short sentences sound like commands or warnings. They are excellent for bulletin material, but five minutes of commands and warnings would alienate an audience.

We do not want to overemphasize the importance of varying sentence lengths because inexperienced writers seldom use too many short sentences. On the contrary, the endless use of endless sentences is a problem that usually stamps the work of the novice.

Note how few names are used in the stories. The source given in the first story is "the Rhodesian military command." In the next, it is "rebel spokesmen." In the fourth, it is "a spokesman for the Energy Department." Only two names are used, President Carter and Frank Fitzsimmons. In both cases, the individuals are first identified by reference to their jobs. For most news stories, what people do is more important than what their names are.

The words you use in your broadcast newswriting should be short. Most long words are too hard to say aloud and too hard to understand. English is a rich language. You can almost always find a simpler word than your first choice if you try. Of course, it must be a word that everyone understands. "Swart" is shorter than "swarthy," but more people will understand if you say "swarthy."

Some important rules for script writing are not evident at first glance.

If you look at the copy carefully, you will see that no words have been split between lines with hyphens. This is to make it easier to read the copy aloud. The rule is do not split words between lines and do not split sentences or paragraphs between pages. Each word must end on the line on which it began. Each sentence and paragraph must end on the page on which it began. If you run out of space typing a word, cross out what you have written and begin again on the next line. If you run out of space writing a sentence or a paragraph, cross out as much of the sentence or paragraph as you have written, and begin it again on a fresh page.

News copy is written on regular 8½-by-11-inch paper. Avoid onionskin or other types of paper that rattle. Otherwise, any type of paper that provides easily read copy can be used. Television copy is often written on "books" consisting of several pages, each a different color, with carbon paper between the pages. This makes it easier to keep track of the many copies of the script needed for television news.

SOME THINGS TO WATCH OUT FOR

Anyone who teaches journalism comes to realize that certain problems crop up in student writing much more frequently than others. Moreover, the common errors change from year to year, just as fashions in clothes do. Some errors get imbedded in lists of things to watch out for, and they remain there long after they are needed. For example, the Associated Press style book resolutely warns against using "suicide" as a verb. Probably there was a time when this warning was needed, but neither of the writers of this book has ever encountered a story in which it was said that someone "suicided."[2] We have compiled a little list of errors that we find frequently committed by students today. The next edition of this book will probably have a very different list because "styles" in errors will have changed.

A   The *A* or *an* means "one of several or many." *The* means "the one and only."

And   A conjunction that traps many writers. The usual problem is *syllepsis* or *zeugma*, two grammatical terms meaning that you are trying to make one word serve two different uses—and one of them won't work. Here are two examples from one story: "He considers Ex-president Carter as the leader and senior spokesman

---

[2] We were wrong on this one. While this book was in the final stages of preparation, we encountered an article in a *Los Angeles Times* travel supplement that described a castle in which someone "suicided."

for the Democratic Party. . . . Elton said it would be too early to tell and wasn't sure if Carter even had the desire to run." The first sentence, as written, reads "leader . . . for the Democratic Party." Correct usage requires that the phrase be changed to "leader . . . of the Democratic Party," so that the sentence becomes: "He considers Ex-president Carter as the leader of and senior spokesman for the Democratic Party." The second sentence literally reads, "it . . . wasn't sure if Carter even had the desire to run." It should be rewritten: "Elton said it would be too early to tell and he wasn't sure if Carter even had the desire to run."

As
A word that should often be eliminated because it has too many meanings for precise usage. For example, does the phrase, "as he was leaving," mean *"when* he was leaving" or *"because* he was leaving"? Most readers would assume the first meaning was intended, yet recently students have taken to substituting "as" for "because." The faddish usage of "as to" should also be avoided.

Bazaar/bizarre
These two words differ in both spelling and pronunciation. There is no excuse for writing about a "bazaar murder case."

Chaise longue
Yes, that's the way it's spelled. It means "long chair," which, if you think of it, is a very good description of what the object is. It's pronounced SHEZ LONG. However, the common SHAYS LOWNJ may be permissible at stations not catering to an educated audience, since the word is probably more commonly given that pronunciation than its correct one. "CHAIS LOWNJ" is not acceptable.

Definite/ definitive
Definite means "established and agreed-upon." *Definitive* means "unquestionably the best example."

Dual/duel
Dual means "consisting of two." A *duel* is a formal fight between two persons.

Due to
This phrase can almost always be replaced by something more exact, such as "because of" or "as a result of."

Emanate/ eminent/ immanent/ imminent
Emanate means "to radiate out from a source." *Eminent* means "prominent." *Immanent* means "having as an inherent quality." *Imminent* means "ready to take place."

En route This phrase means "in transit." It is usually followed by "from" or "to." Pronounce it AHN ROOT, not EN ROWT.

Equal to/equal with *Equal to* means "having the same amount." *Equal with* means "standing at the same position." In nearly all cases, "equal to" can be used in place of "equal with."

Germanizing Our term for running separate words together to form one word. Avoid it. It makes words harder to read. Current student favorites include *enroute, incase,* and *alot.*

Guilty Correct usage is "guilty *of,*" not "guilty for."

Mixed metaphors We cite two examples from a very large file of student efforts—"Kent's deep and soothing voice is a feather in his cap" and "A reason for the station's resemblance to a closed funeral parlor is its infrequent use of film reports."

Proliferate The word means "to produce in large quantities with great speed." "Rapid proliferation" or "increasing proliferation" are redundancies.

Prone/supine *Prone* means "face down." *Supine* means "face up."

Rout/route *Rout* (ROWT) can be either a noun or a verb. You can "rout an enemy" or "put an enemy to rout." *Route* should always be pronounced ROOT. It can be used as a noun ("Take route 66.") or, less frequently, as a verb ("They routed the plane by way of Cairo.").

Throughout The word means "everywhere in." It is not a substitute for either *in* or *through.*

Finally, the following are a few examples of poor student writing we have encountered. And just to prove that no one is perfect, we have also included an error committed by a professional journalist.

There was an actuality of Hughes with poor audio quality followed by no reidentification of Hughes.

Putting "with poor audio quality" after "Hughes" makes it sound as if Hughes, not the actuality, had poor audio quality. The "no reidentification" is awkward and a poor placement of the negative. It would be better to end the sentence after "quality" and write a second sentence: "Hughes was not identified again."

This first F.M. station was built in London, England, and was broadcast through a television station; its waves being thicker and more like television than A.M.

Unfortunately, instructors encounter a lot of sentences like this these days. It would take a book to discuss all the errors in that one sentence. Four things stand out. The student has no concept of what a sentence should be. The student has no clear idea of what he is trying to say. The student did not proofread the material after writing it. Finally, the student obviously has a poor grasp of the meanings of the words he is using.

The newscast included eight stories, opening with two stories dealing with crime.

How can you open a newscast with two stories? One of the two stories must have opened the show. And what was opening—the stories or the newscast?

. . . a change of venue for the murderer. . . .

Unless a person has been convicted, he or she is not a "murderer."

. . . his eyes probably jumped ahead on his copy, saying. . . .

It should be *"in* his copy"—and how did his eyes learn to talk?

In comparison with other stations, I feel that KDEG is. . . .

Poor word placement. It sounds as if the writer were a radio station.

The KDEG news staff deserves alot of credit for their choice of news stories.

"Alot" is a word that doesn't seem to be in the dictionary, but it appears in hundreds of student stories and compositions. This sentence also contains another commonly encountered student error. The verb "deserves" makes clear that the student intends to treat the collective noun "staff" as singular. Therefore, the pronoun "their" is wrong. It should be "its choice." This failure to treat collective nouns consistently has to rank as one of the top problems in current student writing.

Bev Carlson did a story on home appliances which had some pretty shakey camera movement.

Another major student problem, the ambiguous pronoun, appears here. Does "which" refer to "story" or "appliances"? In the usual English word order, "which" would be expected to refer to "appliances."

He did not stumble at all over any words.

Poor word order is a problem here. The sentence should have read, "He did not stumble over any words at all." Or, better yet, drop "at all."

The weather report is very complete.

None is as unique as KDEG's News hour.

Both sentences are examples of trying to modify words that are absolutes. Something that is complete cannot be made more complete. Therefore, to describe a thing as "very complete" makes no more sense than to say that thing is "completely complete." *Unique* means "one of a kind." Despite the popular trend of treating this word as if it merely meant "unusual," it is poor writing to say something is "very unique" or "extremely unique." A thing is unique or it isn't.

Carelessness is the basis of most student errors. For example, one student reporter wrote that the residents of a city with a population of 60,000 owed six billion dollars in unpaid parking fines. You don't need a doctorate in mathematics to see that something is wrong with those figures.

Another problem high on the list of student errors is lack of parallelism in sentence structure. If sentences were kept short, as they should be for broadcast writing, this problem would not arise very often. Unfortunately, that is not the case.

This was followed by stories pertaining to a tornado alert, a defeated proposal to decriminalize public drunkenness in Missouri, and federal administrator Frank Zarb's visit to Kansas City concerning natural gas.

Lack of parallelism is one fault of the sentence above. The phrase that begins with "federal administrator" is not parallel to the other phrases. It should be rewritten: "a visit by federal administrator. . . ." Also, "concerning" is a word most students would do better without. Here it only serves to make the sentence more confusing.

There needs to be some improvements. . . .

Lack of agreement between subject and verb is another major problem of student writers. The sentence should read: "There *need* to be. . . ." The usual cause of these errors is letting a clause get between the subject and the verb. For example:

The first portion of these taped reports were clipped off.

The writer lost sight of the subject, which is "portion," not "reports." The verb must be *"was* clipped."

There are some verbal battles no one can win. The only solution is to retreat and regroup—that is, rewrite the sentence.

There are always at least one or two CBS sound bites.

Changing the beginning of this sentence to "there is" won't make it sound any better. Only rephrasing the whole sentence will solve the problem. The sentence is correct as it stands, but it *sounds* odd because the phrase "at least one or two" has been stuck after the verb.

Nonsequiturs are another common student failing:

A student-operated radio station cannot staff around the clock, but more local leads would be an improvement.

Obviously, the second half of the sentence has nothing to do with the first.

And just to prove that all errors do not come from students, here is one from the columns of the *Los Angeles Times:*

Later, he would recall the advice of a close professor and friend. . . .

The writer has let his adjective stray from its proper location. Obviously, the phrase should read "a professor and close friend."

Exercises
╭╮╭╮╭╮╭╮╭╮╭╮

Exercise 1

Go over this newspaper story, correct any errors, and indicate the changes that would be needed to convert it to broadcast style. Then rewrite the story as a thirty-second radio story.

> Municipal Court Judge Mary Lou D'Annunzio is under consideration for appintment to the Superior Court bench, according to Palmer O. Graft, legal affairs secretary for Gov. Fern.
>
> Graft said Miss D'Annuzio, who was named to the Westfield Court judgeship in October, 1981, was "one of several men and women being considered for the post."
>
> If named, Miss D'Annuzio would be the first woman Superior Court judge in Lemon County.

Exercise 2

Below is a story that appeared in the *Los Angeles Times*.[3] The same story on a broadcast news program the same day was covered in twenty seconds. Rewrite this newspaper story as a twenty-second radio news story.

> ROME—Kidnaped former Italian Premier Aldo Moro has been condemned to death by a "people's court," his captors announced Saturday night in a communique distributed in at least four Italian cities.
>
> "The interrogation of the prisoner Aldo Moro has been completed. There is no doubt that Aldo Moro is guilty and he has therefore been sentenced to death," the communique from the Red Brigades said.
>
> There was no indication if the death "sentence" had already been carried out on the 61-year-old president of the Christian Democratic Party who was kidnaped March 16 in a Rome street ambush in which his five bodyguards were killed.
>
> The communique said, "The responsibilities of Aldo Moro are the same as those for which this state is on trial. His guilt is the same as that for which the Christian Democrats and its regime will be finally beaten, liquidated and dis-

---

[3]Louis Flemming, "Moro Sentenced to Death, Red Brigades Kidnapers Say," *Los Angeles Times,* April 16, 1978, I, p. 1. Copyright, 1978, *Los Angeles Times*. Reprinted by permission.

■

persed through the initiative of the fighting Communist forces.

"Trying Aldo Moro was but a stage, a moment in what is the class war for communism."

Government and political party officials went into night conferences after receiving copies of the communique shortly after 8 p.m. (11 a.m. PST).

Comments were sharp, including a statement that will be printed in today's editions of L'Unita, the official Communist Party newspaper, asserting that the communique is "only the cynical comment of an assassin, totally isolated from the civil conscience."

Until receipt of the communique it had been expected that the Red Brigades would seek to exchange Moro for a number of extremists now in prison, including 15 members on trial in Turin.

Saturday's communique was the sixth to be circulated by the Red Brigades, since it kidnaped Moro.

All the communiques had emphasized the importance of placing Moro on trial before a people's court for the alleged antilabor policies of his party.

Besides the communiques, Moro sent two public letters and at least two private letters to his family. His letters urged, with increasing precision, the importance of agreeing to an exchange of prisoners to save his life. The Red Brigades has said it would seek the release of all Communist prisoners but they have not publicly proposed an arrangement for the release of Moro.

Italian political leaders have taken a hard line against negotiations. That position was reaffirmed by Moro's own Christian Democratic Party last week, although party leaders at the same time urged all possible action to secure his release.

As with the earlier communiques, the Saturday message was hidden in urban centers and the news media were told the locations in anonymous telephone calls. Copies were found here and in Milan, Turin and Genoa in northern Italy.

Police have in custody one Red Brigades' activist, wounded last week when he participated in the murder of a guard from the prison where Red Brigades members are being held in Turin.

Nationwide sweeps by police have turned up a number of extremist hideouts and led to some arrests but none directly tied to the Moro kidnaping.

Moro is regarded as one of the most important political leaders of the nation and a leading contender for election as president next December.

Exercise 3

In broadcast writing, you may have to treat the same story differently at different times. In some programs, there may be only time for headline treatment. In others, you may need to pad out a story a bit to fill up the show on a slow news day. This exercise is designed to get you used to such variations.

Figure 1(p. 66) is an actual press release. It is of minimal news value, but for this exercise, let us assume that you work for a Long Beach radio station and have decided to use the story in a newscast. Assume further that the date on the press release is January 24 of the current year and that you are writing for a news program to be aired on the morning of January 28 of the current year.

Write three radio stories based on the press release. Make one of them twenty seconds long, the second, thirty seconds long, and the third, forty seconds long. Remember that these are news stories, not public service announcements.

Exercise 4

Here is a story written by a student about a fire in the San Bernardino National Forest of California.[4] First mark the errors, then rewrite it as a twenty-second radio news story.

> *Firefighters are still battling a 16-hundred acre brush fire in the San Bernadino National Forest. The fire is believed to be started by arsonist and grew rapidly in the dry heat and desert wind. More than 6 hundred firefighters were called in last night to fight the blaze. Greg Sanders of the U-S forest Service believes that the fire may be contained by 6 PM tonight, depending on whether the winds blow burning embers across the narrow firelines. There have been no injuries of threatened structures in the fire, which is about five miles northeast of Banning.*

---

[4]Reprinted by permission of Michael Hinton.

NEWS RELEASE
CITY OF LONG BEACH
OFFICE OF THE CITY MANAGER

FOR IMMEDIATE RELEASE:

DOG LICENSES FEE INCREASED AFTER MARCH 3

LONG BEACH, CA., JANUARY 24, 1985--Starting March 3, a $3.00 late fee will be added to the 1985 dog license fee of $6.00 for unaltered dogs and $2.00 for spayed or neutered dogs, today announced Dorothy Monnier, director of Animal Control, Long Beach.

Under a state law and city ordinance, a dog kept in the city must be vaccinated for rabies at four months of age and licensed annually for the calendar year.

According to Monnier, licenses can be purchased at the Animal Center, 3001 Willow, Monday through Friday, from 8:00 a.m. to 7:00 p.m. A rabies inoculation certificate, valid for the entire licensing year, must be presented. If the inoculation expires before January 1, 1986, a reinoculation of the dog will be needed before issuing a license.

To qualify for a $2.00 license, a spaying or neutering certificate is required.

All mail applications must be accompanied by a valid rabies inoculation certificate and, if applicable, a spaying or neutering certificate. Licenses will be issued without a $3.00 late fee if postmarked prior to midnight, March 2.

Low-cost rabies inoculation clinics are scheduled for February 3, 10, and 24 from 7:00 p.m. to 8:30 p.m. at the City Sanitation Yard, 2801 East Willow Street.

For additional information, please call (213) 595-5449.

RK:GS:JD

Figure 1

4

Rules and Techniques for Writing and Field Reporting

Let's look at some rules for writing radio news. Virtually all of these rules will also be applicable to television newswriting as well, although there are some additional rules you will have to learn for television.

You can divide these rules into three categories, depending upon the purpose each serves. One group of rules is designed to make it easier for the newscaster to read the copy. Another group of rules is designed to make it easier for the audience to understand the copy. The third group simply provides uniformity. The question, "Shall I do it this way or that way?" always arises when either way will work. To save time, people eventually compile sets of rules that simply tell other people the way something is done in that organization. Newspapers and magazines always have "deskbooks" or "style books," which set out how that publication wants things to be written. An obvious need exists for this because style variations stand out in print. You might do a double-take if you read: "Jones will be in Saint Louis next week. While in St. Louis, he. . . ." You would wonder why St. Louis was spelled two ways in the same article. You might also wonder if you saw both "co-operation" and "cooperation" in the same article, or "per cent" and "percent."

Of course, journalists are much more likely to spot these differences than an ordinary reader would be. But obvious errors and inconsistencies will attract a reader's attention and keep her or him from concentrating on the story. Many broadcast news departments have their own style books, and we have provided one in this book. They are needed. Still, we confess that we cannot answer the student who demands to know why each rule exists. Some rules simply provide consistency. To some degree that makes copy easier to read and helps writers to know how to handle certain problems. However, in the final analysis, such rules mainly suggest a uniform way to treat copy. Certainly, other rules for dealing with the same problems would work just as well.

We have not attempted to list the rules according to their purpose.

From the standpoint of learning and using the rules, it is far simpler to categorize rules according to the types of material they deal with. Most of the rules evolved from the way people use broadcast news. The broadcast audience has only one opportunity to absorb each word in a broadcast story. There is no going back to reread, no pausing to think. Nor does broadcast news reach its audience in the quiet of a library or a private office. Rather, it comes to you at breakfast, while you are eating and reading the newspaper. It comes to you in your car, while you fight the freeway traffic. It comes to you in your living room, while you munch peanuts, read a magazine, and chat with friends and family. If the message is to get through, the words must be simple and direct. The following are some rules that will help you to get your message through.

HANDLING NAMES AND TITLES

Give the full title of an individual on the first mention to assure that your audience does not misunderstand the role of the person being talked about. In subsequent mentions, titles can usually be shortened to save time and make the copy easier for the newscaster to read.

> *Secretary of Housing and Urban Affairs Gloria Mundy was in Lotusville last night. Secretary Mundy told a. . . .*

Give the names of organizations the same treatment as titles. An organization is referred to by its full name first and later by a shortened version. For example, write "The National Safety Council" on first mention and use "the Safety Council," or just "the Council," thereafter. Ordinarily, avoid referring to organizations by their initials. For example, the "A-D-A" could mean the Americans for Democratic Action, the American Dental Association, the American Dairy Association, or even the Average Daily Attendance of students at a school.

A few organizations that are well known may be referred to by initials after they have been identified by their full names in the stories. To make your copy easier to read when you use initials, separate the initials with hyphens rather than periods. Write "F-B-I," not "F.B.I." A single exception is "AFL-CIO," since "A-F-L-C-I-O" is too hard to write and probably no easier to read. Acronyms are written as a single word. Write "NATO," not "N.A.T.O" or "N-A-T-O."

> *The French government is reported to be reviewing the French role in NATO.*

> *The AFL-CIO today endorsed. . . .*

The Fletcher School Parent-Teacher Association has criticized the state board of education. P-T-A members voted to. . . .

Omit middle initials in names—except names the public has become accustomed to seeing with middle initials or when the middle initial may help to distinguish someone in a story from others with the same first and last name.

Write: *Mayor John Marsh*

Not: *Mayor John C. Marsh*

But write: *Actor George C. Scott*

Not: *Actor George Scott*

And write: *The money paid by John M. Jones had been credited to the account of John R. Jones.*

Or you might use "William Y. Smith" because there are so many William Smiths.

Don't use the title "Mr." When you first mention a man, use his first and last name. After that, use only the last name. Make it "Gerald Chan" first and, subsequently, "Chan." A great many stations are now using the same rule for women's names. The first mention is "Mary Grabowski," and subsequently, it is "Grabowski." Stations that take a more old-fashioned approach make it "Mary Grabowski" on the first mention and "Ms.," "Mrs.," or "Miss Grabowski" on later mentions. Use "Ms." if you do not know whether the lady is married or if she prefers to be called "Ms."

There is sometimes a problem in using the names of married women. Many married women today, particularly those in the public eye, continue using their maiden names after marriage. On occasion, you may wish to explain this to the audience, if there is something of interest about the husband. Usually, no explanations are necessary.

In traditional usage, married women were not written of except with their husbands' names. You wrote about "Mrs. Roger Gonzales," not "Selma Gonzales." (Movie buffs may remember the curtain line of *A Star Is Born:* "This is Mrs. Norman Main.") Very few stations adhere to this approach today. Of course, if the lady wishes to be referred to in the traditional way, you should oblige her.

Children and young people also present a problem. It sounds silly to refer to a three-year-old child only by his last name. Sometimes the problem can be handled by using the child's first name. Other times, references such as "the younger Gilpin" or similar phrases will do the trick. Here are some examples:

A Westlake youngster has come up with a cure for people who can't sleep. Six-year-old Tommy Henson. . . . But Tommy insists it will work.

A Clovis woman and her teenage daughter have won a 2-million dollar settlement against the Atomic Energy Commission. Mrs. Luz Contreras and her daughter Connie were injured when. . . . Doctors say Connie Contreras may never regain the use of her legs.

A Cornwall father and son have been selected. . . . The younger Wang is a junior at Cornwall High School.

There are two dying usages of the title "Mr." One is for presidents and living, former presidents of the United States. A good many stations still abide by the rule that the president should always be "President Phillips," "the president," or "Mr. Phillips" (or, perhaps at sometime in the future, "Mrs. Phillips"). However, it is clear that an increasing number of stations, perhaps a majority, now would simply say "Phillips" after the first mention of the name. We think that there's still reason to preserve this very small courtesy for our highest elected official. For example, during President Gerald Ford's tenure in office, you could never be sure whether a story was going to be about the government or the auto industry.

The other use of "Mr." is the most confusing of all. In correct usage, a Protestant minister should be called "the Reverend John Kimball" when mentioned the first time in a story and "Mr. Kimball" thereafter. But the rule is rarely followed today. Protestant ministers are now usually called "Reverend Kimball." And other titles are frequently used: "Dr. Kimball," (even for clergy without doctorates), "Pastor Kimball," "Brother Kimball," and so on. Your only safe course is to ask the minister, or someone acquainted with the minister's church, what the proper term is. If you can't get an answer, stick with the formal approach and call the minister "Mr."—or "Mrs." or "Miss," if that's the case.

Our advice regarding the treatment of Protestant clerical titles also applies to the titles of other religious leaders. Christian clergy at the pastoral level can usually be designated "the Reverend Oscar Saintly" on first mention, regardless of religion. The first name and "the" are required. Although common, it is still technically wrong to write "the Reverend Jones," "Reverend Jones," or "Reverend John Jones." After the first mention, you normally refer to Roman Catholic, Eastern Orthodox, and some Protestant Episcopal priests as "Father Jones." (So far, *Mother Jones* remains a title only for a radical magazine.) As we have already mentioned, the correct form for Protestant ministers, after the first mention of the name, is "Mr. Jones" (or "Mrs. Jones"). It is also correct to write "the Reverend Mr. Jones." Long-winded as this form is, some writers prefer it because it reminds the audience that the person referred to is a member of the clergy. If the individual holds some other religious rank, such as monsignor, bishop, or cardinal, you will have to check the correct title. Usually, after the first mention of the person, you may simply use the rank as the title—"Bishop Saintly," "Cardinal Redhat"—but the first mention can be tricky. For example, an Episcopal bishop is "the Right Reverend," but a Roman Catholic bishop is "the Most Reverend."

You must check the usage. There are simply too many religions and religious titles in the United States for anyone to know them all. And some religious leaders can be highly offended if their titles are not correctly used.

"Junior" is now used for both women and men, if a parent and child have the same name. However, it should be used only when it is needed to clarify the identity of a person in a story. If you write a story about someone named Leslie Ogawa and her mother's name is also Leslie Ogawa, there is no need to use "junior" unless the mother is also well known or both women are mentioned in the same story and you need to distinguish them. In formal usage, the "junior" is supposed to be dropped after the "senior" family member dies. However, in newswriting, we usually continue using the "junior" as long as the name of the "senior" person remains well known to the public. For example, we still write about Will Rogers, Jr., even though his famous father has been dead more than forty years.

Many style books recommend that you drop the commas around "junior" for broadcast writing. The theory is that a comma indicates a pause to the newscaster, and no pauses are wanted here. Our opinion is that the commas on either side of "junior" make the copy easier to read, and we do not think many competent newscasters will be led to put in unneeded pauses. Obviously, it is a debatable point, and you will have to conform to the style of the newsroom in which you work. We do agree with other style books that the "junior" or "senior" should be lowercase. This makes it doubly clear to the reader that "junior" is not someone's last name. (You don't think anyone has "Junior" as a last name? Look in the telephone directory. If you live in a fairly large community, you'll find several Juniors.)

SYMBOLS AND ABBREVIATIONS

Limit your use of abbreviations to "Mr.," "Mrs.," and "Dr." (Technically, "Ms." is not an abbreviation.) You can also abbreviate Fort and Saint when they appear in commonly used place names, such as "St. Louis." Write out everything else, for example, "5th Street," not "5th St.," and "Father Kelly," not "Fr. Kelly."

Write out all symbols. Write "2 plus 4," not "2 + 4." Write "10 dollars and 6 cents," not "$10.06." Write "2 minus 5 is minus 3," not "2 − 5 = − 3." Write "number 5," not "#5." And write "10 percent," not "10%."

DEALING WITH NUMBERS

Simplify arithmetic for your listeners. Why write "67 percent" when you could make it "two-thirds" or "two out of three"? Round off numbers. Precise figures will be lost on the audience. No one will remember that the budget was "6-million-275-thousand-827 dollars and 48 cents." Instead, write "more than 6 and one-quarter million dollars," or simply, "more than 6-million dollars." Your audience won't remember that "the study found that 65 out of the 609 people asked. . . ." So tell them: "More than 600 people were surveyed. The study found that about 10 percent of them. . . ."

Never give out telephone numbers unless you are specifically authorized to do so by the person or group whose number you are using, and then do so only if the number is essential to the story. Too many crank calls are received by people whose telephone numbers are broadcast. Giving a telephone number on the air is somewhat pointless, anyway, because the members of the audience are not sitting there poised with pencils in hand to write the number down, and few have total recall. If a telephone number is given, it should be repeated at least three times. And you should allow time for your audience to get pencils and paper by indicating early in the story that the number is to be given, then delaying the actual giving of the number until the end of the story. First, give the number digit by digit—then repeat the digits in logical groupings. Indicate groupings by the use of hyphens:

The number is 5-5-5-1-2-3-4.

That's 5-55-12-34.

Read "0" as "zero," not as "oh." Remember that, in many broadcast markets, there may be several telephone area codes, so be sure you include the area code. On television, always back up the spoken information by showing the number on the screen.

As you can see, a great many precautions have to be taken when telephone numbers are used. They should be used only when there is no question that they are needed.

Approximately the same rules for telephone numbers apply to addresses, but addresses are used a bit more frequently in electronic news. It is usually best to identify the location of a story by a general area or just a street name instead of giving the complete street address. Tell your audience about "the fire at the Sliding Hills residence" or "the fire at the Main Street factory," not "the fire at 27-83 West Main Street."

There are some occasions when a street address must be given, such as when the audience needs to know the location of an event or when an address might help to further identify someone with a very common name. In the case of a person in a story who has a common name, we still would probably limit the address to a street name and not give the house number. For example: "John Jones of East Melon Street." Where a complete address is needed, break the number into logical groupings with hyphens. Instead of "2-7-8-3-2 West Basura Vista," Make it "27-8-32," which the newscaster would read as "twenty-seven eight thirty-two."

Numbered streets provide a particular problem. The rule is to write out whichever of the two numbers—house number or street number—is shorter and use digits for the longer number. For example: "82 Fifth Street," but "Eighty-two 110th Street." And if a word separates the house number from the street number, you may use digits for both numbers: "82 Fifth Street," but "82 South 5th Street."

Remember that addresses and phone numbers should be used only when they are essential to the story. Giving a telephone number or address over the air can leave the person at that address or telephone number open to harassment and abuse from weirdos in the audience. Giving the address of someone who has died or is in the hospital may be an open invitation to burglars to check out that address. In several cases, individuals have filed suit against stations for giving out their telephone numbers without permission. Presumably, almost any use of an address or telephone number in a news program would not be the basis for legal action, but you should be aware of these problems whenever you consider using addresses and telephone numbers in a story.

Finally, in giving out a specific location, you may attract undesirable crowds to a scene. The information you provide could make it more difficult for firemen to put out a fire or police to quell a disturbance. Therefore, it is usually best to give only general locations in situations of this sort.

We have already noted that the ages of individuals are seldom needed in a story. If there is reason to give an age, do not use newspaper style: "Clara Feldman, 38." Instead, write: "38-year-old Clara Feldman." If you want to give a little more emphasis to the age, you can write: "Clara Feldman, who is 38." These two forms are easier for the audience to remember than the terse newspaper style.

We have also noted that times should usually be given in general, rather than precise, terms. It is easier to remember "about 6 this morning" than "at 5:54 this morning." Write a time in a broadcast story as you would write it in any other copy: "about 4 o'clock" or, if the precise time is needed, "at 3:58." As a general rule, the numbers "one" and "eleven" are always written out in broadcast copy to avoid confusion with the letter "l." Follow this rule for approximate times as well ("about eleven this morning"), but simply use digits where you are giving exact time ("11:02" or "8:11"). While we usually read the number "0" as "zero" to avoid mistaking it for the letter "O," customary usage dictates that the number "0" be pronounced as "oh" when it appears in a time. The exact time "12:02" should be read "twelve-oh-two," not "twelve-zero-two."

Treat times over fifty-nine minutes as hours. Although "60 Minutes" is a good name for a television program, "one hour" is better broadcast writing. Make it "one and one-half hours," not "90 minutes."

Dates, too, should be used sparingly. "Last December 9th" can be written as "late last year." If you are writing in April about "next May 6th," you can simply say "next month." Give exact dates only when they are needed in the story. But, if it is important that the audience know the date of a coming event, give the date at least twice in the story, preferably three times, and in television, show the date on the screen as well. Your audience will also find it easier to remember a date if you connect it with its day of the week:

> *April 10th is the last day Lotusville residents can renew their on-street parking permits. That's next Tuesday, and City Clerk Joe San Filipo says. . . .*

Write out dates using "nd," "rd," and "th" to remind the newscaster to read them as ordinal numbers. Write "June 6th," not "June 6." Write out "first" and "eleventh," as in "October first." However, make it "21st" and "31st," not "twenty-first" and "thirty-first."

If the year is included in a date, broadcast newswriters often insert a hyphen before the last two digits because that is the way years are normally read aloud. We usually say "nineteen-eighty-seven," not "nineteen-hundred eighty-seven." So a date is often written as "March 12th, 19-87." Inserting the hyphen is a good idea, although we feel it is a minor point, and no harm is likely to be done if you forget it.

The word "a" is to be avoided where "one" is meant because "a" sounds too much like "eight." Always write "one hundred," not "a hundred." While there is little likelihood of misunderstanding, careful writers usually use "one" instead of "a" in phrases such as "one-half."

Except in the special cases cited above, use digits to write all numbers up to 999 except for one and eleven.[1] Write "one-thousand," "2-thousand," and so on. Where more specific numbers are needed, combine digits and written numbers: "2-thousand-63" or "one-thousand-85." However, for combinations of thousands with hundreds, write the numbers as we usually speak them: "eleven-hundred," "12-hundred," and so on, not "one-thousand one-hundred" and "one-thousand 2-hundred." If this seems a bit confusing at first, just think of the way you say aloud the name of the current year and the way you say the name of the film *2001*. Round, even thousands are written as "thousand." But combinations of

---

[1] Many writers prefer to use digits only up to ninety-nine. There are some good arguments in favor of this practice, but we feel it slows down the writing process too much. In many newsrooms, all numbers up to ten, eleven, or twelve are written out. We see little advantage in this except that it may help students who have already become used to that style in print journalism courses.

thousands and hundreds are written as "hundreds." Continue this practice through "99-hundred." Write everything above that as "thousands."

When you reach the millions and billions, many writers follow the wire-service practice of inserting the capital letter "M" in parentheses before the word "million" and the capital letter "B" in parentheses before the word "billion." This helps the reader to avoid carelessly misreading the word, and it provides a double check against possible typographical errors. Write "one (B) billion" or "6 (M) million."

A word of caution about the words "billion" and "trillion." They do not represent the same amounts in all countries. "One billion" in the United States means 1,000,000,000, but in Great Britain and Germany, it means 1,000,000,000,000, while 1,000,000,000 is called "one thousand million" or "one milliard." The discrepancy continues throughout the numbering system, so that "one trillion" is 1,000,000,000,000 in the United States, but 1,000,000,000,000,000,000 in Great Britain or Germany, and so on. The words "billion" or "trillion" in stories from other countries should act as a warning signal in your mind to check out the figures as carefully as possible for errors.

Write out fractions. Make it "two-tenths," not "2/10," and "4 and six-eighths," not "4 6/8." Remember that such numbers are hard to remember, so avoid them or simplify them whenever you can.

Write decimal fractions as digits, but write "point" for the decimal point. For example: "The market closed at 8-63 point 2-5 today," which would be read aloud, "The market closed at eight sixty-three point two five today." Again, avoid specific numbers whenever possible.

Use digits for sports scores and election returns, and write out the word "to" instead of using a hyphen between two totals or scores. Make it, "The Aardvarks trounced the Clams 10 to 3," not "10-3." However, be aware that this system, too, can sometimes create problems. The word "to" may be mistaken for "two" in some instances. A safer approach is to state sports scores with the names of the teams and elections results with the names of the candidates. For example, because "Aardvarks defeated Clams, 20 to 17" might be misunderstood as "22-17," the copy should be written as follows: "The Aardvarks defeated the Clams. It was 20 runs for the Aardvarks to 17 for the Clams." If you reread the last sentence carefully, you'll see another possibility for misunderstanding. Had we omitted the word "runs," the phrase "20 for the Aardvarks" might be understood as "24 the Aardvarks." Keep in mind that "one" sounds like "won," that "two" sounds like "to" or "too," that "four" sounds like "for" or "fore," and that "eight" sounds like "ate." On occasion, you may have to rewrite copy to prevent confusion. Two other ways you might approach the problem of keeping scores easy to follow are these: "It was Aardvarks 10 . . . Clams 5," or, "The Aardvarks finished with 17, the Clams with 8."

Always write out the first word of a sentence, even though it may be a number that would otherwise be written as a digit. Your copy will be easier to read, and you will prevent possible confusion with decimal fractions. For example, write, "It was 4 o'clock," but, "Four o'clock came too soon."

QUOTING NEWS SOURCES

The best way for a broadcaster to quote someone is to have that person's statement on audiotape, film, or videotape and to play it for the audience. Having the newscaster read the statement only confuses the audience. It is hard to tell when quoted material begins and when it ends. Therefore, you should avoid written quotations whenever possible. Use them only when they are essential to the story. Most quoted material can be paraphrased. For example, this sentence could be confusing when read aloud: "The president said, 'I expect the unemployment rate to rise slightly.'" Simply change it to "The president says he expects the unemployment rate to rise slightly."

Sometimes you must use a quotation. If no tape or film is available, and if the statement and its precise words are important, then you have no choice but to quote. Your job then is to do everything possible to let your audience know exactly when the quotation starts and ends. In television, a brief quotation can sometimes be shown as a visual on the screen. However, usually you must rely upon your writing skills and the reading skills of the newscaster to get the message across. Open the quotation with a phrase such as "in her words," "quoting now," or "the exact words he used were. . . ." It once was common to say "quote" at the beginning of a quotation and "end quote" at the end. This is somewhat awkward and is seldom used today. However, we see no reason not to follow this approach if more subtle approaches do not do the job.

Quoted material should be kept as brief as possible. If a long quotation cannot be avoided, then interject phrases such as "still quoting" or "and still quoting from the document."

ELIMINATING PRONOUNS

Get rid of every pronoun you can in your copy. Remember that repeating a noun is not bad writing for broadcasting and that every pronoun you use is an invitation to ambiguity. Here is a typical example of the difficulty careless use of pronouns can create for an inexperienced writer: "Kowalski gave the gun to Brown. He laughed." Who laughed? Kowalski or Brown?

REPORTING FROM THE FIELD

Not all broadcast writing is "written," in the strictest sense of the word. Since this is a book about writing, we have not devoted much space to other aspects of broadcast journalism. It is not that we think they are unimportant. Rather, we think they are so important that they must be dealt with at greater length than we can provide in this book. It is essential, of course, to know how to work with a microphone and tape recorder. You must have a good sense of the visual aspects of a television story, and, unless you work exclusively in larger markets, you should probably know how to shoot and edit videotape and film for news. You may even have to learn how to process film in some stations. We aren't going to try to cover those subjects here.

There is one aspect of "unwritten" journalism that several readers have urged us to include in this book. That is the reporting of material from the field—either live or recorded for later use. The growing use of live remotes in television and the increasing emphasis on field reporting for radio make these important elements of journalism.

Field Reporting for Radio

The basics of field reporting are similar for radio and television, although the mechanics are vastly different. In radio, a reporter often takes a tape recorder into the field and records interviews and other material. For features, this material will normally be taken back to the studio, *dubbed* (rerecorded) onto reel-to-reel tape, and then edited for use on the air. The finished product is usually rerecorded onto audio carts for ease of cuing on the air. The reporter prepares a script to be read with the cart by the newscaster, or the reporter may provide the narrative on the cart with the edited actuality material.

For news stories of important events that are taking place, the reporter may either report the story from the scene as a remote broadcast or relay the story by telephone to the station, where it is recorded, edited, and rebroadcast later. Such material may be transmitted to the station by a radio link with the reporter's car or van. However, it is usually preferable to transmit such material via telephone because the quality is better and the transmission more reliable. (If it is known in advance that a remote broadcast will be used—as in the case of a sporting event—special telephone lines are installed for the remote to guarantee the best possible sound quality.)

A simple voice report can be transmitted to the station by regular telephone from any reasonably quiet location, and the station should be equipped with amplified phone lines for recording and air purposes. However, if the reporter has recorded an interview or sounds that are part of the story, then the task of transmitting the recording is more complex. Simply holding the telephone mouthpiece to the tape recorder speaker is not very satisfactory. Reporters used to solve this problem with an ingenious—and illegal—device consisting of a plug, some audio wire, and some alligator clips. The mouthpiece of the telephone was unscrewed, the alligator clips were clamped to the terminals in the mouthpiece, and the plug at the other end of the wire was plugged into the output port of the tape recorder. The result was usually a good quality transmission of the recorded sound. But the telephone company never looked kindly on this method and, in recent years, has installed telephones with mouthpieces that cannot be unscrewed. Several alternative devices have appeared—most of which consist of a small speaker that can be attached over the mouthpiece and plugged into the tape recorder—and quality of these acoustic couplers is variable.

Whatever transmission technique is available, the reporter will pick the various segments of sound she or he wishes to use in the story and feed those back to the station, where they are recorded. Then the reporter transmits the narrative for the story and the various segments are edited together into a *package* by another member of the news team back at the station.

"Writing," in this case, consists of preparing the material that goes with the recorded segments of the story. As often as not, this material will simply be prepared in the form of notes, since there is seldom time or appropriate facilities to write a complete script. Because the material read over the telephone is being recorded, it is possible to do another *take* if the lack of a complete script causes problems. A good reporter should be able to deliver enough material for several stories or several versions of the same story, so that different versions can be used on different programs during the day. Stations can rarely afford to have a reporter tied up with just one story.

A reporter's "script" will include both the material fed to the station and instructions on how the reporter would like it to be assembled into a story. It might all go like this:

REPORTER: Charlie? This is Sandra. I got the mayor opening the park. You want to put this on tape for me?

NEWS STAFFER: Okay. Wait one . . . okay. What do you want to feed first?

REPORTER: There's a lot of good background noise—merry-go-round music, kids shouting. I'm going to feed you about 20 seconds worth.

NEWS STAFFER: Okay. Run some of it so I can get a level. . . . That looks good.

REPORTER: Right. I'm recuing it, and I'll roll now for about 20 seconds. . . . (Tape rolls.) Got it?

NEWS STAFFER: Let me check it. . . . Sounds good. What's next?

REPORTER: I'm going to feed my story now. It should run about thirty seconds. You want a level?

NEWS STAFFER: Yeah.

> REPORTER: Lotusville got a new park today. Mayor Irma Phogg was on hand to cut the ribbon and officially open the new forty-acre Kilroy Park. . . .
>
> NEWS STAFFER: Okay. Give me a five count.
>
> REPORTER: Right. Five. . . four. . . three. . . two. . . one. . . . Lotusville got a new park today. Mayor. . . .

After the reporter feeds the story, the news staff member at the station replays part of the feed to make sure it has been recorded correctly. The two then compare their timings of the story to see how long it runs. The reporter may have to confer with the person at the station about making minor cuts in the recorded story to bring it down to a desired time length. The reporter would then give instructions for editing the story. These instructions are usually recorded on the story tape and also written down for security. The instructions might run something like this:

> REPORTER: Open it with about two seconds of natural sound, then fade it under my voice. Take out the sound about ten seconds in, where I say, "Meanwhile, over at the picnic grounds. . . ." Cut in the audio of the mayor after my cue, "was very pleased." Use the cut that begins, "I don't think any city. . . ." and dump it where she says, ". . . in this entire state." It should run fourteen seconds. Then tack on my closer. If it runs more than thirty seconds, see if you can trim a little.

That, briefly, is one way you can "write" a story in the field. Your material would be edited at the station, a lead would be written for the newscaster to read, and the story would be aired while you are still in the field working on another story.

You need to keep track of the material that you have recorded, making notes about sounds and important statements, noting the number on the tape counter at each important place. If possible, you should keep rough timings. Later, exact timings will have to be made for each segment to be used. You must keep track of what is on your tape because it is a waste of time to transmit the entire tape. And you should only transmit the segments you know you will use—or segments you think might later be of use to someone else back at the station. It is important that you edit while you collect sounds and get interviews. Although you should never risk missing something important by recording too little, it is clear that the less you record, the easier your tape will be to work with.

Field Reporting for Television

Television reporters employ techniques somewhat similar to those used by radio reporters. In some cases, the equipment in your station van may be complete enough for you to edit your videotape in the field. More often, however, you will have to transmit material back to the station for editing. Often it is possible to plan out a story well enough in advance so that no editing is needed. For example, you can prepare a stand-up opening statement memorized from notes. Then you can write out in detail the rest of the material you intend to read over the video picture. You can station yourself in a location in which the camera can focus on you for the stand-up and then pan away to whatever it is you are talking about while you continue reading your script into the microphone.

Video pictures may be recorded in the field for later editing or they may be microwaved back to the station if you have the appropriate equipment and are in a suitable location. With this type of set-up, you might do a live insert into a show in progress or you might follow a procedure similar to phoning in a radio story. You might do your stand-up, then move to another location and have the camera shoot while you read your story over the picture. Both sound and picture would be transmitted back to the station where they would be recorded and the parts of your story assembled for later use on the air. Or you might read your stand-up, then continue reading your script on camera. This material would be recorded, but only your voice would be used from the material in which you are seen reading the script on camera. Your voice would be used over other material you send back. You would feed other recorded segments to the station for recording and provide instructions for assembling the story.

As you can see, despite the differences in technology, radio and television require similar techniques. We have not attempted to give a detailed explanation of these techniques, but we hope that this brief overview will give you an idea of how to approach these forms of electronic news "writing."

Exercises

Exercise 1

Reporters don't always have to go looking for news. It often comes to them. Many individuals and organizations depend on free publicity from the news media to further their goals. Most of these individuals and organizations—companies, government agencies, special interest groups, and politicians—employ people to write newsworthy material for direct publication and broadcast.

Congressman William Proxmire of Wisconsin is the U.S. Senate's champion press release user. Congressman Les Aspin, also from Wisconsin, is Senator Proxmire's counterpart in the House of Representatives. Figure 2 is a press release that was issued by the office of Senator Proxmire as a part of his ongoing "Golden Fleece Award" program to point out wasteful governmental spending and keep the name of William Proxmire in the minds of the American public. Write a sixty-second radio story from the release.

Exercise 2

Figure 3 is the initial police report of a major assault. Police report forms vary from city to city, but most include the same information given in this one. (This one is fictional, however.)

Write a short, forty-second, radio news story from the material presented in this report. There are several things to remember while writing this story. First, the investigation is continuing, so you can mention that fact and should avoid coming to definite conclusions. Second, the assault involved a minor and she is the victim of an attempted rape. Either of these conditions usually excludes a victim's name from being mentioned in any news accounts of the crime. Why is this so? You might discuss this policy in class. Is it still justified?

Exercise 3

Cruising the city, looking for the scoop that will make you a media star, you hear the police scanner on your car's dashboard squawking something about a murder in a bar. You check out the bar first, then head for the police station.

At the station, you collect some police paperwork, including the two statements given here (Figures 4 and 5). Write a forty-five-second radio news story from these statements. Remember the accused is considered innocent until proven guilty. (These statements are fictional.)

Exercise 4

Tape record a television newscast and a radio newscast for the same day. Pick a story that was used in both programs and compare the radio and television versions. Write a brief comparison of the two stories along with your explanation of the differences.

OFFICE OF

S E N A T O R   W I L L I A M   P R O X M I R E

WISCONSIN

FOR IMMEDIATE RELEASE

Senator William Proxmire (D-Wis.) announced today that "I am giving my Golden Fleece of the Month Award for a $2 million prototype police patrol car. The car ended up as an earthbound spaceship on wheels. This experimental car would make James Bond green with envy. It should leave the taxpayers purple with rage.

"The 'Fleece' winner for this month is the Law Enforcement Assistance Administration (LEAA), which spent the money to develop this car. Fortunately, this is one space capsule that never got off the ground. Because its load of problems exceeded even its load of gadgets, plans for field testing the model car were halted. But this welcome relief came only after $2 million had been drained from the federal treasury to pay for this ill-conceived project.

"What we have here is an idea which might originally have had some merit. But the car was so loaded down with one gold-plated item after another that ultimately it became a Golden Fleece."

Proxmire makes monthly "Golden Fleece" awards for the biggest, most ridiculous, or most ironic example of wasting federal tax funds.

Proxmire sits on the Senate Appropriations Committee, which oversees LEAA's budget. He also serves as chairman of the Senate Committee on Banking, Housing and Urban Affairs and the Joint Economic Committee's Subcommittee on Priorities and Economy in Government.

"What was the purpose of LEAA's so-called 'Police Patrol Car System Improvement Program'? According to that agency's draft summary final report on the program, the objective was:

incorporating into the police car the expressed requirements of the police community for a number of technical improvements and the evaluation and demonstration of an improved police car to enhance capabilities, utility, safety, economy, and, ultimately, police officer productivity.

"In view of this seemingly noble goal, why does LEAA deserve the 'Fleece' for this month? There are at least three good reasons.

"First, let's look at what LEAA tried to cram into and onto its model car and what this would mean in practical terms, for the police officer trying to use such a vehicle.

"A policeman who was thrust behind the wheel of this 'wonder car' would have a lot on his mind besides crime prevention and law enforcement. In addition to driving the vehicle and thinking about the usual things found on a normal car, he would have to worry about his multiple spark discharge ignition system while grasping his hand-held voice/digital terminal while reading his heads-up display while listening to his audio recorder while looking at his wide-angle periscope rearview mirror.

"If this did not keep our beleaguered patrolman busy enough, he would be further occupied by the need to check out his tire sensor, his brake wear sensor, his catalytic convertor/exhaust temperature sensor, and seven different condition sensors.

(more)

Figure 2

"On top of this, he would have to be concerned about keeping tabs on his carbon monoxide monitor, using his voice/digital transceivers, and operating his microcomputer mass memory, while at the same time keeping a watchful eye on his digital cassette reader and his keyboard.

"Rather than 'too little, too late,' this is an example of 'too much, too soon.' The result of this equipment overkill would be, in effect, a gold-plated police car suitable, perhaps for a potentate or a playboy, but not, in my view, for the average working patrolman in this country.

"Moreover, anyone who believes that a car with all these gadgets would get more miles per gallon and have lower maintenance costs, as the contractor claims, would also have to believe that Tampa Bay won the Super Bowl and the tooth fairy is alive and well in Keokuk.

"Second, LEAA itself, in the draft report referred to earlier, cites a number of shortcomings and problems in its prototype car.

"Third, a critique of this LEAA program by an outside, nonofficial analyst provided further reasons why it was a wasteful and unwise expenditure of federal funds. Two points, in particular, stood out.

"This observer reported, first of all, that the median price of the LEAA-recommended, police-car package would have been $49,078 per automobile, above and beyond the sticker price of the car itself. This amount that local police departments would have had to pay per car was based on an assumption that a city or county would initially invest in twenty prototype cars, choosing what LEAA calls 'sophisticated features' midway between the lowest-priced and highest-priced. Where in the world would local governments get that kind of money, even if these cars were worth every penny?

"And second, this critic of the LEAA model car project charged that working police input was ignored by LEAA in developing the prototype. This charge was supported in a General Accounting Office report on the LEAA. Clearly, this failure on the part of LEAA is indefensible, especially when we stop to realize that the kind and amount of equipment in a police patrol car may mean the difference between life and death for the officers in that vehicle.

"Recently, I was one of two United States senators to vote against reauthorizing LEAA. I wanted to abolish the agency entirely. I still do, as I recently indicated to the president in soliciting his help to bring this about.

"If I am successful in getting rid of LEAA, the taxpayers will not be burdened with paying for projects like this one. In the meantime, I intend to tell the American people about LEAA's wasteful spending practices. And that's why LEAA gets the 'Fleece' for this month."

Figure 2 (continued)

INVESTIGATION REPORT NO.   AA 071 321157

OFFENSE CLASS: att. rape   TIME OF OCCURRENCE: 10:30p   DATE: 10/21/81
                assault
                               TIME CALL RECEIVED: 10:40p

Location of offense: 25 E. Second St.

  Cross street: -----

Complainant: Patricia Kelly   Sex: Female

        Age: 17 DOB 7/3/64   phone: 692-0986

    Address: 25 E. Second St.

    Vehicle: Make/model _____ Body _____ License _____

              Color _____

DESCRIPTION OF INVESTIGATION TO DATE:

   Interviewed victim's boyfriend and victim at Lydia Hall Hospital.
Victim was asleep in her home and awoke to find a man had climbed through
an open window. The man was described only as large and Caucasian. Victim
fought, screamed when man tried to rape her. Man stabbed her repeatedly
and fled through the open window. Victim's screaming woke up her boyfriend,
Richard Rothfritz. He was asleep in another room in the house. When he
arrived in the victim's bedroom, the assailant was already gone. No damage
to house except for blood stains on bedclothes and mattress. Fingerprint
crew will go out there Friday to check for prints. Victim is in critical
condition at hospital, which prevented extensive interview with her. Photos
were taken at the house. Responded to house initially on call from Rothfritz,
who called the department after hearing the victim screaming, then went to
hospital after ambulance had taken victim there.

By: Badge No.   103   Date: 10/21/81

Typed name: Sam Chase, Officer, CID

Signature: *Sam Chase*

File:

Figure 3

STATEMENT

My name is Charles Rogers. I am a white male, born Oct. 18, 1936. I live at 1414 Evelyn Drive, and I work as a truck driver for Mrs. Bartlett's Bread Co. I am giving this statement voluntarily.

Wednesday night, me and a bunch of other guys were drinking beer at the Dew Drop Inn on Telephone Street. I guess I got there about 6 o'clock. I had been putting quarters in the jukebox most of the night. None of the other guys wanted to put money in to play the records. One of the guys at the table, Jake Cobb, I think his name was, had been mouthing off for a little while about how he didn't like the songs I had been playing. I had been playing a bunch of Loretta Lynn and Tammy Wynette songs and he said he was tired of hearing a bunch of women sing.

Well, the jukebox quit playing so I got up to go put some more money in it and Cobb walked over to the jukebox with me and said why didn't I play some Charley Pride or something like that. I told him it was my money and I would play what I damn well pleased. He reached for one of the buttons on the machine and I grabbed his arm and I guess we rassled around a little bit. The bartender, Sam, came over and broke it up and told Jake to leave.

I been drinking at the Dew Drop Inn for a couple of years I guess. This other guy's only been coming in there for about three or four days, but he's got into a couple of arguments before. He pulled a pistol on my friend, Roy Arbuckle, last night after they had been drinking for a while. Well, anyway, after a couple of hours this Jake fellow came busting through the front door hollering something about that guy that don't know nothing about music. He started coming toward my table and he stuck his hand in his pocket like he was going for his gun, so I pulled my pistol and cut loose. I think I shot at him two or three times. I must have hit him because he kind of reeled out the front door and fell in the parking lot. I gave my pistol to Sam and waited in the bar until the police came.

I can read and write the English language and I have read the above statement and it is true and correct to the best of my knowledge.

Charles Rogers

CHARLES ROGERS

WITNESS: *Fernando Gonzalez*

WITNESS: *Jack Livingston*

Figure 4

STATEMENT

My name is Sam McManus. I am a white male, age 52. I live at 777 Ocawa
Circle. I am the night bartender at the Dew Drop Inn, 2082 Telephone.

Wednesday night, I was working in the bar. Several customers had been
at a corner table since about 6 p.m. The customers included Chuck Rogers,
one of my regulars, and a guy by the name of Cobb, who has only been in
here a few times.

Chuck had been playing the jukebox most of the evening, or giving me money
and telling me what songs to play. He was playing mostly songs by Loretta
Lynn and Tammy Wynette.

About 8 p.m., Chuck and Cobb got up and went over to the jukebox. They
started scuffling and arguing about something and I went over and broke
up the fight. I told Cobb to get out until he could behave himself. He
had caused regulars some trouble a couple of times before. He pulled a
gun on a guy in here last night. At least that's what some of the regulars
said. I was in the back when it happened.

About 9:15, maybe a little later, Cobb came back in. He just blew through
the front door, acting real drunk and hollering at Chuck. So then he
started heading for Chuck's table and reached into his pocket and that's
when Chuck pulled a pistol and shot at him about four times.

The other guy, Cobb, staggered out the front door. Chuck gave me the
pistol and I called the police. I guess I had served five or six beers
to each of the guys.

I can read and write the English language and I have read this statement
and it is true and correct to the best of my knowledge. I have given this
statement voluntarily.

SAM MCMANUS

WITNESS:

WITNESS:

Figure 5

5

Special Considerations for Television News

All of the rules discussed so far apply to both radio and television. Now let's examine some rules that apply only to television.

SIX RULES JUST FOR TELEVISION

1. Write Many Words for the Newscaster and Few for the Videotape

The television newscaster dominates the picture when the camera is trained on her or him. The newscaster speaks with authority, and the audience listens. Segments with the newscaster on camera help to maintain rapport between the newscaster and the audience. They also provide a place for various types of stories for which there is no videotape or film: late-breaking stories, nonlocal stories for which there is no syndicated videotape, stories too short to be worth videotaping, stories with unsatisfactory videotape, stories with no particular visual aspect, and stories that the news department simply failed to get on videotape or film. (No one's perfect.)

On-camera stories usually allow the writer the greatest flexibility in writing, and these stories can generally be made more concise than stories accompanied by film or videotape. They are the easiest type of television news story to write because nothing has to be synchronized with visuals on videotape or film. You can write this kind of story much as if it were a radio news story.

In contrast, you must keep your writing to the minimum when you are working on a story that is to be read while the audience is viewing film or videotape. The newscaster no longer dominates the scene. The picture rules now. Words must be chosen and arranged to work with the pictures. The viewers don't need much spoken material because they can absorb much of the story by seeing it.

2. View the Videotape before You Write the Story

There are occasions when deadlines give a writer no choice except to write a story and hope the film or videotape that comes in later will have the pictures the writer has talked about. This approach is risky at best. The visual material may not fit with what has been written—or, worse, there may be something in the visual material that the writer has not included in the script. That means the visuals must be edited or the audience must guess what is being shown.

There are three ways for a writer to work with visuals. One, the script is prepared first, then the visuals are edited to match the script. Two, the film or videotape is edited first and the writer is provided with a *spot sheet,* which lists the shots in a story, the order in which they appear, and their running time. Three, the writer prepares a generalized spot sheet for the film editor. Which of these ways will be used most often depends upon the traditions that have grown up at a particular station. All three systems work.

Preparing the script first. At some stations, the writer prepares the script first, then the film or videotape editor edits the visuals to match the script. Many stations carry this process a step further and have the writer sit down with the editor and select the shots to be used.

Let's look at an example of this sort of story, which was written by reporter Wayne Satz of KABC-TV, the ABC-owned television station in Los Angeles. It was the lead story on the 5 o'clock segment of Channel 7 Eyewitness News, March 15, 1977.[1]

Satz had been covering the story for several months. It involved a long-standing feud between the Los Angeles County Board of Supervisors and the County Assessor, Philip Watson. The supervisors had hired a special investigator, Carmine Bellino, to make a study of Watson's assessment practices. On the day of this story, Bellino made his report to the supervisors.

The story presented a number of problems. To obtain permission to shoot in the supervisors' council chamber, the camera crew had to accept restrictions upon the use of lights and the placement of cameras. These restrictions limited the types of film shots available for the story. Watson himself was in the hospital with a serious heart condition and could not be interviewed. Deputies in Watson's office were unwilling to be interviewed on so delicate a subject while Watson was not there. The story itself was somewhat complex to explain to the audience. Here is the way Satz handled it:

---

[1] Photos and story © Copyright American Broadcasting Companies, Inc. 1977. Reprinted by permission.

JOHN HAMBRICK (ON CAMERA)

Good evening. I'm John Hambrick with Chuck Henry. Here's what's happening at 5 o'clock. The results of a 4-month study of the Los Angeles County Assessor's Office were given to the Board of Supervisors today. Investigator Carmine Bellino and his staff spent about one-hundred-thousand dollars examining the assessment practices of Philip Watson. Well, today they told the supervisors what they thought about how the office functions.
Wayne Satz was there, and he is here now to fill us in on that report.

WAYNE SATZ (ON CAMERA)

John, Bellino's study more-or-less said the supervisors were right. Yes, said Bellino, the county assessor went after homeowners a lot more vigorously than owners of commercial property—probably because Assessor Watson found that easier to do. And, yes, Bellino said Watson had interfered with the assessment process in certain questionable ways. No reaction from Watson to any of this just yet.

SATZ (SOVT/VO/Nat. Sound Under)

Bellino told the supervisors he'd confirmed that Watson's office intentionally emphasized homes over buildings.

BELLINO (SOVT)

Carmine Bellino
Special Investigator

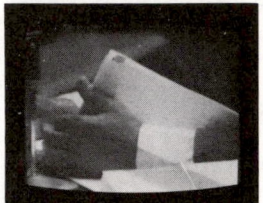

And another comparison of 120 commercial-industrial properties with the adjoining residential properties over the period from '71 to '76, showed a decrease in commercial-industrial assessments of one-point-5 percent while residential increased 40 percent. One of the reasons, of course, it's more difficult to appraise commercial-industrial. It takes . . . you need more experienced personnel.

SATZ (Voice Over)

Bellino also confirmed that some building owners who'd given money to Watson's campaigns were enjoying underassessments . . . and so are some who didn't.

Bellino said the Forum in Inglewood was underassessed by almost one million dollars last year. And there were new charges against Watson—that he cancelled an audit

of a friend, that his office deceived the State Equalization Board, that he stepped in . . . against the advice of the county's lawyer . . . to reduce the valuation of certain water companies by some 10 (M) million dollars. What the staff has learned, Bellino said, is that assessments can be manipulated because the assessor doesn't gather all the information he should.

BELLINO (SOVT)

So it's very important that the documentation be complete in these files because that's one way the assessor can manipulate the decision of the appraiser, and it can be an avenue that leads to underassessments.

SATZ (ON CAMERA)

Now Mr. Watson, who's still hospitalized because of his heart condition, knows that supervisors—as well as news reporters—will be interested in his response when he's ready to respond. Neither the supervisors nor Bellino is prepared to say Watson's done anything criminal here. They just generally agree that Bellino ought to keep on lookin' at the tax assessor's office.

John. . . .

| JOHN HAMBRICK (ON CAMERA) | Assessor Watson is having more trouble with the county supervisors. (Hambrick continues with a second story about Watson.) |

(The material you have just read is a transcript of the story so you can follow its verbal logic. The actual script would look different. Bellino's words, for example, would not appear in the actual script.) The story begins with a rather long on-camera introduction. First the station anchorman gives a brief history of the controversy. This is necessary because no good newsperson should assume that the audience knows the background and details of any story, however much publicity the story may have had. In this case, it was important for Satz to explain the story carefully because it had been building for many months, and probably was not one about which the public was well informed.

After the anchor's introduction, Satz spent more time on camera stressing the key element of the story—the investigation had found irregularities in the assessment practices of Watson's office. The usual rule in writing is to get to the film or videotape as soon as possible, but the complexity of this story, combined with a lack of good visuals, made the long, on-camera introduction preferable.

The film portion of the story begins with Satz reading his copy over the film. The pictures were relatively unimportant to the story; therefore it made sense to write the story first and then have the film editor match the visuals to the copy. The first job was to select the film sections with sound on them that Satz wanted to use in the story. Of the many minutes of Bellino's testimony that the camera crew had recorded, Satz picked three segments that summed up Bellino's main points. The first emphasized that residential property assessments had been raised sharply over a five-year period while assessments on nearby industrial property had been reduced slightly. The second pointed out that it is more difficult to assess industrial property than it is to assess residential property. Because these two statements were closely related, Satz chose to link them together in one single audio segment. The third segment emphasized that inadequate collection of data made it easy for the assessor to manipulate the assessed value of property.

A writer must work closely with the film editor to avoid problems when selecting sound-on-film segments. One common difficulty is "lip flap": a second of lip movement without sound at the start of some sound-on-film cuts. It occurs because the sound track is twenty-eight frames ahead of the picture with which it corresponds.

A camera crew had obtained pictures of one of the allegedly underassessed buildings to illustrate the story. However, the lacking element was Watson himself, or someone to speak for him. The best shots the camera crew could come up with were of the door to Watson's offices and a portrait of Watson. This was weak visual material for the story, but it was all that was available.

Satz and the film editor decided to "double chain" the story. This meant that the material with Bellino's voice on it would go on one reel of film (the *A reel* or *A roll*), and the material showing the door and Watson's portrait would go on a second reel (the *B reel* or *B roll*) that would be cut electronically into the story at an appropriate point. Actually, some of the natural sound from the A roll would be played *under* even when Satz was speaking. This effect would make the film seem more realistic.

Knowing the material he had to work with, including the content and running times of the sound-on-film cuts, Satz was now able to write his script, emphasizing the key elements of the story and using the audio cuts and B Roll to add impact to the most important points. Note that the copy written to be read on camera is lengthy, but the copy read over film is brief, allowing the pictures and sound to carry most of the story. However, Satz used his own words to summarize points that would have taken too long to cover or that might have been difficult for the audience to follow if he had used the actual audio.

Satz got quickly into the first sound-on-film cut of Bellino, using a brief six seconds of voice over film. This method is good practice. Sound-on-film material usually is more interesting than voice-over material.

Notice, in the picture, the shot of Bellino's hands is a *cutaway* inserted by the film editor to avoid a *jump cut* between the first and second audio cuts used. (The term is explained later, for now just keep in mind that combining two sound-on-film or sound-on-videotape cuts showing the same speaker may create a jump cut.)

After another brief section of voice over, the picture dissolves to the B Roll pictures, which show the underassessed building and the portrait of Watson. The picture then dissolves back to the supervisors' chambers for the last sound-on-film cut, which ends the filmed portion of the story. Satz then concludes the story on camera. Satz, who holds a law degree, is very careful to point out that no accusations have been made claiming that Watson has done anything criminal. (Technically, since all the material reported came from the public hearing of a governmental body, the reporter should be protected from libel actions by the defense of *privilege*, but caution is always in order. In any case, fairness and good reporting would call for reporting that no criminal acts had been alleged.) The anchorman then leads into another story about Watson, following the logical procedure of linking stories with related subject matter.

The advantages of writing a script and then allowing the film or videotape editor to match visuals to the script are that it allows the reporter more time for writing and reporting, and it allows the film or videotape editor to assemble the visuals—the job she or he is the best trained to do.

If the writer has used correct line lengths in writing the script, the film or videotape editor should be able to estimate fairly closely the reading time of each section of the story. A film editor usually has markings on her or his editing bench that indicate how many seconds a given length of film runs. The film can be measured like yard goods—four seconds for this part of the story, twelve for that part. Using this technique, the film editor can assemble film for a story very quickly. Or, the reporter may record her or his story on magnetic film and the film editor, using any of several devices available for synchronizing sound tracks to film, can match precisely the pictures to the reporter's words. If this technique is used, the sound and pictures must later be combined by recording the sound track onto a *magnetic stripe* on the film, or the film and sound track must be run in synchronization on an interlock projector, a projector designed for running separate picture and sound tracks in synchronization.

With videotape, most editing consoles can be set to indicate the running time of a specific segment. Segments can be selected to match times estimated by counting the lines in the script. Or the reporter can prerecord the narration on videotape and videopictures can be edited into the videotape to synchronize with the voice track.

Preparing the pictures first.   At other stations, the film or videotape is edited first. The writer is then provided with a spot sheet that lists the shots in the story in the order in which they appear and specifies the running time of each shot. Frequently, when this method is used, the writer first participates with the editor in selecting and assembling the shots.

In some cases, the words must be written to match the pictures. Most stations subscribe to at least one syndication service that provides stories to the station via coaxial cable or satellite. These stories are videotaped by the station, usually in the afternoon, for use on later news programs. Information about the stories is transmitted to the station via teletype, usually complete with a transcript of the narrative spoken by the reporter. However, some stories contain only pictures, and it is up to the news department to write copy to match the pictures, using the teletype material and other news sources as the basis. On other occasions, the producer of the local news may feel that the job done by the reporter on the syndicated story was inadequate or, often, new events have occurred in the story since the syndicated material was transmitted. In such cases, the producer may decide to replace the narrative written by the original reporter with new material written by the local news department. Since the pictures have already been edited, it is rarely practical to re-edit them for local use (although stories are sometimes shortened). Here is a script that was written at KABC, Los Angeles, for a story from the ABC syndication service.[2]

---

[2]Photos and story © Copyright American Broadcasting Companies, Inc. 1977. Reprinted by permission.

This is what a shot list of the videotape would look like. (A number of abbreviations are used. You will become familiar with them later. SOVT means sound on videotape. CU means close-up. OC means out cue. LS means long shot, and MS means medium shot.)[3]

SPOT SHEET

:00–:04	Wide shot of hearing, officials at table.
:05–:08	Shots of audience.
:09–:24	SOVT CU of man speaking. Says no competition among big oil companies. OC: ". . . the energy field."
:25–:29	Wide shot of officials at table.
:30–:33	LS back of bearded young man addressing officials.
:34–:47	SOVT MS bearded young man speaking. Says that energy is being wasted at hearing by having curtains drawn and lights on at hearing. OC: " . . . all these lights."

Here is a transcript of the completed story.

JOHN HAMBRICK (ON CAMERA)

The Federal Energy Administration has begun a round of hearings to get the views of John Q. Public on solving energy problems. One of those meetings was held in New York today.

JOHN HAMBRICK (SI VT/VO)

Those at the New York meeting sounded familiar themes—hopes for solar energy, fears about nuclear energy, above all,

---

[3] Spot sheets may be prepared in two ways. Usually, if the film or videotape is unedited, the running time of each individual shot is listed. Sometimes this system is also used for edited stories. For example, if the first shot of a story runs five seconds and the second shot runs four, the spot sheet might look like this:

:05   shot one
:04   shot two

However, for edited stories, the cumulative running time of the shots is usually used, and at some stations this system is also used for unedited material. For example:

:00–:05   shot one
:06–:09   shot two

Special Considerations for Television News

though, suspicion regarding the oil companies.

UNIDENTIFIED SPEAKER (SOVT)

I'd like to see a breakup of the oil companies where they don't completely dominate the energy field and that they own the oil companies, integrated . . . there is no distribution of oil other than theirs . . . where they own the coal mines, and where they own the production of nuclear energy. There is no competition in the energy field.

JOHN HAMBRICK (SI VT/VO)

One young man just looked around him and found something valid to complain about.

UNIDENTIFIED YOUNG MAN (SOVT)

And I can't see why this room here, all these curtains are closed, all these curtains are closed. On a sunny day we have all these lights on—at an energy hearing, mind you. All right? I mean, it starts. You know, this is . . .

this is stuff like this. You open those curtains, you'll have sunlight. You won't need all these lights.

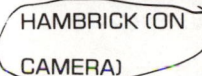

HAMBRICK (ON CAMERA)   (reacts)

The story is brief (forty-seven seconds). The writer has only two brief sections for which to write voice-over-videotape; the first is eight seconds long, the second is nine seconds long. Both sections are needed to prepare the viewer for the two sound-on-videotape segments that follow. The background of the story has to be told in the short, on-camera introduction. Because the story took place in New York, but is being shown to a Los Angeles audience, the writer is careful to give the location of the story three times in the opening of the story. New York is mentioned just before the videotape begins, and is mentioned again in the first sentence read over the videotape, while the words *New York City* are shown over the videotape through the use of a character generator.

The writer does an economical job of summing up the hearings in a single phrase, "familiar themes—hopes for solar energy, fears about nuclear energy, above all, though, suspicion regarding the oil companies."

This leads directly into the attack on the oil companies by the first speaker. The second voice over serves only to set the audience up for the comments on the second sound-on-videotape segment.

Note, incidentally, how confused and nearly incoherent the material in the sound-on-videotape segment is. It is typical of everyday speech—full of repetitions, incomplete thoughts, and grammatical errors. When heard, it makes more sense than when written down and read. Nevertheless, it should remind you of our warning not to take the concept of "conversational writing" too literally. (Incidentally, the reason the drapes were drawn and artificial light used at the hearing may have been to accommodate the television news cameras. Mixtures of daylight and artificial light can cause problems of color balance.)

This story was a simple one, presenting relatively few problems. All that the writer had to do was make sure that the copy written to be read over the videotape took the necessary reading time. Usually the writer tries to write the copy a second or two short. It is obviously better to have the copy a bit too short than to have it run too long. If it is too long, the newscaster will not complete reading it before the sound-on-videotape segment begins. However, waiting for the sound to begin can also be disturbing, so reading time for copy should be only slightly shorter than the time of the silent videotape. Again, if you have your margins set correctly on your typewriter, you should have a good estimate of your reading time from your line count.

If you find that you cannot cover adequately the material for a story in the time provided by silent videotape in a story, you can always move some of the key elements to the introduction. You also have the option of putting some material in a *tag* to be read on camera after the vidotape portion of the story.

Generally, writing copy for pre-edited videotape or film is relatively simple. However, it can limit the writer's freedom in the construction of the story. Keep in mind that some of the time before any sound-on-videotape or sound-on-film segment must be spent preparing the audience for what they are about to see and hear; names and locations need to be specified and topics have to be explained. Usually, the more sound-on-videotape or sound-on-film segments there are in such a story, the tougher the writer's role becomes. However, even a story with no sound-on-videotape or sound-on-film segments can be tricky. Remember, the copy must match the pictures. You must not confuse the audience by talking about one thing while they are watching something else on the screen. That does not mean that every word has to match every picture, but the less difference there is between pictures and sound, the easier it will be for the audience to follow.

Preparing the generalized spot sheet first. In some cases, the writer will prepare a generalized spot sheet for the film editor, not specifying each shot to be used, but listing the types of shots wanted at various points in the story and the running times for the various segments of the story. The editor then prepares the videotape or film while the writer writes the script.

Whichever of the three methods is used for preparing a story, the writer will normally pick out special audio sections, such as statements from speeches or interviews, before anything else is done. These audio sections are carefully timed, and the rest of the story is constructed around them.

As you can see, whichever method is used, it is essential that the writer see the film or videotape first.

3. Let the Picture Tell the Story

It is pointless to try to write words to compete with good pictures. Within limits, you can even leave segments of videotape or film stories with no narration. However, there is some danger in having no narrative if there is absolutely no sound on the videotape or film as well. (The audience will begin to wonder if something has gone wrong at the station or with the television set.) Use your narrative to provide additional information that is not provided by the picture or use a narrative to clarify something that may not be obvious in the picture. Also, as we mentioned earlier, certain types of information need to be repeated so the audience will be sure to grasp the story. Here you can reinforce the picture with words.

Let's take a couple of examples. Suppose your story includes a segment showing Governor Fern roller-skating. It is not enough to write simply: "Here's Governor Fern roller-skating." It would be better to provide extra information: "One of the governor's favorite hobbies is roller-skating." And, of course, it would be even better if you had a videotape of the governor saying, "Roller-skating is my favorite hobby." You should be especially careful to specify what's on the screen if it is something hard for the audience to figure out. Suppose the governor's hobby was tying dry flies for trout fishing. You might have some very good close-ups of the fly-tying on videotape or film, but the audience still might be puzzled by the image. You would have to explain your visuals with narrative. It is also good practice to use words to back up pictures that establish the locale of a story. You might have an opening shot in a story showing a building with an easy-to-read-sign that says "City Hall." And you might back up that sign with words to make sure the locale is clear to your audience: "At City Hall this morning . . . ."

Essentially, then, this rule is simply an extension of our earlier rule about redundancy versus repetition. The matter here is not one of remembering to repeat in words what is seen on the screen, but of determining whether that repetition is necessary or redundant.

4. Make Use of Natural Sound

You can avoid the problem of too much silent footage and make your story more interesting at the same time by leaving natural sound on the film or videotape whenever it does not interfere with the narration or other important sounds.

5. Throw a Few Words Away

You face the same problem with television news that you face with radio news. The audience is not "tuned in" all the time. You have to be just as cautious about putting important material in the lead here as you would be in radio. Moreover, you don't want any very important pictures on the screen during the first or second shot.

Television news writing may have to be either "tight" or "loose," and sometimes it must be both in the same story. The reason is that you must accommodate the pictures. Sometimes there isn't enough visual material to cover all that you need to say about a subject. Other times, you may have trouble coming up with enough written material to cover the pictures on the screen. As we noted, you do not have to keep the newscaster talking every second. However, you can frequently use the time needed for the audience to view specific pictures to add interesting material that would not normally be provided in a broadcast story. A typical example of this is when you identify people on the screen. It takes about one second to say, "This is Senator Maize." But the audience should have three or four seconds at the least to look at the senator's picture and get used to what he looks like. A one-second shot would be ridiculous. So, you write four seconds of copy to go with the senator's picture: "Iowa's Senator Milo Maize, who is vacationing in Lotusville, was a guest at the one-hundred-dollar-a-plate dinner."

In short, every word of your copy doesn't have to be vital to the story—but there should be a reason for every word you use.

6. Let Your Copy Follow Visual Logic

The most important difference between radio and television writing is that the television writer must understand visual logic. Your words may look all right on paper and sound all right when you read them aloud, but there is no guarantee that they will work with the pictures. The arrangement of the words in your story will be dictated by the visual logic of the film or videotape.

Let's take an obvious example. Action within a sequence of film or videotape shots should seem to occur normally. *Cuts* from one shot to the next should, when possible, "match action." That means that if the person seen on the videotape is raising her or his right arm at the end of the first shot, that action should seem to continue uninterrupted in the second shot. The right arm should not be shown descending at the start of the second shot.

That, you may say smugly, is the tape editor's problem. Well, it is and it isn't. The editor has only so much freedom with the pictures if they are to match up reasonably with your copy. You may have arranged your story so the tape editor has no choice but to use a *jump cut,* that is a cut in which there is a noticeable and disturbing lack of continuity with the preceding shot. This situation occurs commonly when the writer has selected several segments of a speech or interview to be edited together. Since the shots were taken at different times, the action is not continuous, and frequently it is noticeably discontinuous. There are ways of dealing with this, but the writer must be aware of the problem.

We noted earlier that, as a writer for television, you must allow time for things to be seen on the screen. It would be acceptable in a radio script to write, "Guests at the dinner included Hollywood stars Tab Key, Brick Wall, and Sunday Brunch"—but that won't work for television. A "three-shot" (one shot showing three people) on a television screen makes the people in the shot too small for easy identification. You need a close-up for each person, and you need about four seconds of each close-up. So instead of the two seconds it might take to mention the three stars, you must write twelve seconds of copy—four seconds for each face so the people in your story can be identified in their close-ups.

You face the same problem if you list a series of locations visited by somebody. This line would present problems for visual presentation: "On the campaign trail, Governor Larry Fern visited Mumford, Frisbee, and Salty Gulch today." If we want to see the governor at each location, additional time must be provided in the script.

Another point of visual logic is that times and locations should change in understandable sequence. It may make sense in a radio story to switch back and forth in time or in location, but such switching about in television is visually confusing. You do not want to skip from a night-time rally to an interview done that morning, and then back to the night-time rally. Switches in time and location are possible, but they are usually best handled by making each different location or time a separate story.

New stories on film or videotape usually need certain material at the start. The location of a story is often set with both words and pictures. Most stories will also call for an *establishing shot.* This is a shot—generally, a *wide shot*—that fixes all points of reference in the subsequent pictures for the audience. In essence, the establishing shot tells the audience where it is standing while watching the event. Establishing shots can be omitted, especially in the case of simple interviews, but there is always a risk of the audience becoming disoriented if you do not write your script so there is a logical place for an establishing shot at the start of the story. If no establishing shot is used, the audience may assume it is viewing the scene from one location, then later becomes distracted and confused when a shot that could not have been taken from that location appears in the story.

The writer must also be aware that once the establishing shot is chosen, all other shots must conform to its orientation. There may be shots the writer would like to use but cannot include because they would disorient the audience.

It is important that persons seen in a story be identified as soon as possible. The audience should not be left guessing whose picture is on the screen. Nor should the writer provide material to be read about one person while another person's picture is on the screen.

In short, it isn't enough to write the word—you must also "write" the picture. You must see clearly in your mind what the screen will look like for every line of your copy. "Writing" the picture is really more important than writing the words, and when the two conflict, it is usually the words that must be changed.

WORKING WITH TELEVISION CUES

To "write" with pictures, the television newswriter must learn a new set of *cues*. These cues are included in the script to describe what picture should appear on the screen at each point in the script. They are used by the videotape or film editors, the director, the producer, and other key members of the news department to translate the script into pictures. Unfortunately, there is almost no uniformity in the terms used. Each station has its own system, and sometimes different writers at the same station will use different terms for the same thing. Moreover, some of the terms used are trademarked names for equipment. ("Chromakey," "Videfont," and "Vizmo" are examples.) This is awkward for the writer who has come from another station that uses equipment that is made by an unfamiliar manufacturer and has a different name.

The following list represents cues that are in fairly wide use:

A ROLL	The first of two rolls of film (or, rarely, videotape) run in an A-B ROLL story. The process lets the director dissolve or cut back and forth between two reels of film, the A ROLL and the B ROLL. The audio usually comes from the A ROLL but can be switched back and forth between the reels. A typical use of this process would be in a speech or interview. The story would begin with the sound and picture of the speaker on the A ROLL; then the pictures in the story would be switched and the material on the B ROLL would be used to illustrate what is being said while the story's sound continues to come from the A ROLL.
B ROLL	The second of the two rolls in an A-B ROLL story. This roll usually contains silent footage, which is shown while the sound track from the A ROLL is played.

CG   Stands for "Character Generator," the general term for electronic titling equipment such as the Videofont.

EASEL   Same as STAND.

FLIP   Same as STAND.

FULL SCREEN   Since slides may be used in several ways, some stations precede the SLIDE cue with FULL SCREEN to indicate the slide will occupy the entire screen. The complete cue looks like this:

> FULL SCREEN
> SLIDE #N-753-82
> Gov. Fern

HARDWALL News programs using Chromakey often keep some picture showing in the Chromakey area at all times. The HARDWALL cue is used to indicate that the Chromakey area is to be left blank.

KEY   Short for "Chromakey"—the name of a commercial process for matting color video images. An image from any video source (usually a slide, film, or videotape) is matted into a specially colored area (usually blue) seen on the screen. To the audience, the effect is similar to RP or VIZMO, but more picture sources are available than for RP, which can only project still pictures.

LIVE   The newscaster is seen on camera. You can specify the person reading the copy by making it SAM LIVE.

MOC   Short for "Microphone on Camera." Same as LIVE.

MONITOR   The video material shown on a large video screen incorporated into the news set.

OC   Means "Out Cue." That is, the last three or four words heard in a cart segment of a radio story or the audio segment of a television story. Also refers to "On Camera," as in "Mary OC" or "Anchor OC."

RP   A visual, almost always a slide, projected from behind a translucent screen on the set.

> RP
> SLIDE #N-753-82
> Gov. Fern.

SI FILM   Means "Silent Film." The film is run with the audio input from the film chain turned off, whether or not the film has a sound track.

SI FILM/VO	Same as SI VT/VO, but film, rather than videotape, is the visual medium.
SIL FILM	Same as SI FILM.
SIL VT	Same as SI VT.
SIL VTR	Same as SI VT.
SI VT	Means "Silent Videotape." This videotape is to be shown with the audio from the tape turned off.
SI VT/VO	Means "Silent Videotape with Voice Over." The videotape is to be run with its audio turned off. Audio is supplied by a newscaster reading in the studio.
SLIDE	The picture on the screen is created by a 35 mm. slide in a projector that is part of the electronic gear usually called the "film chain." Since several slides may be used and stations usually have large libraries of slides, each slide must be further identified. The identification often looks something like this:

> SLIDE #N-753-82
> Gov. Fern

SOC	Means "Standard Out Cue." These are the words specified by a news department for its reporters to use when signing off a story. For example: "Reporting from the Long Beach City Hall for KLON, this is Alice Wong."
SOF	Means "Sound On Film." The film is to be run with the audio supplied by the film's sound track. Some stations limit this cue to film with an optical sound track.
SOMT	Means "Sound On Magnetic Track." This cue means essentially the same as SOF, but it is used at some stations to specify that the film has a magnetic, rather than optical, sound track.
SOT	Same as SOVT.
SOVT	Means "Sound On Videotape." The videotape is shown with its own audio.
SOVTR	Same as SOVT.
STAND	Refers to materials, such as photographs, mounted on cardboard and set on a stand or easel in the studio so they can be shot with a studio camera. If more than

one such visual is used, each should be numbered and identified. For example:

> STAND #1
> State Map

If more than one STAND visual is to be used, it is preferable to insert a non-stand shot between them. Otherwise, more than one studio camera may be tied up. The locations of the studio cameras have to be taken into consideration. If only two cameras are used for the show, tying up both for STAND shots can cause serious problems.

SUPER Short for "Superimposition." One video picture is superimposed upon another. All elements of both pictures are present on the video screen, but the brightest elements predominate. Thus, white lettering on a black background, if *supered* over a second picture, shows as white lettering on the second picture, leaving the rest of the second picture essentially unchanged. Superimposition is mainly used in news to provide titles similar to Videfont.

> SUPER SLIDE
> #T-825-82
> "Helga Thompson"
> "Robbery Victim"

VCR Short for "Video Cassette Recording." Since most video cassette equipment is not designed for air use, this cue is most likely to be used in classroom projects or for cable news programs.

VF Short for "Videfont"—a commercial character-generating system. This system allows written material to be inserted into the television picture from a typewriter-like keyboard. It can be used to identify persons or locations shown on the screen or sometimes to identify an off-camera voice. The exact content of the material to appear must be spelled out. If the material is not to run across the bottom of the screen, then its desired location in the picture must be specified.

> VF: "Helga Thompson"
> "Robbery Victim"

VIZ Short for "Vizmo"—a commercial system for video rear projection. This electronic system permits use of rear projection for videotape and film as well as still pictures. It also permits limited forms of animation.

VTR Short for "Videotape Recording." Since most video recordings have sound on them, at some stations this cue is used instead of SOVTR.

THE TELEVISION NEWS SCRIPT

Now let's look at a typical television news story. This story was used on KNXT, the CBS-owned station in Los Angeles.

24 lines

NIGHT RAIN 4-15 AVB --- 4

JONES

Rainwater on the

Hollywood Freeway

tonight caused north-

bound traffic to

VTR: 27 SOT UNDER back up all the way

SUPER: HLLYWOOD from the downtown area

to the Vermont Overpass

in Hollywood.

Upwards to two feet

of water collected

on the freeway before

work crews were able

to drain it off.

Some of the lanes

were open . . . but heavy

Saturday night traffic

still XXX made driving

from downtown to

Hollywood XXXXX

VTR CONT difficult through

NIGHT RAIN 222 AVB --- 4A

VTR CONT
JONES

the evening.

At this hour, all

northbound lanes are

officially open but

traffic is still

WIPE TO VTR

congested.

The top line of a script for a television news story contains the *slug*—that is, the name of the story, the date of the broadcast, and the initials of the writer. In the upper right-hand corner, the page number is typed in. This is generally done after the story is written, since the writer probably has no way of knowing for certain where the story will go in the final script for the program. Page numbering is done only after the script has been assembled in what is expected to be its final form. Often the page numbers are penciled in instead of typed. This makes it easy to erase and change the numbers when required.

The same treatment is given to the name of the anchorperson designated to read the story. In the example given, the name "Jones" was typed in after the script had been arranged in its final form. The writer often has no way of knowing in advance who will read the copy.

Notice, in the example, that the lead is written in the past tense. Present tense is preferred for most broadcast writing, but there is considerably greater use of past tense in television news. Stories on film or videotape are, by their nature, past events. There is little point is describing them in present tense. However, it is fairly common for the material read on camera, including on-camera leads to film or videotape stories, to be written in the present tense. The writing later switches to the past tense when the tape or film appears on the screen. Because the event described in the sample news story script is over and done with, the lead is past tense.

The copy for the script is typed in oversized type that is about twice the size of the largest type available on a regular typewriter. This makes it easier for the newscaster to read on the TelePrompTer. Manufacturers give various names to their large type faces. "Bulletin" is one commonly used. Most of these type faces are "6 pitch," meaning there are six letters to the inch. A good many 6-pitch typewriters have no lowercase letters and will only type in capitals.

The material to be read aloud is typed on the right-hand side of the page. The left-hand column is reserved for cues. The writer "writes" the pictures in the left-hand column and the words in the right-hand column. The lengths of the lines of copy in the right-hand column are usually carefully set so that an estimate of the reading time required can be made by counting the lines. When a script is written in oversized type, each line of type usually takes about one second to read.

In the example shown, the first cue comes about four seconds into the story. The cue "VTR :27 SOT UNDER" means that the videotape for the story should appear on the screen at that point, that the tape runs for twenty-seven seconds, and that the sound from the videotape (SOT) is to be heard softly below (UNDER) the narration.

Immediately below this first cue is a second cue: "SUPER: HLLY-WOOD." That means the word "Hollywood" is to be superimposed on the picture at the bottom of the screen. Here is a good example of using the picture to back up the words. The on-camera lead tells us that the event happened on the Hollywood Freeway. When the tape runs, we see the word "Hollywood," and we hear the word "Hollywood" used again by the newscaster in the seventh line of the script.

At the bottom of the first page of our sample script is the cue "VTR CONT." This cue simply means that the videotape does not end at the end of this page, but continues running as we turn to the next page. If you count the copy lines from the tape cue, you will see that by the time the newscaster reads to the bottom of this first page, about sixteen seconds will have passed since the tape first appeared on the screen. Since the cue indicates that the tape is twenty-seven seconds long, it could run another eleven seconds.

At the top of the second page of the story, the original slug is repeated, but "222" has been typed in place of the date. This is simply one way of showing that this is the second page of the story. Notice that the typed page number in the right-hand corner is "4-A," not "5." It is the custom at most stations to number the stories rather than the individual pages of the script.

The cue "VTR CONT" appears again at the top of the second page of the story to remind everyone that the videotape is still on the screen. The name of the anchorperson has also been typed on this page. Nothing is left to chance.

The final cue, "WIPE TO VTR," requires a bit of explanation. The writer wanted to combine this story with another story about the effects of heavy rain in the area. Rather than return to the studio newscaster for a lead into the second story, the writer chose to go directly to the videotape of the second story by using a *wipe* from the first videotape to the second. To the viewer, a wipe gives the impression that the second picture pushes the first one off the screen. The new picture starts at one side of the screen and progressively moves across the screen, replacing the old picture. Two videotape machines are required, with appropriate electronic synchronization equipment and appropriate switching equipment in the studio—no problem, of course, for a CBS-owned station in Hollywood.

If you count all the lines of copy from the first cue, you will note that the script only takes twenty-two seconds to read, although the videotape runs twenty-seven seconds. This is common practice. A tape or film is usually edited with a pad of five seconds or so—a bit of extra running time in case something goes wrong. Here the five-second pad allows for the wipe with no worry about the first tape running out.

Now let's look at the content of the copy itself. We've already commented on the use of the past tense and the repetition of the story's location with words and picture. The location is given in words before it is shown on the screen. That prepares the audience for what is to come. It would not be good television newswriting to show a picture first and leave the audience to guess where it was until the script followed with an explanation. Note that no attempt is made to be precise with numbers. "Upwards to two feet of water" is close enough. And notice that the writer has simply used the "X" key on the typewriter to cross out mistakes. There is rarely time in electronic news to retype copy, and proofreading symbols are useless for the newscaster, who must be able to read the corrected copy at a glance. Haste led the writer to use "upwards to." The correct idiom is "upwards of."

Above all, note how brief the story is. This story is devoted to an event that could affect many of the viewers, and it closes with a statement of the current state of the problem. Yet the entire story takes only twenty-two seconds to read. This is typical of television news. Minimal detail is provided, but the viewers learn enough to decide whether or not they should attempt to drive on the Hollywood Freeway at this hour, and, with the story that follows, they are also given some idea of the effects of the rain they have been having.

The next story, prepared by a broadcast journalism class at California State University Long Beach, was simple enough. Dr. Wallace Moore, a retired professor at the University, had modified a Honda automobile to run on solar power. On a sunny day, Moore drove the car to a campus parking lot. The students videotaped the car and a "news conference" with Moore.

The students made a number of mistakes in covering the story. First, they interviewed Moore for about forty-five minutes. When the videotape was rerun later to begin preparation of the script, the students quickly realized that they had given themselves too much material to work with. While it is always better to have too much than to have too little videotape, it takes a long time to go through forty-five minutes of tape to pick out one or two usable cuts. The news conference gave each student a chance to ask questions, but a one-student interview that kept the videotaped material short and to the point would have been more practical. Second, after shooting the car in one location, it was decided to move it to a second location where the light was better. Since there is no visual logic in seeing the car in two places in the same story (unless it is shown moving from one to the other, which would waste time), the material videotaped at the first location could not be used in the final versions. Time and effort had been wasted by not checking for a good shooting location to begin with. Third, the parking lot proved to be a poor place to shoot the story because it was noisy and there were frequent interruptions by cars driving in and out. Fourth, the student camera operators ruined a great many of the shots with poor focus, poor lighting, and poor framing. Moreover, they had obtained a good close-up of the solar panel on the car's roof, but had not gotten a wide shot from a high angle that made it easy to see where the panel was located on the car. (Such a shot should precede the close-up.) Fifth, the student reporters degraded the quality of some of the sound through poor microphone placement.

That seems like a long list of errors, but they are not unusual errors for student projects. You should keep all of them in mind and avoid them when you prepare your stories. However, even in the best of news departments errors and technical problems occur. The preparation of a television news story always begins with an assessment of what visual and audio material you have for the story that can be used on the air. On pages 114 and 115 is a series of still photographs made from the unedited videotape of the story. The shots are in the sequence in which they appear on the videotape. (Unless a story is *cut in the camera*, the sequence in which the shots occur is not usually the sequence in which they appear in the story on the air.)

In this case, shots one through nine had to be discarded because of the movement of the car to the new location. Shots eighteen, twenty, twenty-one, twenty-eight, and thirty-two had to be eliminated because of poor quality. About half of the shots were usable visually, but some of these also had to be eliminated because of poor audio. However, not all the shots that were poor visually were a total loss since the possibility remained of using the audio from some of these shots over other pictures.

While the long news conference turned up a great many facts about the car and its inventor, these were the most important:

1.   The car was a hybrid. Its gasoline engine under the hood had been left intact and could be used for driving the car. An electric motor, powered by batteries, had been installed in the rear of the car to provide electric propulsion.

2.   A panel of solar cells on the roof of the car could be used to charge the batteries, but it was more efficient to plug the built-in battery charger into a regular electric outlet while the car was parked overnight.

3.   When powered by batteries, the car had a range of about twenty miles and could hit a top speed of about thirty miles an hour.

4.   On a sunny day, the car could be driven by the power from the solar cells alone, but the top speed was about three miles an hour.

5.   Moore said it had cost him about $10,000 to modify the Honda. (Some equipment had been provided to him free by battery manufactur-

ers.) He thought a mass-produced car that included the features of his car could be marketed for $10,000 to $12,000. He said he had been approached by some manufacturers, but had made no deals to have his patented solar car produced.

6.   Moore said his primary motivation in developing the car had been to help reduce pollution. He said air pollution had contributed to the death, from emphysema, of one of his best friends.

The first job, of course, was to select the audio cuts—the sound-on-videotape material that would be used in the story. Two cuts were selected. The first was Moore discussing the relative merits of charging the batteries from the solar panel and charging them from an electrical outlet. This was chosen because there were plenty of visuals that could be B-rolled (shown over Moore's voice) to illustrate what he was talking about. (Regrettably, a close-up of the cord and plug could not be used because of poor focus.) Obviously other cuts could have been used, but this one both told the story in the voice of the interviewee and provided good visual illustration of what was being said. It was also one of the cuts in which Moore was most concise. B-rolling the pictures over his voice made it easier to edit Moore's statement and tighten it further.

The second cut chosen was the statement about Moore's reason for creating the car. This was not a very important aspect of the story, but it was brief and it had emotional impact. Moore's concern came through clearly in his statement about the death of his friend. This cut helped to acquaint the audience with Moore and made him a sympathetic character. Since the auto itself was clearly of limited practicality, it was important to demonstrate that Moore's intention was sincere and that he was not an eccentric tinkering with gadgets.

The choice of audio cuts can be determined by many factors. The primary factor is the quality of the audio and the picture. Other factors include the importance of the statement to story, the conciseness and clarity of the statement, and the audio and visual contribution of the statement to the overall impact of the story.

Once the audio cuts had been selected, they had to be carefully timed, the out cues carefully recorded, and a summary of the statement prepared for the fill, or backup copy, for that cut. The first cut ran forty-eight seconds and the second cut ran twenty-two seconds.

The next task was to write the on-camera opening, the voice-over-videotape material, and—if desired—an on-camera closing. The producer (the instructor) decided the total running time for the story should be about two minutes. Since the audio cuts used up one minute and ten seconds, the rest of the story would have to be told in fifty seconds, or—using a two-second line—about twenty-five lines. Of course, those lines had to be written with thought to the visuals that would accompany them. Here is one way the story could be written:

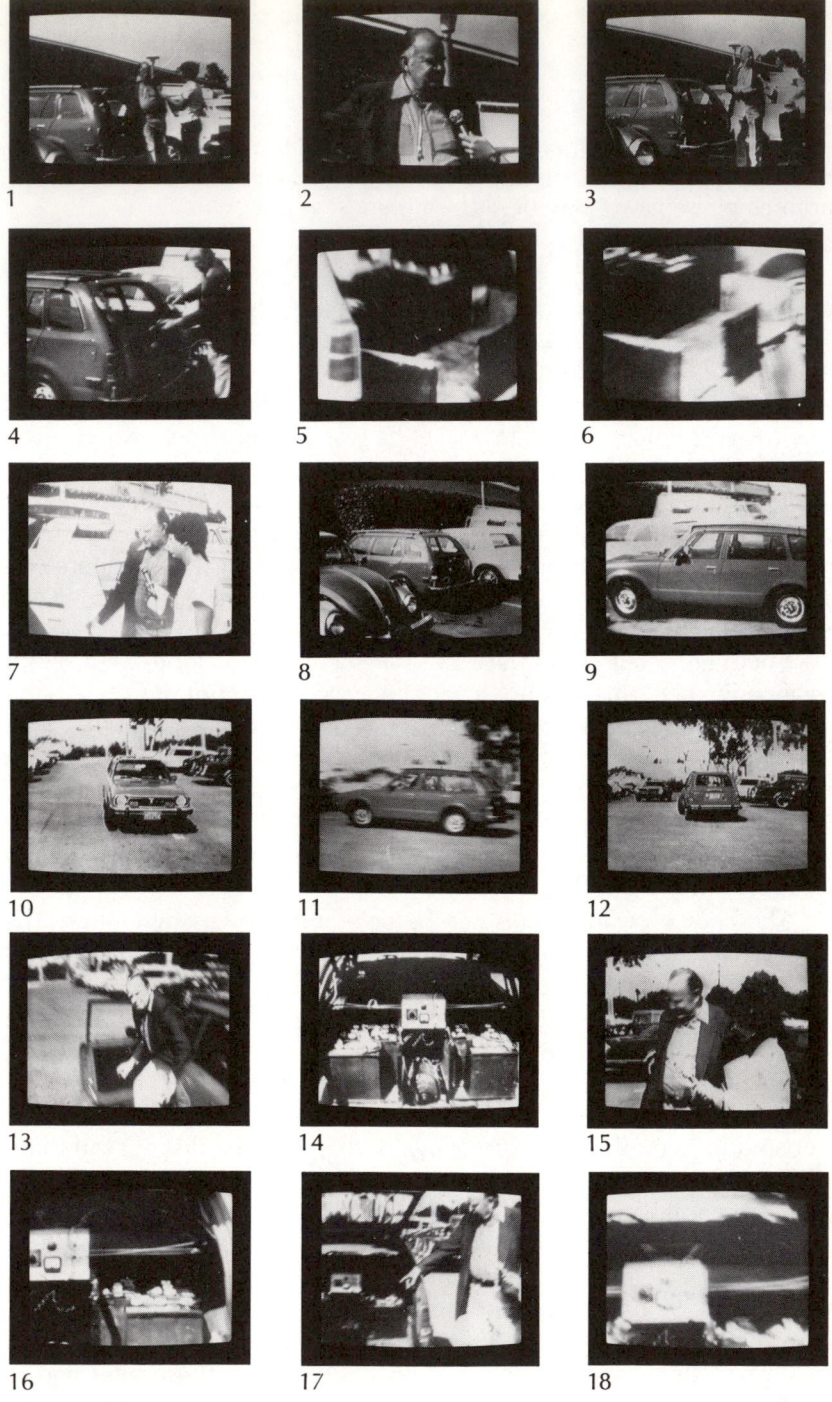

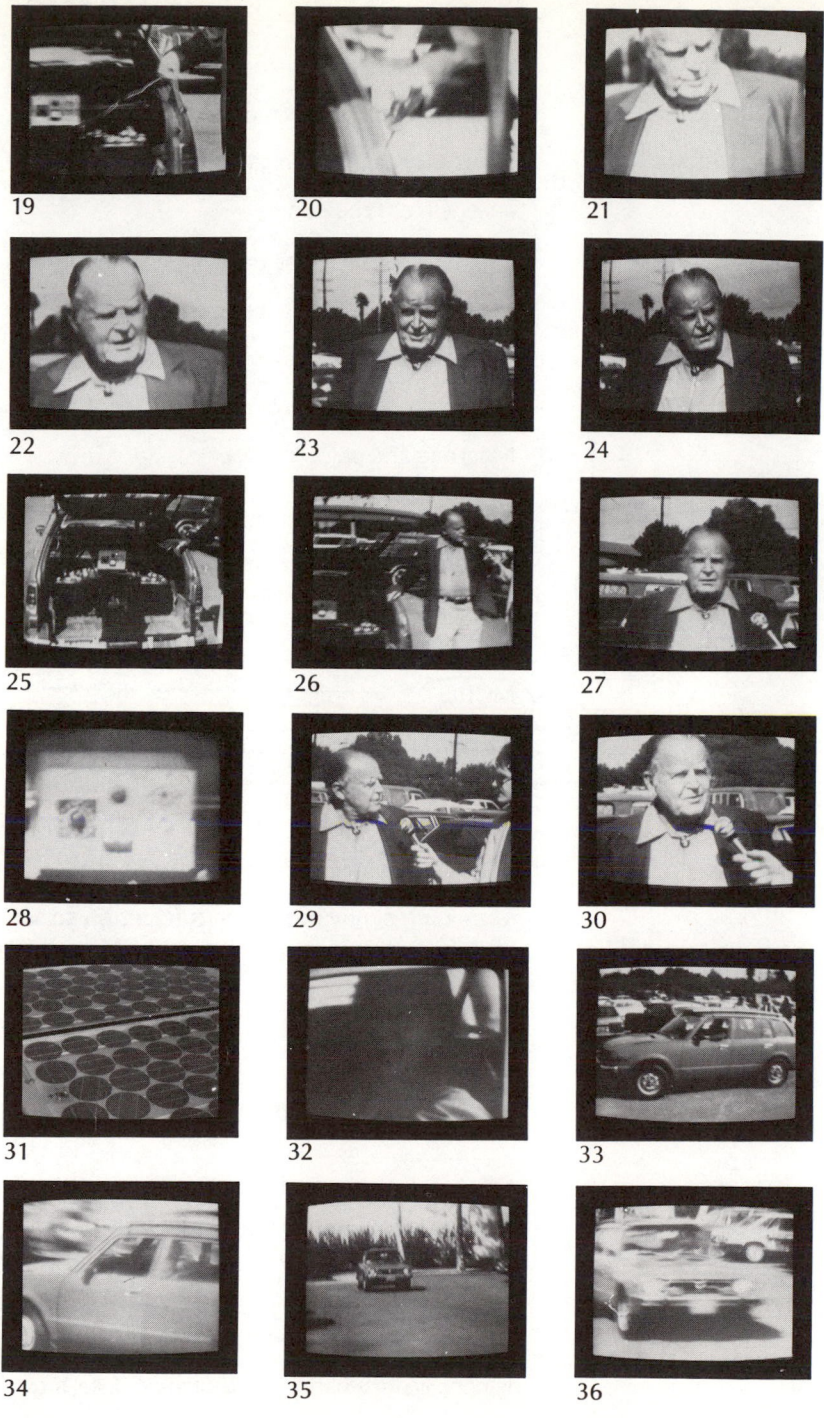

19 20 21

22 23 24

25 26 27

28 29 30

31 32 33

34 35 36

SOLAR CAR—6 O'CLOCK NEWS—3/28/81—YEE   *49 lines*

KELLY ON CAMERA KEY: Solar Car Slide	With gasoline prices soaring, a Long Beach man has come up with a car that runs on electricity—and even takes some of its energy from the sun.
SI VTR/VO CG: "California State University Long Beach"	The car has a regular gasoline engine for long trips, but for short trips around town, it can zip along at 30 miles an hour, powered by batteries. Retired college professor Wallace Moore is the car's inventor.
SOVTR (:48) CG: "Dr. Wallace Moore" "Inventor"	OC: " . . . not very efficient." FILL: Moore says the batteries can be charged from the solar panel, but it is more efficient to recharge them from a regular electrical outlet.

MORE ⟶

SOLAR CAR—6 O'CLOCK NEWS—3/28/81—YEE—FIRST ADD

SI VTR/VO	Dr. Moore says the car has a range of about 20 miles on fully charged batteries, and—yes—on a sunny day it can run just on solar power—but the top speed is a snail-like 3 miles an hour. The retired Cal State Long Beach administrator says his purpose is not saving fuel, but saving lives.
SOVTR (:22) CG: "Dr. Wallace Moore" "Inventor"	OC: " . . . clean up the air." FILL: Moore says he hopes cars like his will cut down air pollution. He says smog helped kill a good friend who suffered from emphysema.
SI VTR/VO	It cost Moore about 10-thousand dollars to modify his 19—76 Honda. There are no

immediate plans to market the car

commercially.

The on-camera lead-in provides the story's news peg—rising gasoline prices, and it alerts the viewer to the subject of the story, an electric car that uses solar power. This is backed-up with art work suggesting a solar car Chromakeyed into the area behind the newscaster. The lead does not overplay the solar angle, since the car really uses solar energy only in a minor way. The location of the story is provided in the lead. In the first sentence over videotape, it is explained that the car is a hybrid. This material would play over a shot of the car driving up. The character generator is used to remind the viewers of the locale. The maximum speed and limited range of the car are mentioned. This would play over a shot of Moore getting out of the car. A close-up of Moore would play over the line that identifies him and leads into the first audio cut.

While the first audio cut is playing, the picture would dissolve from Moore speaking, to shots of the solar panel, the batteries, and the plug-in battery charger. (The close-up of the cord and plug is not usable, so the charger must be shown alone.) Prior to the dissolve to the B roll, Moore is reidentified to the audience with the character generator.

The second voice-over segment adds further details about the car, which play under more shots of the vehicle and its features. Note that the name of the speaker has been repeated immediately after the audio cut to remind the viewer who was speaking and to get Moore's title of "doctor" in again. We return to a close-up to lead into the second audio cut.

The second audio cut runs with no B roll. It is relatively short and strong visually. Moore is again identified with the character generator.

Moore's second statement could have made a strong ending to the story. However, there are still a few facts that would add to the story, and using a voice-over end to a story can help avoid a *tight out*. Often if a story ends with an audio cut, the director must immediately switch back to the studio cameras or else unwanted material may be seen on the screen—for example, Moore's lips still moving although the rest of the sound on the cut had been erased (degaussed). Instead, the writer chooses to end this story with a shot of Moore getting into his car and driving off. This gives time for a few more details and gives the director a closing shot, which he can cut away from at any time. Customarily, the videotape editor would see to it that this shot of the car driving off runs at least four seconds longer than the reading time for the last voice-over material. Thus, if there are any problems, the director has some extra time or *pad* in the videotape before it ends. Moore is identified once more, following an audio cut, and in both identifications following an audio cut, Moore's name has been introduced in a natural, unobtrusive manner, avoiding statements such as, "That was retired college professor Wallace Moore, inventor of the solar car." Such identifications belabor the obvious.

Finally, the writer should write the line count in pencil in the upper right-hand corner of the script and circle all material not meant to be read aloud. (Note that the line count should include thirty-five lines for the running time of the two audio cuts.)

A copy of the script and some of the pictures that were used in the final story follow. Look over the script and the pictures, and consider how you might have written the story. There is no single way to write a video news script. Different audio cuts could have been chosen, different pictures used, and different facts emphasized. The point is to understand that writing television news stories requires a clear picture in your mind of what you are going to do both visually and in words. The two elements must blend together to give maximum emphasis to both. It is not something that you learn overnight. It takes practice to develop a good grasp of the way the words and pictures play together. Don't be discouraged by, but learn from, the mistakes you are bound to make. The students made many errors in preparing this story, and yet, the final product was a reasonable, creditable story.

It will probably be useful to you to reread this chapter carefully several times. Then go on to the exercises. You are on your way to becoming a television newswriter.

SOLAR CAR—6 O'CLOCK NEWS—3/28/81—YEE   *49 lines*

KELLY ON CAMERA KEY: Solar Car Slide	With gasoline prices soaring, a Long Beach man has come up with a car that runs on electricity—and even takes some of its energy from the sun.
SI VTR/VO CG: "California State University Long Beach"	The car has a regular gasoline engine for long trips, but for short trips around town, it can zip along at 30 miles an hour, powered by batteries. Retired college professor Wallace Moore is the car's inventor.

SOVTR (:48)

CG: "Dr. Wallace Moore"
"Inventor"

OC: " . . . not very efficient."

FILL: Moore says the batteries can be charged from the solar panel, but it is more efficient to recharge them from a regular electrical outlet.

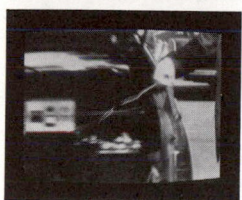

MORE →

SOLAR CAR—6 O'CLOCK NEWS—3/28/81—YEE—FIRST ADD

SI VTR/VO

Dr. Moore says the car has a range of about 20 miles on fully charged batteries, and—yes—on a sunny day it can run only on solar power—but the top speed is a snail-like 3 miles an hour. The retired Cal State Long Beach administrator says his purpose is not saving fuel, but saving lives.

SOVTR (:22)

CG: "Dr. Wallace Moore"

OC: " . . . clean up the air."

FILL: Moore says he hopes cars like his will cut down air pollution. He says smog helped kill a good friend who suffered from emphysema.

SI VTR/VO

It cost Moore about 10-thousand dollars to modify his 19-76 Honda. There are no immediate plans to market the car commercially.

Exercises
xxxxxxxxxxxx

Exercise 1

Write two stories from the following set of facts. Write the first story for radio and the second for television. Assume that each story will be used on a program aired at 6 o'clock in the evening, local time, on February 26. Choose your own slug for the story. The radio news program you are writing for is the "Romak Reporter." The television program is "Newswatch." Each story should run about forty-five seconds. (Each might run a minute or more with actualities.)

There was an eclipse of the sun on February 26. The eclipse was visible throughout the northwestern United States and western Canada. The area in which a total eclipse could be seen, barring cloud cover, stretched in an arc from Oregon, up through Idaho, Montana, and into Canada. The eclipse was the last total solar eclipse to be visible in the United States this century. The last previous total eclipse took place in 1962. The next total eclipse will be visible in the United States in 2017. There was a great deal of public excitement about this event, with enthusiasts travelling great distances to watch it. Some even arranged to be aloft in aircraft above the area, in case clouds obscured the eclipse. Scientists studied the eclipse to learn more about the sun's corona and the way it may affect the weather on Earth. A group of Druids from Berkeley, California, travelled to Bellingham, Washington, to view the eclipse. Bellingham, which was in the area destined to view a total eclipse, is the location of an exact copy of Stonehenge in England. Stonehenge is thought to have been built by the ancient Druids as a location for studying or worshipping the sun, planets, and stars. The modern Druids at Bellingham, Washington, performed strange rites and ceremonies during the eclipse. The eclipse began about 7:00 A.M. PST, reached totality at 8:02, and was over by 9:00 A.M. An eclipse occurs when the moon passes between the Earth and the sun, casting its shadow on part of the earth and hiding the sun from our view.

Exercise 2

The television station you work for subscribes to a daily feed of television new stories that the station's network sells to its affiliates. Each subscriber videotapes the daily feed and uses whatever stories it wants on its local news program. Most of these stories are edited news stories with sound. However, on February 26, the network supplied both an edited story on the eclipse and a six-minute sequence of unedited material, which your station could edit and use instead of the edited network story.

You are writing for the 6 o'clock, evening edition of "Newswatch," and your producer has asked you to create a fresh story and have the six minutes of network videotape edited to conform to your story. Using the information from the preceding exercise, write the story. Open with four to ten seconds of MOC (newscaster reading on camera), and finish up with thirty to forty seconds of SI VTR/VO (your newscaster reading while the edited, videotape story is shown on the screen).

When you have completed your script, take another sheet of paper. In a column running down the left side of the page, type the last word of each line of your story. Write opposite each word what videotape scene the audience will be seeing while that line is read. Do not run any shot less than four seconds nor more than eight seconds. Let the last shot begin four seconds before the end of the reading time and run three to four seconds longer than the estimated reading time. This provides leeway for the newscaster who reads a bit fast or a bit slow. Do not try to make words and pictures synchronize too closely. Check the style book in Appendix A if you need to use more than one page. The video editor will select the shots to match your story from the log shown below. Remember, you need not use the shots in the order in which they appear in the log. Any shot can be shortened in editing, but none can be made longer.

Shot List

TIME:		STORY: Eclipse
From:	*To:*	*SI SOVT*
00:00	00:30	CU eclipse beginning
00:31	01:25	CU sun total eclipse
01:26	02:15	CU sun end of eclipse
02:16	02:40	CU map showing path of eclipse
02:41	03:25	Various shots loading scientific equipment on plane
03:26	04:05	Various shots scientists boarding plane
04:06	04:22	LS plane takes off
04:23	04:35	Various shots interior of plane
04:36	04:45	CU of scientist peering into telescope in plane
04:46	04:58	LS of Stonehenge replica in Bellingham
04:59	05:20	Various shots procession of Druids
05:21	5:30	MS Druid priests praying to sun
05:31	05:40	CU Druid priest praying
05:41	05:55	LS Druid priestess dancing
05:56	06:15	LS Druids marching around Stonehenge

Exercise 3

The following story was used on ABC's syndication service.[4] It is a feature story, with little hard news in it, and the reporter was Greg Dobbs in Chicago. The news peg was pending congressional legislation that would have extended retirement age for many people and would have eliminated mandatory retirement for others. The laws were later passed by Congress.

Write the story for pre-edited videotape. However, to make sense of this story, write it as if the legislation were still pending. Since there is not much hard news in the story, you may have to write loose rather than tight to find enough to say in this story. However, do not invent facts; stick with the material supplied. There are four sound-on-videotape segments in this story. You will have to time your script precisely to make it work. Remember, it is better to be a little short on copy than to run too long. Write to leave yourself four or five seconds of "pad" on the end of the videotape.

The story has an unusual visual ending. Apparently the only visual record of George Morton receiving his gold watch was a black-and-white photograph. The reporter and the video editor opted to end the story on a video shot of that photograph. Obviously, this is not an ideal ending for a video story, but reporting sometimes consists of making the best of what is available.

Background. Congress is considering legislation to extend retirement ages and end mandatory retirement for many occupations. In Chicago, an insurance firm, Bankers' Life and Casualty Corporation, has had a company policy for over 25 years that persons of any age may be hired and may continue to work so long as they perform their jobs correctly. At present, Bankers' Life has 120 people over sixty-five years old on its payroll. Among them, shown in the videotape, are Loretta Davidson, a seventy-five-year-old switchboard operator, and Herschel Bold, a seventy-nine-year-old who distributes mail and memos in the building. Bold had been forced to retire from a job with another employer when he was sixty-five. He came to work for Bankers' Life when he was sixty-nine. Shown in a photograph is George Morton, who also retired from work with another employer at sixty-five. After coming to work for Bankers' Life, Morton stayed on for twenty-five years, and was awarded a gold watch for his service. The story also includes a statement from a Bankers' Life official who was not otherwise identified in the actual network story. For purposes of this exercise, he will be identified as Arthur N. Littlejohn, a vice-president of Bankers' Life, who is in charge of its midwestern division. Substitute your name for Greg Dobbs's.

---

[4]Photos and story © Copyright American Broadcasting Companies, Inc. 1977. Reprinted by permission.

Shot List

????–????   MS Anchorperson on camera. Make the on-camera lead-in as long or short as you feel appropriate.

0:00–0:08   VTR, Natural Sound under, MS of Loretta Davidson operating the switchboard. CG: Reporter's name.

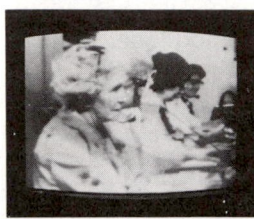

0:09–0:18   CU Davidson, Sound Up Full, CG: "Chicago."
FILL: Davidson says she works to "stay in her right mind."
  OC: " . . . my right mind."

0:19–0:27   Nat. Sound Out. MS Bold delivering mail.

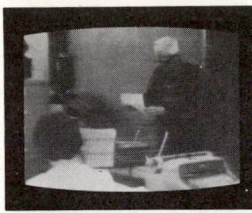

0:28–0:33   CU Bold. Sound on Videotape
FILL: Bold says he wants to keep productive.
OC: ". . . some line."

0:34–0:48   Silent Videotape. Series of shots of older workers in office.

0:49–0:56   CU Littlejohn. Sound on Videotape. FILL: Littlejohn says older workers do the job better.
OC: " . . . or others."

0:57–1:05   Silent Videotape. More shots of older workers.

1:06–1:18   Silent Videotape. Still of George Morton. Tilt down to watch and back up. Camera is on watch case from 1:09 to 1:13.

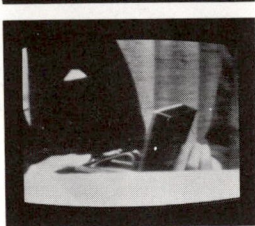

Exercise 4

The following is a set of stills printed from a film story shot by a student. The details are fairly simple. A university is preparing for its annual art festival. Some of the art students are studying metal sculpture and a cameraperson has gone to the metal-working area of the art department to chronicle the artists at work. The metal is heated in a forge and then beaten on an anvil. (As you can see, some of the pictures are underexposed or poorly composed.) The camera operator finished the roll of film by shooting an identifying shot of the sign outside the art department and a metal sculpture of the type on which the students were working.

Write a one-minute script for this story. Very likely you will want to rearrange the sequence of the various shots as well as eliminate the unsatisfactory ones. Keep visual logic in mind. Indicate which shots would be used where by writing the number of the shot at the start of the line of copy where that shot would be used.

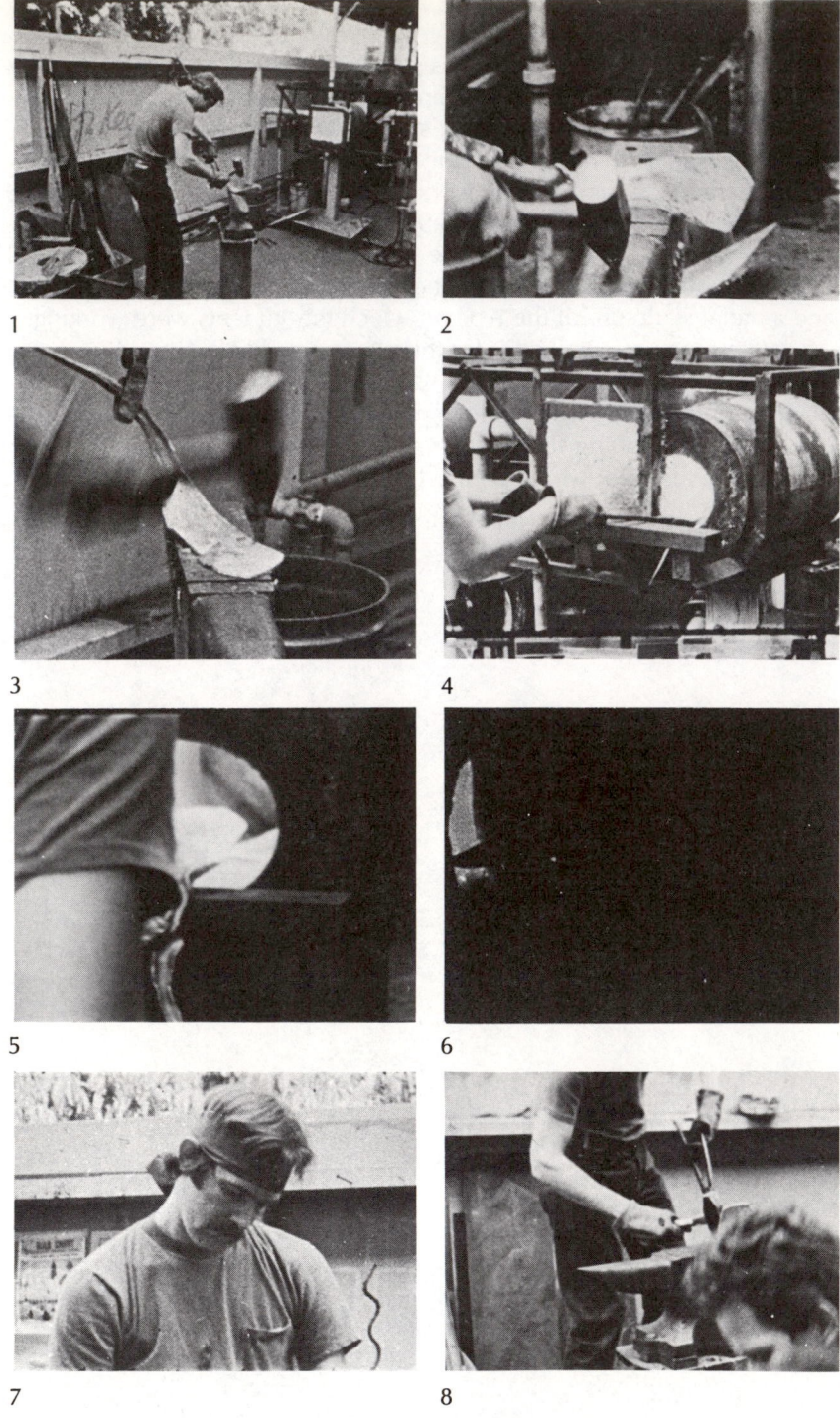

1

2

3

4

5

6

7

8

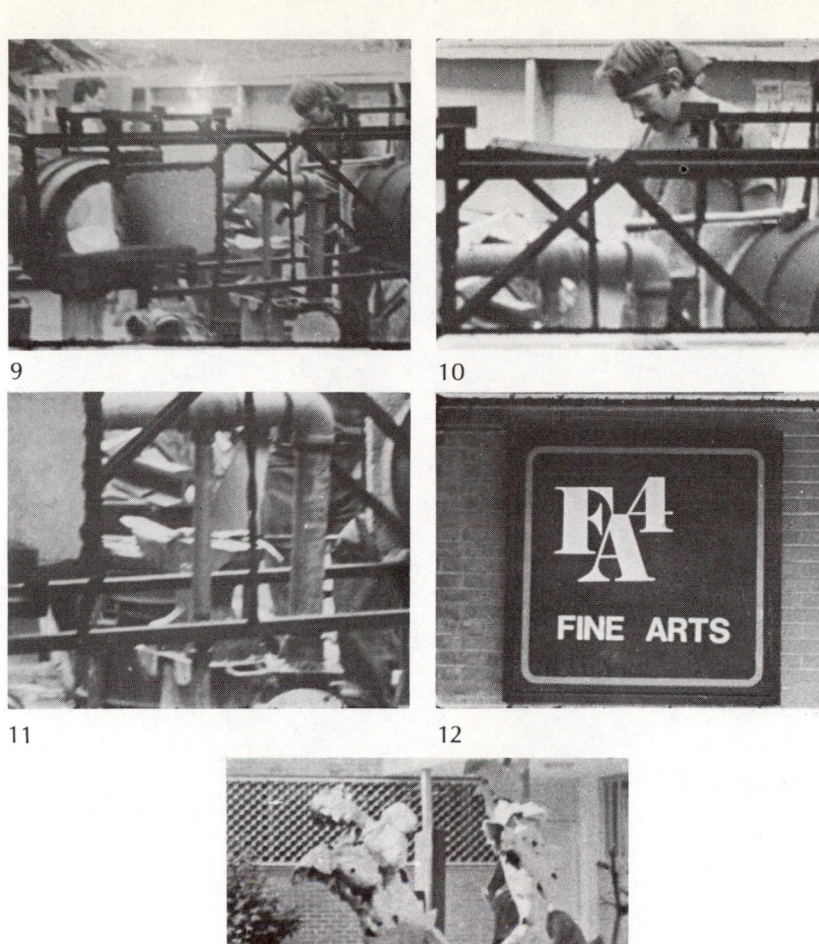

9

10

11

12

13

Electronic News Editing

All forms of news must be edited, but the editing procedure is most important for electronic news. We indicated earlier that the editing process for electronic news begins with the cutting out of facts and then proceeds to the deletion of words and phrases. However, it is a mistake to assume that editing is always the elimination of material. Editing also involves changing existing copy and sometimes adding new material. The first goal of the editor is clarity. Brevity should never be attained at the cost of clarity.

CHECKING THE FACTS

Electronic news editing begins, like all news editing, with the careful checking of the facts in the story. Broadcast news must be prepared under the tightest of deadlines, and errors are bound to slip in from time to time. A good newsroom should be equipped with several standard reference works. But the most important reference library is in the editor's head. The editor must be able to spot errors and must have a feeling for material that needs to be checked out, even though it does not appear obviously wrong. News editing requires a good knowledge of current events, and it also requires some knowledge of the types of mistakes certain reporters are most likely to make. The editor learns from working with the news staff that one reporter is sometimes careless about getting names correct while another is likely to get figures wrong. The editor takes extra pains to watch for those mistakes when working with material produced by these reporters.

However, many broadcast news staffs are too small to assign one person to the job of editor. Instead, each reporter and writer must be her or his own editor. The first thing a good writer in any field does with a finished story is sit down and edit the copy carefully. Don't be taken in by plays, films, or television programs in which the reporter rips a sheet of paper from the typewriter and races to the editor's desk with it. Even under the tightest deadline, a good writer checks the copy.

Editing for electronic news must also include a check into matters such as correct pronunciation. For television, it is important to be sure that pictures are correctly identified.

KNOWING THE LAW

The editor, even if the writer is the editor, must have a good sense of the legal aspects of journalism. Are any of the statements in a story libelous? Do they invade someone's privacy? Do they violate any of the rules of the Federal Communications Commission, the Federal Trade Commission, or a host of other agencies? Inexperienced writers often labor under the misapprehension that they are not responsible for libelous statements if the statements are direct quotes or on tape. Be advised. A libel is a libel. If you disseminate it to the public, even by using someone else's words, you can be sued—and so can your station, the owners of the station, the newscaster, the news director, and anyone involved in the dissemination of the libel.

EDITING FOR THE LISTENER

For both radio and television, the editor must pay careful attention to the way the copy sounds. There are hundreds of stories in broadcasting about sentences that looked all right on paper, but came out sounding very differently from the ways they were intended. We've mentioned that two words can sound like one to the listener—for example, "a tax" can wind up sounding like "attacks." There is also the danger that a sound will become detached from one word and seem to belong to another—for example, "and effects" is difficult to distinguish from "and defects." And many words in English are pronounced the same way, but spelled differently. "Two," "to," and "too" are examples.

Carelessly placed words can change or obscure the meaning of a sentence. There is an apocryphal tale of a television news editor who failed to delete this line from a story: "The president flew back to Washington this morning, leaving his wife, who has a cold, behind." If that sentence seems all right, you are not ready to write for electronic news. It may seem strange advice, but to write and edit television news copy, it is very helpful to cultivate a dirty mind. If you can't catch every possible double meaning in a story, you are leaving yourself open to all manner of problems, including lawsuits.

Word placement can entirely change the meaning of your stories in more subtle ways, too. Compare these two sentences:

Doris went alone.

Doris alone went.

Sometimes, a broadcast news editor must indicate a pause for the newscaster or identify a word that must be stressed in order to make clear the meaning of a sentence. Ideally, of course, a broadcast news sentence should be constructed so that its meaning does not depend upon a special emphasis or pause. However, sometimes there is no alternative. Note how a shift of emphasis changes the meaning of this sentence:

He *will do it.*

He will *do it.*

KEEPING YOUR COPY UNBIASED

A broadcast news editor must alway be on the alert for seeming bias in broadcast writing. It is easy to skim over copy without taking into consideration what the audience will see as its apparent "slant." After all, most news is not slanted deliberately. But it is very easy for a story to have the appearance of bias, especially to those in the audience who hold views opposite to what they think the slant of the story was.

Because broadcast newswriters must prepare copy for such a large audience, it is difficult to say anything without offending someone. We are not suggesting that you must avoid offending everyone in the audience. Broadcasters are often accused of that, and in some cases it is true. But your news will be meaningless if your goal is to offend no one. What you must do, instead, is make sure that you have done everything in your power to treat each issue fairly. Because you are certain to be the target of criticism, the only thing you can do is to prepare your copy so that when you are accused of bias, any fair-minded person who saw or heard the story will reject the charge.

HELPING THE NEWSCASTER

The editor must edit the copy to make it easy for the newscaster to read as well as easy for the audience to understand. For example, the editor should draw wavy lines under tricky words to call attention to them, like this: "Genero says Buddy isn't an ordinary outdoors horse. He calls Buddy a house horse."

The editor must also see to it that all the cues are properly marked on the script. The cues must be placed correctly and easy to read. Without the cues, nothing gets on the air.

UNDERSTANDING VISUALS

Editing requires a good sense of the visual rhetoric and, also, the rhetoric of the ear. The editor has to recognize that editorial decisions cannot be made on the basis of the copy alone. The picture and the sound dictate much of the script. What appears at first to be a good place to cut copy may turn out to be a poor place because the extra copy is needed for the picture at that point. Moreover, the selection of pictures and sounds is dictated by many factors other than the words on the film, videotape, or audiotape. For example, a desirable statement on videotape may prove to be unusable because of problems with the picture. Or an audio cut for radio may have to be deleted because of background or other recording problems. An individual's vocal inflection is a consideration in the selection of any statement. A person's speech pattern may be such that a statement may seem to have been cut off in mid-sentence. The editor must be aware of all these problems and make editorial decisions on the basis of the total story—the copy, the sound, and in television, the picture.

RULES FOR EDITING

Here are some general rules for electronic news editing. They should look familiar to you. Essentially, they are the same rules you have already learned for broadcast newswriting. After all, the job of the editor is to put the copy into the condition in which it should have been written in the first place.

1. Edit less formally for broadcast writing than you would for print. Remember that the words are meant to be spoken. Read the copy aloud so you can get a feel for the way it sounds.

2. Be suspicious of pronouns. In any form of writing, pronouns can be dangerous. The writer knows which noun each pronoun in a sentence stands for, but a reader or listener may find the sentence anything but clear. The problem is considerably more serious for broadcast writing than it is for print because the audience has only one chance to get the meaning of a statement. There is no way for listeners to go back and try to figure out what the writer meant. You can write surprisingly good broadcast copy by eliminating most pronouns and simply repeating nouns. When you are editing copy, you should pay special attention to pronouns and be certain that there is no question about their meaning.

3. Remember to simplify and round off all numbers. Delete numbers not essential to the story. Try to put remaining numbers in easy-to-grasp form. For example, instead of "66 point 7 percent," write "two-thirds" or "two out of three."

4. Check to make sure all qualifying statements have been placed at the beginnings of sentences where they are more likely to be heard by the listeners.

5. Place transitional words, also, at the start of sentences. For most forms of writing, it is considered better style to put such words as "however"

later in the sentence. But for broadcast writing, such words must begin a sentence so the audience knows at once the direction the sentence is taking.

6. Ruthlessly cut out all but the most essential details. Print is well adapted to providing details; broadcasting is not.

7. Keep in mind the wide range of sensibilities of your audience and the powerful impact of broadcasting in comparison to print. Avoid gruesome or disgusting details. Be sure all pictures are in good taste. Even some common sights—for instance, a person receiving a hypodermic injection or having blood drawn for a blood drive—can upset many viewers. You must also avoid material that might cause your audience to panic or become violent.

8. Read the copy aloud and listen for any awkward sounds. "S," "th," and "ing" can cause difficulties. A common word like "aluminum" can trip up a reader from time to time. Word combinations like "quartz wrist watch" can also prove troublesome.

9. Pencil out most attempts at clever plays on words. Puns, tongue-twisters, and similar word games are sure to cause difficulty for the newscaster and confusion for the audience. Worse, the audience may become so absorbed in the sound of the words that the meaning is lost. Keep it simple.

10. Get rid of lists, especially lists of names or numbers. The audience cannot remember so much detailed information.

11. Eliminate names whenever possible. Local names are generally good to use, as are names of famous people. All other names can usually be deleted and the person's job or role in the story substituted for the name. Remember, what the person does is usually more important than the person's name. This rule is particularly handy when the name is a difficult one to pronounce. For example, it is simpler for all concerned if you write, "the head of the Polish delegation" instead of "Wladislav Brznewski."

12. Watch for careless uses of abbreviations. Make sure that only very well-known ones—such as "Y-M-C-A"—are used or that names of organizations are spelled out in full before any abbreviated form is introduced in a story.

13. Make sure that pronunciation guides are provided for any words that may prove difficult. Remember, even fairly simple words can sometimes cause problems, so provide a pronunciation guide if there is the slightest possibility that the word may be mispronounced. Pencil in needed guides above the difficult words, using uppercase letters for accented syllables and lowercase letters for unaccented syllables. Use a simple phonetic system that will be easy for everyone to understand. Don't expect newscasters to know the International Phonetic Alphabet (IPA) or to understand the diacritical markings used in dictionaries. Instead, use guides like this:

CHUM-lee
Lady Cholmondeley will be in Lotusville for a week while. . . .

14. Edit long stories down as much as possible. The audience has a short attention span. You will do better to strive for a news program with many brief stories than one with a few long ones. Try to keep radio stories under forty seconds and television stories under one minute. Of course, there will be times when this isn't possible, but never let a long story pass without giving it an extra look to see if more cannot be cut out.

These are the basic rules for marking broadcast copy. Forget about any copyediting marks you may have learned for other uses. Simply cross out completely any word that needs to be changed and neatly print the correct word above it. Be sure everything on every page is clearly marked and easy to read. Time permitting, retype any page that has too many corrections.

ARRANGING THE STORIES

The final job of editing a script for a news program is the arranging of the stories in the script. Remember, only when the final arrangement has been made do you number the stories. Follow the rules outlined in Chapter 1.

Try to arrange stories so that they form logical groupings. You must lead, of course, with the most important stories of the day, but it is not necessary to arrange stories in descending order of importance. Nor is a strict division of stories into national, international, and local news necessarily a good idea, although some programs stick to that format. Rather, you should try to arrange the stories as they might come up in a conversation. Your arrangement should be as if each story reminded you of the next. You might work something along this line: the big story of the day is the president's new policy on the Middle East. That makes you think about a story on oil prices. Oil prices make you think about a story on increased prices for heating gas here at home. That reminds you of a story on the cost of living here in Lotusville—and so on.

Special attention needs to be paid to the stories that lead into and out of commercials and those that come at the end of the program. You should be aware of the material that will be in the commercials and try to avoid pairing certain stories with certain commercials. For example, it would be very poor taste to go directly from a story about a tragedy that cost hundreds of lives into a funny commercial.

Never put a long story or one that uses film, videotape, or an audio cart near the end of your program. There is no unobtrusive way that you can get out of such a story once it has begun, so if the newscaster suddenly realizes that time is running out, there is no alternative except to stop in the middle of the story—not a very professional way to end a show.

The closing of a program is usually part of the regular format of the show. So there is not much to edit in most cases. Some shows have a format that calls for always ending the show or going into a commercial with a light story (sometimes called a *kicker*)—one that is humorous or has plenty of human interest. Selecting such stories and fitting them into the logical pattern of the rest of the show can sometimes be a problem.

Many shows combine all of the sports news in a single package near the end of the show. This makes sense, but some sports stories could be aired earlier in the program if they fit the "conversational logic" of the story sequence. On the other hand, if your station has a separate sportscaster to read sports news, you might be invading her or his turf by putting sports stories elsewhere in the news. In many cases, the sports copy is prepared by the sports staff, independent of the regular news staff. This situation calls for careful coordination by the editor in putting together the final script—especially in checking the timing and making sure there is no duplication of stories.

ARRANGING FILMS AND VIDEOTAPES

If your television news program uses film instead of videotape—or if you have limited tape facilities—you may encounter special problems in selecting material for the end of your program. All newsfilm for a single show is usually spliced onto one or two reels. In some cases, all the videotape stories for a program may also have to be recorded onto a single roll of videotape. In such a situation, your selection of the final stories for the program should be based on the premise that the final story may never get on the air. If, while the program is being broadcast, the director finds that the program is running overtime, it is the director's right to order some stories eliminated to put the show back on schedule. There is no "fast forward" on most motion picture projectors, so it rarely makes sense to cut out a film story that is in the middle of the show. It takes the same time to run through that story to the next one even if the story is not used on the air. So, the story most likely to be cut from the show if the program is running overtime is the last story. To a lesser degree, this same situation may occur with videotape stories if they are all on the same reel, although it is possible to fast forward videotape. Sometimes it may make sense to postpone the dropping of a story until near the end of the show, when it is clear just how much time is needed, so even without the special problems just mentioned, the last story is usually the one that gets cut if cuts must be made. Therefore, when putting a script together you should usually put the least important film or videotape after all other film or videotape stories.

TIMING SCRIPTS

Timing, of course, is an integral element of editing broadcast news copy. Once the editor has chosen the stories to be used, times must be estimated as accurately as possible. If the program is running a bit long, the editor can often go back and cut a line from one story and another line somewhere else and get the script back to the proper length. If that won't work, one or more stories will have to be cut. And, if a deadline is very tight, it will probably be quicker to cut a whole story than to try to edit the script down to the correct running time.

Whenever you edit copy, you must be sure to change the estimated running time of any story that has been lengthened or shortened by your editing.

You may be called upon to *backtime* your script. The responsibility for backtiming the script falls on different shoulders at different stations. At some, it is the producer's job; elsewhere it may be the job of the news editor, the newscaster, or some other staff member. The idea is to mark at the top of those stories falling near the end of the show, and sometimes those leading into commercials, what the time on the clock should be when the newscaster starts to read that story. At some stations the entire script is backtimed. Then everyone can keep track of how much the show is running ahead of or behind schedule. Sometimes just the time is written at the top of the page. Sometimes the notation is made "AT 03:20" or "NLT 03:20," meaning the story should begin at, or no later than, three minutes and twenty seconds into the show. If the entire show is not backtimed, the producer and director will probably backtime all the stories in their own copies of the script because they have the ultimate responsibility for keeping the show running on time.

ADDING PAD

The editor's final job in arranging the script is to prepare the pad. As we have already explained, the end of each script should have several minutes worth of short, not-too-important stories in a separate section. (Sometimes a few pad stories may be placed in a special section before a commercial.) These are stories the newscaster reads only if the program is running fast. They are used to fill time until the beginning of a part of the show that must start at a specified time such as the sign-off. You must see to it that the pad stories are easy to read and all very brief.

No story or script is ready for the air until it has been edited. A common error of inexperienced broadcast journalists is to continue writing right up to *air time,* leaving little or no time for careful editing. Always set your deadline for copy so that you have adequate time to edit what has been written. The time spent editing is just as important as the time spent writing. Even if you only "rip and read" from a wire service, you must edit. If anything, editing is more important then because it is your only chance to catch errors in the wire copy before it goes on the air. A good news show depends just as much on good editing as it does on good writing. Learn to do both well.

Exercises
ᴀᴀᴀᴀᴀᴀᴀᴀᴀᴀ

Exercise 1

Put together a one-minute radio newscast from the following news items. Assume that the line lengths of the copy are correct for radio and that you can use the full sixty seconds of the minute for news. Do not worry about opening or closing material or commercials. Since most of these stories run about four lines, you will have to select the four stories you think have the most news value. Arrange them in the order you think they should be used on the air. Try to make your selection cover a variety of news topics that would be of interest to your audience. Be prepared to defend your selections in class.

AN ISRAELI FREIGHTER TODAY WILL BECOME THE FIRST ISRAELI VESSEL TO GO THROUGH THE SUEZ CANAL IN A QUARTER CENTURY. THE VESSEL, NAMED THE ASHDOD, IS LINED UP WITH A NORTHBOUND CONVOY THAT IS TO LEAVE SUEZ CITY IN EGYPT LATER TODAY.
—0—

THE LAST AMERICAN MILITARY PERSONNEL LEFT TAIWAN TODAY . . . ENDING 28 YEARS OF U-S MILITARY PRESENCE ON THE ISLAND. A MUTUAL DEFENSE TREATY WILL NOT BE TERMINATED UNTIL THE END OF THIS YEAR.
—0—

THERE WAS AN ANTINUCLEAR DEMONSTRATION IN TOKYO TODAY— INVOLVING ABOUT 300 PEOPLE. THE DEMONSTRATORS ARE DEMANDING THAT ALL NUCLEAR POWER PLANTS IN JAPAN BE SHUT DOWN FOR SAFETY INSPECTIONS.
—0—

THE MOUNT SOUFRIERE (SOO-FREE-AIR') VOLCANO ON THE ISLAND OF ST. VINCENT IS ACTING UP AGAIN—AFTER TWO DAYS OF RELATIVE CALM. VOLCANIC TREMORS STARTED UP AGAIN THIS MORNING—AT THE RATE OF TWO OR THREE EVERY MINUTE.
—0—

FEDERAL SAFETY OFFICIALS SAY THAT ABOUT ONE-MILLION FORD MOTOR COMPANY CARS BUILT BETWEEN 1970 AND 1973 HAVE FUEL TANK DEFECTS WHICH COULD RESULT IN DEATHS AFTER REAR-END CRASHES. THE CARS AFFECTED ARE FORD MAVERICKS AND MERCURY COMETS.
—0—

THREE ISRAELI CHILDREN WERE INJURED BY A BOMB OUTSIDE A SCHOOL IN TEL AVIV YESTERDAY. THE BOMBING CAME AS THE ISRAELI CABINET VOTED TO REINSTITUTE CAPITAL PUNISHMENT FOR TERRORISTS.
—0—

ANTINUCLEAR DEMONSTRATIONS WERE HELD YESTERDAY IN COLORADO, NORTH CAROLINA, OKLAHOMA, AND NEW MEXICO. THE BIGGEST WAS AT THE ROCKY FLATS NUCLEAR WEAPONS PLANT IN

COLORADO, WHERE 284 PEOPLE WERE ARRESTED FOR BLOCKING
ACCESS ROADS.
—0—

A GROUP CALLED TEAMSTERS FOR A DEMOCRATIC UNION ARE URGING
STRIKING STEEL HAULERS TO ACCEPT A NEGOTIATED CONTRACT, END
THEIR THREE-WEEK WALKOUT, AND RETURN TO WORK MONDAY.
—0—

THE ISRAELI CABINET VOTED SUNDAY TO REINSTATE CAPITAL
PUNISHMENT—AND INSTRUCTED PROSECUTORS TO DEMAND THE DEATH
PENALTY FOR TERRORISTS CONVICTED OF SO-CALLED INHUMAN CRUELTY.
—0—

TESTS ARE SCHEDULED FOR LATER TODAY TO MAKE SURE THAT A NEW
REACTOR COOLING PLAN PUT INTO EFFECT YESTERDAY AT THE CRIPPLED
THREE MILE ISLAND PLANT IN PENNSYLVANIA IS WORKING.
—0—

Exercise 2

Edit the following short news stories. Correct any misspelled words and typographical errors. Do not make the stories any shorter.

These stories are written in radio news format. Rewrite them (after editing) in television news format. Assume that the news set at your station has a Vizmo screen in back of the newscaster, that the freighter story is on videotape and the Vins story is on film.

On a separate sheet of paper for each story, describe what the television audience will see on the screen as each line of copy is read. Each script should begin MOC with appropriate cues for Vizmo. The freighter script will wind up with SI VTR/VO and the Vins story with SI FILM/VO. It is up to you to decide how much of each story will be tape or film.

In converting these radio stories to television format, what differences occur in the script? Do you need more words? Fewer? About the same number? How much difference does the addition of visuals make in each story?

From your standpoint as a professional who must judge the news value of each story you might use on the air, to what extent is each story a "media event"? Would these stories have occurred without news coverage? How much hard news value has each? Be prepare to discuss these questions in class.

FREIGHTER

(Suez City, Egypt)—A freighter named the Ashdod became today the firts ship flying the Israeli fla g to transit the suez canal since the creation of the of the Jewish state in 1948.

The 45-hunderd ton cargo ship, sailing empty, entered the waterway at its southren end this mornng as th seventh ship in a 34-vessel northbound convoy. It paid the usual $9,000 transit fee for the 15-hour trip.

The Ashdodd blew it's sirns severaltimes as it entered the cannel. An isreali flag flew from a mast and another one was painted on the funnel. An egyptian flag few from the ship's bow, asis customerry with all ships using the waterway.

It was a fist test of the implementaiton of the egyptian-israeli peace treaty.

VINS

President Reagan brouught justreleased so viet disident Georgi Vins with him as he as he attended Snuday worship service in Washington. Reagan told members of teh Church that it si sinfull to remain si lent about government injustices . . . and said he beleives God wood dislike the kind of pa triotism requires that silenc about government evils.

3 of the other 4 soviet dissidents were released saturday in exchange four 2 russian spies attended rallys on the east coast-sunday. but the best nown of them—Aleksander Ginzburg—set out for Vermont were he'll spend som time with his longtime collegue . . . nobel prize winning author Alexander Solzhenitsyn.

Exercise 3

Edit these television stories:

GARBAGE STRIKE—6 O'CLOCK NEWS—5/5/79—KENNEDY

BOB ON CAMERA KEY SLIDE: GARBAGE STRIKE	Rotting lemon peels are diappearing from Lemon County. . . . Trash pickup for a million reisdents now is back to near normal. . . . One third of the striking garbage workers crossing their own picket lines today to return to their jobs. Still no formal settlement in the eighteen-day, fourteen-city walkout . . . but the trash companies appear to have won.

STRIKE—6 O'CLOCK NEWS—5/5/79—MARSH

BOB ON CAMERA	In another labor dispute, eleven hundred
KEY SLIDE: EDISON	Lotuslandia Edison Company maintenance
LOGO	employees today delayed a thretened midnite
	walkout until next Tuesday. . . . Labor-
	management netogiations on a new contract
	have been under weigh for six months.
	The hand-up is a company-proposed rotating,
	seven-day week.
	Edison says

STRANGLER—6 O'CLOCK NEWS—5/5/79—JONES

BOB ON CAMERA	Farmdale Police are continuing there
KEY SLIDE:	investigation of a prime suspect in the
STRANGLER	Southside Strangler killings.
	The body of strangler suspect John Minton
	was realesed by authorities to a private
	funeral home. . . . But at the same time,
	services were held for his apparent victime

| KEY SLIDE: COLE | . . .Mary Cole, whom police say died wiht him |
| | a in a double shootout. |

Exercise 4

Type the following story, using double space and correct margin settings. Edit the story down to about thirty seconds. Do not rewrite the copy; simply cross out any unnecessary material and pencil in whatever additional material is needed.

118 YR OLYMPICS

(ATHENS)— —LOS DIABLOS OFFICIALS AND MEMBERS OF THE
INTERNATIONAL OLYMPIC COMMITTEE AGREE THE CHANCES OF LOS
DIABLOS BEING CHOSEN AS THE SITE OF THE 1984 SUMMER OLYMPICS
ARE BLEAKER THAN EVER.

LOS DIABLOS IS THE ONLY CITY ASKING TO HOST THE GAMES BUT THE CITY HAS RUN HEAD ON INTO THE I-O-C OVER THE ISSUE OF WHO CONTROLS OLYMPIC COSTS—THE I-O-C OR THE LOS DIABLOS CITY COUNCIL.

DESPITE BEHIND-THE-SCENES NEGOTIATIONS FOR THREE DAYS, THE MAIN CONFLICT REMAINS UNRESOLVED.

ANTONIO CALLA, THE PERSONAL ASSISTANT OF LOS DIABLOS MAYOR SAM WHITE, ADMITTED THE DIFFERENCES WERE STILL "VERY SERIOUS." WALT WONKA, A CITY COUNCILMAN WHO IS SKEPTICAL OF THE LOS DIABLOS BID, SAID HE WAS "NOT CONFIDENT" OF LOS DIABLOS BEING CHOSEN.

A SOURCE ON THE I-O-C's NINE-MAN EXECUTIVE BOARD MADE IT CLEAR THERE WAS LITTLE ROOM FOR MANEUVER.

7

How to Observe

Every good writer must be a good observer. You must train yourself to look for details that would ordinarily be missed, and you must develop the skill of turning those observations into words and pictures.

Broadcast newswriting is necessarily brief, and we achieve that brevity by cutting out facts and details. So training yourself to be a careful observer may seem a waste of time. It isn't. As with any art form—and good writing is an art—what you can do within the confines of the medium demonstrates proficiency. To write well for radio, you must help the listener see the scenes you describe. To write well for television, you must know which visual elements of a story are important and how to use words to describe the elements that are missing or difficult to make out on the screen. As a reporter on the scene, you must observe carefully what is happening. As a writer in the studio, you must study the audiotape, videotape, or film material skillfully to select what is most important. So, begin your career as a broadcast news writer by learning how to be a good observer.

BECOMING A GOOD OBSERVER

You can start learning how to be a good observer by asking yourself what you feel about the event you are going to observe. It is no secret that people tend to see what they want to see. Two witnesses of the same event can give strikingly different accounts of it. So ask yourself what *you* want to see. Next, ask yourself what you expect to see. That should help you to guard against your own inclination to make events match your desires or expectations. As James Thurber observed in one of his fables, "You might as well fall flat on your face as lean over too far backward."[1] Be aware of your prejudices when you cover a story, but don't eliminate an

---

[1] "The Bear Who Let It Alone," in *The Thurber Carnival* (New York: Harper & Brothers, 1945), p. 253.

observation simply because it jibes with your preconceptions. After all, reporters face similar events day after day. What they expect concerning an event is usually what happens. As long as you are on guard against forcing something different to conform to your preconceptions, you will be safe.

Next, consider your point of observation. Ask yourself how someone viewing the event from a different location might see it. Is it possible you have missed something important? You may decide that you need to move to a different location or move around while reporting.

For broadcast reporters, moving to a different location is not always easy. You have equipment to consider, and you need good placement for microphones and cameras. The best place for the equipment may not always be the best observation point. Microphones must be as close to the subject as possible, and long cables can create problems. Cameras can be bulky and are usually better operated from a tripod. That means they are usually assigned positions in back of other reporters to keep them from blocking the view. Video recorders can also be relatively bulky and hard to move about. Positioning equipment so that a cable or microwave signal can get to the desired receiver also limits your location. If time permits, it is a good idea to look around at any event you are reporting and at least check out different viewpoints with your eyes and ears, even if you cannot get to them with cameras and microphones.

For example, consider what happened to a campus radio station reporter who had covered a noon rally to protest the governor of Florida's policies on higher education. After hearing the story reported on the radio, one student wrote an angry letter to the program's producer asking whether or not the reporter had actually attended the rally. The reporter had estimated the crowd at 100. The critic said the crowd had numbered at least 300. The reporter had described the crowd as relatively tranquil, the applause as meager. The critic held that the rally was exciting and that the crowd had been "electrified" by the speakers. The letter ended, "Is it possible that your reporter's political interest led him to misinform his listeners—and perhaps even himself?"

Of course, the bias may be all the other way. People who write such letters are likely to have political interests so strong that the evidence of their eyes and ears is suspect. Hoping to see a large crowd, they are likely to see one. Wanting a speech they approve of to win loud applause, they are likely to hear that applause. Only a crowd that is thin almost to the point of invisibility, or applause that is nearly inaudible, will convince these strong partisan observers that their cause has failed—and even then they are likely to blame the radio for inadequately publicizing the event.

That is how the reporters reason when they are on the defensive: partisans see what they want to see and hear what they want to hear. But that is not the end of the matter. Even reporters who are scrupulously nonpartisan, or try to be, cannot turn themselves into machines for reporting and interpreting events. With the best will in the world, no reporter can completely overcome human inadequacies. Neither can you.

In the case of the campus radio station reporter at the noon protest rally, consider the likelihood that both the critic and the reporter were misled by their eyes and ears. The critic, a partisan, was standing up front near the speakers. Looking around, he saw a closely bunched crowd, with listeners almost touching one another. In his position, he was surrounded by those who supported the speakers. Their applause was loud and their comments approving. By contrast, the reporter, seeking a detached perspective in keeping with his role, stood farther away from the speakers. In his position at the back of the crowd (where the listeners gave one another more space and some sprawled on the ground), the reporter got an impression of thin ranks of people showing little interest. The people near the reporter were neither pressing forward eagerly nor applauding loudly.

From these differing perspectives, it is not surprising that the reporter and the critic received quite different (and, ultimately, inaccurate) impressions. But it is easier to blame the reporter than the critic. Instead of stationing himself in one place, the reporter should have moved around the scene to obtain a more faithful impression of crowd response. Instead of judging the size of the crowd from his limited viewpoint, he should have counted small samples in both the closely packed and the thinly populated areas to obtain a better estimate. Then, of course, he should have made it clear in his story that both the crowd response and the crowd size reported were estimates.

Estimating the size of a crowd is one problem reporters frequently face. You have several ways of handling it. You can go to an official source and cite that source in your story: "Police say there were only about forty demonstrators." Or you can cite conflicting sources: "Police say there were only about forty demonstrators, but organizers of the rally claim that over 200 people were there." Or you can make your own estimate. But no matter what sort of estimate you use, someone will probably disagree with it—after all, that's why it's an estimate and not an exact figure.

One technique reporters use for estimating crowd size is to divide the crowd visually into equal-sized rectangles. Then they count the number of people in several of these rectangles, calculate the average number of people in a rectangle, and multiply the average by the total number of rectangles. If some parts of the crowd have noticeably fewer people, you can count those areas separately.

CHOOSING YOUR WORDS WITH CARE

Because broadcast writing is usually tight writing, adjectives and adverbs are looked on with some suspicion by broadcast writers. We recommend

Mark Twain's advice: "As to the adjective—when in doubt, leave it out." This means that when you do use an adjective, you must be doubly certain that it is the right one. The first question to ask yourself is whether an adjective is really needed; the second question is which adjective says exactly what you mean.

There are many things about persons and events that your audience will have a hard time discerning from a brief electronic news report. For example, you would ordinarily want to have on audiotape or videotape the most important segment of a speech. That segment might have been received with tremendous applause by the audience. But it is also possible that the audience was not very enthusiastic and the one segment you have selected as most important does not correctly tell the broadcast audience how those present at the event reacted to the speech as a whole. That should be explained. And it will have to be explained in very few words. What is your best description of the audience's response—cool? reserved? restrained? apathetic? low-key? There are dozens of adjectives you might use, but which is the very best one? The words we have suggested here are not strictly synonymous. (There is an old saw that the only true synonyms in the English language are "gorse" and "furze." Try looking them up in the dictionary.) If you say the audience was "cool," that may suggest an undertone of mild hostility. On the other hand, if you say it was "reserved," that suggests the audience wished to remain somewhat aloof from the speaker or the speaker's views. Each word you choose carries with it a sort of halo of related ideas. You have to know your language well to understand the full meanings of the words you select and their connotations for your listeners.

Observing, then, is a double process. It is seeing things with as little distortion as possible and describing what you see with as much verbal precision as your abilities permit. Verbal precision is useless without good observation, and good observation can be crippled by imprecise writing.

One poorly chosen word can change the meaning of a story. How powerful a single word can be was shown clearly in this experiment conducted in a college classroom. The professor gave each of his students a written description of a guest lecturer. The descriptions were alike with one exception: one group of students read that the lecturer was "rather cold," while the other group read that the lecturer was "very warm." The students did not know that the descriptions varied.

After the lecture, the students were asked to rate the guest. The evaluations of those who had read the "warm" description rated him as more considerate of others, more informed, more sociable, more popular, better natured, more humorous, and more humane than the evaluations of the students who received the "cold" description. Also, 56 percent of the students who had read the "warm" description engaged in discussion with the lecturer; only 32 percent of those who had read the "cold" description did so.

The students were misled, of course, by the written descriptions they had received. As a broadcast newswriter, you are a writer of descriptions. Your audience may be affected by your words just as the students were affected in this experiment. When you describe someone, you must think carefully about each word you use and what effect it may have on your audience.

How often must you, as a broadcast newswriter, describe someone? In nearly every script you write. And a single word like "warm" or "cold" can describe a person so strikingly—even if incorrectly—that many of your viewers will carry away the thought. When you are writing a news script describing workers on strike, how should you describe them—as "militant," "quiet," or what? Selecting a proper description is not easy. But if you omit any description, your audience may be misled by what they see or hear.

OBSERVING FOR TELEVISION

You might assume that the camera can do all the observing for you in television. But the audience can be misled by what the camera shows. Thirty years ago, communication researchers Kurt and Gladys Lang conducted a study that clearly pointed out the problem. They chose as the subject of their study the television coverage of a parade in Chicago to welcome home General Douglas MacArthur. President Harry S. Truman had relieved MacArthur of his command in the Korean war after a dispute over the way MacArthur was carrying out the declared policy of the United States in that war. MacArthur was supported in his dispute with Truman by most Republican members of Congress and some conservative Democrats. There was heavy media coverage of the situation, and MacArthur's return was one of the first events to be covered extensively by the new medium of television.

The Langs stationed thirty-one observers along the parade route in Chicago. Other observers monitored the television reports of the parade. The following is a typical account by one of the observers along the parade route:

> I had listened to the accounts of the general's arrival in San Francisco, heard radio reports of his progress through the United States, and had heard the Washington speech as well as the radio account of his New York reception. . . . I had, therefore expected the crowds to be much more vehement, contagious, and identified with the general. I had expected to hear much political talk, especially anti-Communist and against the administration.
>
> These expectations were completely unfulfilled. I was amazed that I did not once hear the president criticized, or as much as an

allusion to the Communists. . . . I had expected roaring, excited mobs; instead, there were quiet, well-ordered, dignified people. . . . The air of curiosity and the casualness surprised me. Most people seemed to look on the event as simply something that might be interesting to watch.

In sharp contrast were the impressions of the television viewers. One observer who was monitoring the television coverage reported:

. . . the last buildup on TV concerning the "crowd" gave me the impression that the crowd was pressing and straining so hard that it was going to be hard to control. My first thought, "I'm glad I'm not in that" and "I hope nobody gets crushed."

No one was in real danger of being crushed, despite the television impression. A parade observer reporting from streetside on the same scene said only:

Everybody strained but few could get a really good glimpse of him. A few seconds after he had passed most people merely turned around to shrug and to address their neighbors with such phrases: "That's all," "That was it," "Gee, he looks just like he does in the movies," "What'll we do now?"[2]

In short, then, the camera does lie—or, in any case, those who report with cameras can juggle scenes in such a way that reality and reportage are quite different. Another, more striking aspect of the Langs' study was that the television viewer found the general the center of attraction throughout the telecast. The camera followed him and maintained the viewer's focus on the interplay between heroic figure and enthusiastic crowd. The cheering seemed constant and even seemed to reach its crest as the telecast ended. Meanwhile, the reality along the streets was much less exciting. The spectators caught a brief glimpse of the general, and that was all.

When observing for television, the rule is this: unless you describe what happened from the standpoint of an observer, you and the rest of the news staff are lying.

SOME GUIDELINES FOR OBSERVATION

The following guidelines will help you be a good observer.

---

[2] Kurt Lang and Gladys Engel Lang, "The Unique Perspective of Television and Its Effect," in *Mass Communications*, ed. Wilbur Schramm, 2nd ed. (Urbana, Ill.: University of Illinois Press, 1960), pp. 544–60.

Assume Some Distortion Will Creep In

Not even the best reporter can be free of all distortion. But if you assume that some distortion is inevitable, you will be on the lookout for it and you will be better able to keep the distortion to a minimum.

Keep Your Emotions in Check

It is very unlikely that there is really such a thing as a "dispassionate observer." Newspeople, too, get caught up emotionally in some of the events they cover. We are all human, and we all have emotions. Reporters must deal with every aspect of human life. Some events are bound to anger reporters. Others must make them weep. Most reporters do develop a tough hide. They make a practice of joking about things that other people would find disturbing. This is not cynicism; it is a defense mechanism. Without this defense, the task of reporting some stories would be almost too grim to contemplate. But don't be mistaken. Despite the joking, reporters feel the same emotions as anyone else. Professionalism demands that those emotions be kept in check.

This is more important for a broadcast reporter than for a print reporter. You may be reporting on the air live. Even if the material is not live, broadcast deadlines are tight. There is little time to cool off and reconsider. There is far less editing and rewriting in electronic news than there is in print. And there is far more likelihood in broadcasting that your first impressions of a story will get on the air. You must set emotional distance between you and the event you cover. You must not be carried away by the enthusiasm of the crowd, you must not be outraged by statements or actions, you must not let pity keep you from doing your job, and you must not let fear diminish your abilities to report.

No one manages this all the time. You have to remind yourself that your job is to get the story on the air. After that, if you want to cry, have the shakes, break something, or shout obscenities—okay. But always remember—the story comes first.

Concentrate on the Significant Details

Time after time we have alluded to the way people mentally "tune in" and "tune out" news. This is normal human behavior. No one pays attention to everything that is going on around her or him. We would get little done if we did. St. Teresa of Avila is said to have complained that her meditations were sometimes disturbed by the sudden realization that a chair needed dusting or a picture frame needed straightening. Even saints need to tune out the things going on around them. But when you are observing, you must be tuned in.

It is a tough job. Marshall McLuhan has popularized the concepts of "matrix" and "linear." Print, he says, is linear. One word neatly follows another. But life is a matrix. Everything comes at us at once. We have to select some things to concentrate on and ignore the rest. The trick for the good observer is to know which things to concentrate on.

The good observer does not allow one event to absorb all of her or his attention. Instead, the observer scans the scene with both ears and eyes. The observer pauses, concentrates on one item, then goes on to another. After initially scanning the scene, the observer sets up a rough hierarchy of segments of the scene to watch. Some segments obviously have more potential than others. Some can be observed once and mentally filed away. If there is a sign hanging behind a speaker, the wording of the sign will not change. You note it once and then cross it off your mental list of things to concentrate on. On the other hand, if there is a heckler in the audience, it is a good bet that the loudmouth will not be satisfied with making just one disturbance, so you pay more attention to that area of the room. Try to get a look at the heckler. Does the person appear angry, distraught, mentally disturbed, drunk, or just boisterous? What is the heckler's race, sex, age, and physical appearance? Do any of these characteristics seem to tie in with what the person is saying? Is the person carrying a sign or wearing any symbols that indicate a particular viewpoint? Does the heckler appear to be alone or part of a group?

That is just one element of your observation. What about the person making the speech? How would you describe that person? Tall, short, thin, fat, dark, light, young, old? How is the speaker dressed? How does the speaker move? Does the speech seem well-prepared? Does the speaker seem ill at ease? What about the speaker's gestures?

You know that you will probably use little, if any, of this information in your story, but that is not the point. The point is that you have it available if you do happen to need it. Remember, you can't go back and observe the event after it's over if you decide later that you need some other item of information.

REPORTING "LIVE"

Some of the best examples of the broadcast reporter as an observer are live descriptions of events given by reporters as the events occurred. This book, of course, is about writing, and such reports are not written. Yet they can vividly illustrate how skilled broadcast reporters train themselves to observe and describe events.

Here is an excellent example—CBS reporter Bruce Dunning's description of one of the last flights to carry refugees out of DaNang before it fell to the North Vietnamese communists in 1975:

> We're trying to get them on as quickly as we can. They're holding onto the air-stair. There's a sea of humanity jamming on. Impossible to stop the crowd. People are falling off the air-stair. They've

got about a half dozen people on the plane. They're . . . uh . . . caught. Another dozen . . . they're running along, grabbing at the air-stairs. Our plane is surrounded here. I don't know how the hell we're going to get out. We're loading the people on as fast as we can. Women and children are obviously being left behind. All around the plane there are people with children, women standing around, but it's the men who don't have any who are getting on fastest. They're the ones that are jamming up the stairs. We've gotten on about three or four children and a couple of women, and that's all. They've torn apart the railings. The plane is rolling. People are still trying to crawl up the stairs. They're falling off on the runway behind. We're leaving behind a stream of people. The plane is picking up speed, heavily overloaded. The tail is sinking badly. We're trying to get everybody up front. They're taking off on one of the most rough runways—take-offs I've had, but this World Airways fella has done a fantastic job. The men on board are cheering. But it's hardly a case of cheering, I should think. These men left behind hundreds of thousands of women and children that should have gotten on. We only got on about two or three women and a . . . maybe a half-dozen kids. We're up in the air. We're up over DaNang. We seem to have everybody on. This was the most terrifying experience I've ever had in Viet Nam.[3]

This is a good example of the careful observer working under pressure. Dunning's report needed little editing to convert it into print. His descriptions were clear and simple, delivered in short, easy-to-understand sentences. There are few adjectives. But Dunning has made a careful analysis of the scene before him. He has described and emphasized the key points—the crowd fighting its way up the stairs to the plane, the women and children left behind, the perilous takeoff, and finally, the elation of the men who made it, tempered with the sad realization that most of the women and children had been left behind.

The reporter in this case makes an interesting contrast with the subject of his story. The reporter, who kept his head and did what was expected of him by reporting the event, contrasts dramatically with the men of DaNang, who panicked and violated the basic rule of all civilized people in a disaster: women and children first. (Although, to be fair, the reporter was already safely on the plane.)

Of course, most reporting is not so dramatic. But whatever you report, if you train yourself to be a good observer, you will find that you have already taken care of some of the toughest work of writing before you sit down to write.

---

[3] Rebroadcast on the CBS 50th Birthday Program, September 18, 1977. Courtesy Columbia Broadcasting System.

How to Observe

Exercises

Exercise 1

If you can sharpen your observation techniques, you can become a better reporter. Consider the following situations and decide what details you would look for in each one. List at least five areas of observation for each situation.

1. You interview the head of your campus computer center for a story about the many different uses various departments have for the computer. What will you look for at the computer building to flesh out your story?

2. You are interviewing the head of a teachers' union who has recently proposed that all public school teachers be given the right to strike. Your meeting with her is taking place at the airport, where she has a one-hour layover. What kind of details can you gather in a situation like this one?

3. You are spending a day on the road with Pete Durham, a politician who is running for Congress. His assistant is driving both of you through the district. You stop at drugstores, post offices, courthouses, and local businesses and gathering places. What details will you gather on a road trip like this?

Exercise 2

Go with a classmate to an event such as a football game, a rock concert, or a political rally. Then, separately, each of you should write about the event in a one-minute radio news story. Compare your story with that of your classmate. Does your classmate's story seem distorted?

Exercise 3

As an observer, you must go to the busiest building on your campus. Go there at a time when the students are moving from class to class. Take notes on their behavior—how some of them hurry along, while others seem lethargic, and so on. When the next class starts, go into the largest classroom and take notes on how the teacher performs and how the students perform (or fail to perform). From your notes, type at least two, double-spaced pages of description and bring your observations to class for reading and discussion.

Exercise 4

A common failing of beginning writers is to describe interviewees by name only or—God forbid!—by height and weight. For broadcast writing, such descriptions must be tight, and often a person's name *is* all you have time for. But a writer must be an accurate observer. There are stories in which you will need to call into play an ability to observe and describe. To develop those skills, the rules for this exercise are: You must describe an interviewee in one minute without giving the individual's height, weight, or color of eyes or hair. For example, one student described a teacher this way:

His soft, hesitating voice leaves you with the impression that here is a kind man who has been thrust into authority and does . . . not . . . know what to do with it. Oddly, this lack of authority in his attitude is an asset. People who work under him consider him as one of the gang rather than the boss man.

He usually wears a white shirt and a pair of baggy, tan pants. He seems both immaculate and carefree at the same time. His somewhat breathy speech, bright eyes, and hurried walk make him seem to be in a constant rush to get somewhere or finish something. You notice this even when he sits listening to a student. He sits leaning forward on his desk, with his arms supporting his weight and his hands clenched. He is interested in what the students say and hangs onto every word—not only with his mind and quick eyes—but with his whole body. His appeal is that of a shy little boy who finds everything around him vital and interesting.

Your assignment now is this: In fifteen minutes write a one-minute description of a teacher without giving her or his height, weight, or color of eyes and hair.

Exercise 5

Learning to "think on your feet" is an important part of becoming a broadcast reporter. Team up with another student and attend a meeting of one of the bodies of your student government. Take a tape recorder, a note pad, and a stopwatch. Your classmate should carry only a note pad and a pencil. Observe the meeting and take notes. After the meeting, your classmate should leave to type up his version of the story. You go immediately to the nearest quiet location you can find and record a one-minute audiotape story about the meeting. Reverse roles with your classmate for another similar meeting. Compare the written and spoken descriptions of the meeting in class.

If you have access to sound-on-film motion picture equipment or portable video recording equipment, conduct the exercise as a stand-up report. Find a location close to the site of the meeting and report the story directly to the camera. Let your classmate operate the equipment, keep track of the time, and signal you when to wind up the story so you can make it exactly one minute. Take along some large cue cards or sheets of paper and a felt tip pen so that you can make a few notes to be held just below the camera lens. Speak directly to the camera and try not to appear to be reading notes. You will find this very difficult at first, but do not give up. It will become easier with practice. Compare your stand-up story with your classmate's written story.

Exercise 6

Have your instructor pick out a photograph in a recent newspaper or magazine and let everyone in the class study the picture for thirty seconds. Then, within ten minutes, you are to write a one-minute description of the picture. Use radio or television format, as your instructor directs. As much as time allows, each student should read her or his description and let the class discuss how well the description fits the picture. As you consider each description, watch for mistakes, for the omission of important elements, and for the inclusion or overemphasis of unimportant elements.

8

The Interview

Interviewing is the heart of broadcast reporting. Most audio stories used in radio news and videotape stories in television news are interviews.

However, the interview is also one of the most criticized electronic news forms. The primary reason is the necessary brevity of the interview segments used on the air. Forty seconds—often less—is about all that is likely to be used in a radio interview. A television interview may run a minute or more, depending upon the content and the type of program in which it runs. In both media, this is probably only a tiny fraction of the material recorded during the interview.

INTERVIEWING FOR ELECTRONIC NEWS

All news is edited, of course. Newspapers must trim down and select from the material they collect, just as broadcast news departments must. Some experts have estimated that only about 1 percent of the daily news collected finally gets into the newspapers. Newspapers also condense interviews, but they can carry a larger portion of the total interview than broadcasters can normally use. Moreover, newspapers are more flexible in their editing. They can cut out a word here, a sentence there, and sometimes make the printed version more polished than the original interview. Broadcasters cannot edit with that precision. Both for technical reasons and because of limited preparation time, broadcasters must use entire segments of recorded material. They seldom have the option of taking a bit of this portion of the interview and a bit of another portion. It is a question of one segment or the other. That means that qualifications to one statement made in another portion of the interview may have to be left out. When the interview is aired, the interviewee may feel that she or he has been misquoted. A more accurate description would be that the person has been "underquoted"—too little of a statement was used to get its complete meaning across.

The newspaper writer can also help clarify material that may have been unclear, ambiguous, or even incorrect in an interview. The broadcast writer, on the other hand, is stuck with the words exactly as the interviewee spoke them. Moreover, the broadcast newsperson runs the risk of being accused of trying to twist those words if she or he interjects explanations of what was really meant. Experienced broadcast interviewers know that people sometimes unintentionally say exactly the opposite of what they mean. It happens all the time. In the broader context of an entire interview, the real meaning is usually perfectly clear. But if an interviewer does not quickly stop the interviewee and ask for correction or clarification, unintended statements remain in the recorded interview and may get on the air.

Most broadcast reporters are given less time to prepare for stories than newspaper writers. In a smaller market, one reporter may have to conduct several interviews in the same day, plus carry out other reporting assignments. Under these circumstances, the reporter can't do much homework before starting to ask questions.

LEARNING TO INTERVIEW

Despite these problems, the interview is probably the most common form of recorded broadcast news story—and it can also be the best. Well-conducted broadcast interviews, handled by experts, can convey more to the audience than the same material can in print. On radio, the listener can hear the interviewee's tone of voice and note the length of time the interviewee takes to respond to questions. On television, the interviewee's facial expressions and body language add to the meaning of the words. The camera can *zoom* in for a close-up of the subject's face or hands and give the audience a view that even the interviewer does not get during the interview.

To be a good electronic newsperson, then, you must learn to be a good interviewer. It is true that some people seem to have been born with an ability to interview while others are never able to master the art. But anyone who devotes time and effort to the task can at least become a competent interviewer.

DEVELOPING AN EFFECTIVE ATTITUDE

The stereotype of the broadcast reporter as a demanding, rough-talking crusader is generally false. For every reporter who dashes around acting out this role, you will find a hundred others who are warm, personable, and usually more effective. No doubt, some reporters believe that techniques that emphasize verbal force help them in their work, but most reporters do not feel this way. Of course, there are some occasions when any reporter may have to stand firm. After all, part of the job is asking tough questions. But a reporter's main source of information is people. And treating people with respect is usually the best way to get information from them.

However, most students come to the job of interviewing too shy and undemanding. When someone agrees to an interview, we say, elegantly, that the person has "granted" an interview. Nonsense. If the person did not feel she or he had something to gain from the interview, you can be sure the interview would not be granted. As a broadcast writer, you are providing that person with a conduit to the public. In return for that privilege, the interviewee gives you the chance to ask tough questions. Your obligation to the public is to see that the audience gets accurate and reasonably detailed information from the interview. Students, of course, are learning their trade, and some errors are to be expected—but entirely too often a student "interview" turns out to be a situation in which the reporter sits by passively and lets the interviewee say whatever she or he feels like saying and then end the interview. (Students are not the only broadcast journalists guilty of this fault.)

That does not mean that you have to be essentially hostile to your interviewee. A few reporters succeed with that technique, but for most it is a mistake. You can draw more flies (and good responses) with honey than with vinegar. Moreover, a hostile approach will lead your audience to suspect you of bias and unfair reporting. The best approach is to be courteous, but persistent. When the interviewee dodges a question, you should politely point out that your question has not been answered—then you should repeat the question. You may have to do this several times. Or when the interviewee rambles, you should politely bring her or him back to the main point. Remember, broadcast interviews must be short, and it is not amiss to remind the interviewee that answers must be kept short.

You need to tread a careful line between empathy and sympathy. You should not become emotionally involved in the problems of your interviewee, but you should understand the emotions that person is feeling. For example, your job will often require you to interview bereaved parents. Sympathy must not keep you from doing your job, but empathy should make it clear that you do not ask such questions as, "How did you feel when you saw the train run over your baby?"

WORKING WITH THE INTERVIEWEE

You will have better luck with an interview if you learn to set your interviewee at ease. That begins with being at ease yourself. You must deal with the interviewee as an equal. You must be able to converse with the interviewee as you would with an old friend. You must also be aware that some people will find the microphones, lights, and cameras a new and disturbing experience. And you will probably have to remind the interviewee politely about such things as speaking into the microphone, not moving off camera or out of the lights, and not making extraneous noise by doing things such as nervously drumming fingers on the table. You can't expect most people to be really at ease in this sort of situation, so you will have to use all the charm you can muster to get the interviewee interested enough in the conversation to forget the surroundings. Sometimes you can help allay the interviewee's fears of microphones and cameras by subtly pointing out that the equipment is helping to get her or his message across to a large audience and is also helping to protect the interviewee against being misquoted. However, you must use some discretion if you use this approach. In some cases, you may raise new issues that will make the interviewee worry more.

PREPARING FOR AN INTERVIEW

Professionalism for a news writer includes knowing what an interview is: a purposeful conversation. On rare occasions, an interviewer may have to conduct a "fishing expedition," not quite sure what the conversation will uncover. But a reporter must not elevate vague inquiries to the status of a method. Hoping that aimless questions will turn up something guarantees that an interviewer will spend much of her or his career wasting everybody's time. The late John Gunther, author of the famous *Inside* books, chose to begin an article setting forth his trade secrets in this way: "It seems to me that the first essence of journalism is to know what you want to know." This rule may seem ludicrously simple. Many beginners, however, are all too obviously unaware of it. Nothing so deadens interviews as reporters who are not quite sure of what they want. Interviewers must first decide what they want to know—then determine who can tell them.

It is essential to be well prepared for an interview. That means you must do as much research for the interview as your time will allow. As we noted, too often a broadcast reporter has little or no time for such preparation. So you must know where you can get the information you need quickly. You must be up to date on a broad spectrum of current events so that you will know something about your interviewee and your topic even before you receive the assignment.

You should always have the following information before you begin an interview: (1) the interviewee's first and last name—including both the correct spelling and the correct pronunciation, (2) what the person does, (3) the interviewee's official title, and (4) the purpose of the interview. Also, you should prepare a list of questions. Try to have a few "ice-breakers" ready to open the conversation—and try to keep it a conversation, not a monologue on either side. If you start with a few easy questions, you can help the interviewee to feel at ease. Broadcast journalist Russell Porter suggests: "Warm your interviewee up by having him talk about what he wants to talk about. Then induce him to talk about your subject."

CONDUCTING THE INTERVIEW

Don't stick slavishly to your question list while you conduct the interview. The interview may move in a new and useful direction all on its own. You shouldn't try to drag it back to your prepared questions—so long as the interview is going somewhere interesting. Although you should keep your prepared questions in mind so that you can raise one whenever you see that you are reaching a dead end in the conversation or that the interviewee is rambling, it doesn't follow that question number two on your list is the second question you should ask. Question ten may make more sense at that moment. You must use common sense and have a feel for the direction of the conversation. Don't be afraid to come up with questions not on your original list. Better ones usually come to mind as a result of the interaction between you and the interviewee.

Tough questions are usually best saved for last. By that time, your interviewee should be in a more responsive mood. If not, it is still best to hold the tough questions for the end. After all, if they are very tough questions, asking them may really be the end of the interview. Your interviewee may end it right there, and you don't want to run the risk of having your first question also be the last one. Even an interviewee who does not terminate an interview because of a tough question may be made hostile or wary during the rest of the interview. So the start of an interview is seldom the time for tough questions.

There are rare exceptions. Some interviews are destined to be adversary relationships from the outset. There are situations in which there really aren't any "easy" questions to ask about a topic. In such an instance, it's a waste of time to ask irrelevant questions simply to postpone the inevitable. And once in a while, an interviewer has to make it clear from the start that she or he means business, that the interview is not to be just fun and games. These are, as we stated, rare exceptions. The basic rule of delaying hard questions to the end still holds for the vast majority of interviews.

You should neither try to dominate the conversation nor let the interviewee dominate it. What the interviewee says is more important than what you have to say. In fact, your question may be edited out later to save time. But not everything that may pop into the interviewee's mind is necessarily interesting or germane to your topic. Moreover, most stations today like to develop an image for their reporters, which means that some participation by you in the conversation may be desirable in the final edited interview. Unfortunately, inexperienced reporters sometimes forget to keep a leash on their opinions. Interviews and news conferences these days are sometimes ruined by people who are supposed to be reporters, but who turn their privilege of asking questions into an excuse for making a speech. So let's be brutally frank: no one cares about what your opinion on the topic is. If they did, you would be the interviewee.

PHRASING YOUR QUESTIONS

This desire of inexperienced reporters to become the center of attention also leads to another major problem in interviews: the endless question. Some reporters ramble on endlessly and often wind up posing no question at all. Too often today we hear this anguished response from the interviewee: "But what is the question?" In fact, the question you ask may be so complex in its nature that it would take the entire faculty of M.I.T. to answer it, but it must be phrased so that a four-year-old child can understand what you have said.

This is one area in which preparation sometimes backfires for the inexperienced reporter. You can become so immersed in the jargon of the interviewee's field that you forget to phrase your questions so the audience, too, can understand them. It may bolster your ego to be able to converse with an interviewee in her or his "language," but you must not forget about your audience. Worse, a jargon-laden question often lends itself to a simple yes-or-no response. In most cases, the result is a very dull interview. Here's an example of what we mean:

> REPORTER: Does that mean, Senator, that the Administration is abandoning a Keynesian approach to the recession and adopting a purely monetarist policy?

> INTER-
> VIEWEE: Yup.
>
> (Long painful silence as it becomes evident the senator has completed his answer.)

Once in a while, of course, a simple "yes" or "no" can be dramatic. But we usually want a more detailed statement from the interviewee. A better approach would have been:

> REPORTER: Senator, could you explain how the Administration has changed the way it is dealing with the recession?

Or the reporter can lead the interviewee into an explanation through a series of questions:

> REPORTER: Senator, has the Administration changed its plan for dealing with the recession?

> INTER-
> VIEWEE: It has.
>
> REPORTER: Why?

"Drawing Out" Interviewees

When you find that you cannot get your interviewee to respond to each question with more than a monosyllable, a simple technique that usually works is to ask, "Why?"

"Why?" is a question that cannot be answered "yes" or "no." It forces a lengthier response from the interviewee. People like to be asked "Why?" because that question gives them a chance to show off their expertise. Of course, it can also show off their lack of expertise. But that result is equally important to your audience—if not so flattering to the interviewee.

In the preceding sample interview, "How?" would also have been a good question to ask in order to elicit a more detailed response. Don't be afraid to ask "Why?" and "How?"

Acting as Surrogate for the Audience

The broadcast interviewer has to learn to ask "dumb questions." We do not mean pointless, stupid questions. Rather, we mean the interviewer must ask questions that the audience wants the answers to. You may already know the answer to a question or you may think that the question isn't very important, but the members of the audience do not know as much about the subject as you do. You must ask the questions that elicit the answers they need.

As we pointed out earlier, you must know what you want before you begin an interview. That does not rule out interesting new material that comes up in the interview, but most of the time an interviewer knows pretty well what the interviewee will say. That's not editorial bias; it is simply good journalism. You have probably selected your interviewee because she or he is a known spokesperson for a particular point of view or an acknowledged expert in some field. In many cases, you could easily state the position of your interviewee yourself and skip the interview. But hearing the information from a "source" instead of the newscaster makes the program far more interesting. It also adds those dimensions of sound and picture that would be missing if you simply summarized the interviewee's point of view or paraphrased the interviewee's statements. In most interviews, you are not trying to get the interviewee to reveal new information. Instead, you are trying to get the interviewee to state something you already know in her or his own words.

For example, you ask, "Sheriff Katches, were there signs of foul play?" You don't ask that because you don't know. If you don't know the answer to that question, you haven't been doing a very good job of reporting. Rather, you ask that question because you want the answer to come from the sheriff.

Your Responses

The broadcast journalist has some special considerations to keep in mind during an interview. First, you should avoid the appearance of bias. You must not show dislike for your interviewee or disagree with what is said. You should look and sound neutral.

The usual problem with the inexperienced reporter is not showing overt hostility, but appearing to be too much in agreement. We learn in our daily lives to make little friendly responses to people who are speaking to us—even when we disagree with what they say. We nod politely, smile, and make other signs we are listening and want the other person to go on. These responses are habitual in most of us, and we are seldom aware of them. But, on camera, a nod or a smile will appear to the audience as a sign of enthusiastic agreement with what is being said. You must break these habits. You should look interested in what is being said, but you should not indicate approval or disapproval by your actions or words.

Verbal responses, too, are part of our habitual way of listening to people. On radio and television, however, they sound idiotic and unprofessional. Young journalists are often surprised the first time they hear themselves conducting an interview. At every pause in the interview, they hear themselves mumble "Uh huh," "Yeah," "Really?" "I see," "Oh," "I know," or some other pointless phrase. It is often impossible to edit out these silly phrases, and it takes time to do so when it can be done. You must learn to interview without using these interjections.

INTERVIEWING BY TELEPHONE

Radio reporters must develop the special skill of interviewing over the telephone. This is the quickest and easiest way to get an interview for radio. For most stations, telephone interviews are far more common than interviews done on location or in a studio. And at a small station, the staff simply isn't large enough to take the time for the other types of interview.

There are disadvantages to telephone interviews. While a telephone interview can be the easiest kind to get, it is also the easiest kind of interview to dodge. Without ever actually refusing to talk to you, the person you hope to interview can somehow always be out of the office when you call or never get around to returning your call. And, of course, you can't see the person during the interview. There may be a cabal of attorneys and public relations people hovering around the interviewee's desk, scribbling out each response to be read. In fact, you can't really be sure you are talking to the right person. More than one broadcast reporter has been taken in by someone posing as someone else over the telephone. Still, it would be hard to produce a radio news program without using telephone interviews.

There are certain rules that must be followed when you conduct a telephone interview. First, you must inform the person on the telephone that you wish to record the interview for use on a news program. Try to give this information in a casual, reassuring way. Sometimes, it frightens people. Once you have the consent of the interviewee, you can turn on your recording equipment.

Next, you will have to ask a few unimportant questions to set the interviewee at ease while you set the proper levels on the recording equipment. Don't tell the interviewee that these questions are just to get an audio level. If you do, you may find that the interviewee's voice suddenly grows louder or softer when you begin the actual interview questions. Remember to remind your interviewee to keep responses short. This is particularly important for radio news.

Listen carefully for extraneous noise. Most newsroom telephones have a push-to-talk switch, which cuts off the mouthpiece of your telephone when the button is not held down. This is a bit tricky to learn to use, but it is an invaluable aid to keeping out background noises from your end of the line. Just remember to depress the button immediately before you start to say something and release it as soon as you have finished speaking. Listen also for noise on the other end of the line. You may have to ask your interviewee to move to another telephone in less distracting surroundings.

Sometimes you will encounter interference on the telephone line. Tell the interviewee that you will call back on another line. Then hang up, and redial or rekey the number. If you try this several times and still get interference, call the operator and see if you can get a better line. You should, of course, have a specially amplified, balanced line at your station for conducting such calls. Regular lines and nonprofessional recording devices will produce poor results.

When you have completed the interview, ask the interviewee if you can call back if you need additional information. Do not, however, offer the interviewee any veto power over the content of the interview. What goes into the interview is your responsibility.

It is good public relations for your station to remind the interviewee of your station's call letters and frequency and to indicate when you think the interview material may be used. However, never promise an interviewee that the material will be used at a specific time—or that it will be used at all.

EDITING INTERVIEW MATERIAL

You can usually achieve the tightest interview story by editing your questions out of the interview. You can paraphrase your questions if they are needed in the script. However, there are times when a question must be left in or when station policy dictates that the reporter must be seen or heard in most stories.

You cannot clean up broadcast interviews, cutting out stammering and minor imperfections. You must select whole segments of the interview for use. For radio, you will rarely use more than one statement from an interview in a given news program. However, time permitting, you can often prepare several stories—each of which uses a different segment of the interview—and use one story on each of several news programs. This way you can get more mileage out of your interviews.

If you do use more than one *cut* from an interview, make it clear to your audience where one segment ends and another begins. For television, the change in the picture is usually an easy way to let the audience know you have shifted to a different segment of the interview. For radio, it is best to insert some phrase between two audio cuts—for example, "But later, the senator qualified that statement." Not every use of two cuts edited together may require such a transition, but you should always be on the alert to make sure you do not mislead the audience into thinking that two statements from two different parts of an interview were originally made one after the other. In some circumstances, joining two statements without using a transitional phrase can change the meaning of one or both of the statements.

CBS News has a rule that is followed by many stations today. It forbids the presentation of interview material in any sequence other than that of the original recording. In other words, you may edit out material between two cuts, but you may not reverse the order of those cuts in your story. This helps to prevent distorting statements by quoting them out of context.

You can also mislead your audience by intercutting two interviews in a story. It is logical to include statements by spokespersons from both sides of a controversy. Sometimes interviews of two opposing spokespersons are edited so that pro and con statements are provided on each major issue. This creates the illusion of a "debate"—but you should take pains to make sure your audience understands that it is not a real debate, that the two speakers were not in the same room and could not respond directly to each other's statements. In an actual debate, the speakers might have made very different statements. Be sure your audience understands that it is listening to statements taken from two separate interviews. Some news directors will not allow this type of story because they feel it is inherently misleading.

WRITING THE INTERVIEW STORY

What we have said so far in this chapter may seem to have little to do with the topic of writing. But you cannot write an interview story until the interview has been completed and the segments to be used have been selected. The writer's first job after the interview is completed is always to listen to the interview and select and time the segments to be used. The rest of your story is built around these segments.

You must decide what the key points of the interview are. You will probably use an audio- or videotape cut of only the most significant statements. However, other statements in the interview may be important enough to paraphrase in your story. In that case, outline those statements you intend to use, keeping details to the minimum. And remember, you want to avoid direct quotes that have to be read by the newscaster.

The following basic rules should be kept in mind as you are writing broadcast interview stories.

Identify Interview Participants

Be sure that everyone seen or heard in a story is clearly identified in advance. In television, use the character generator or some similar device to put the interviewee's name on the screen while the interviewee is speaking. It is also a good idea to include some brief identification of the interviewee's role in the story. For example:

Annette Matsuda
Arson Expert

The interviewee can be reidentified in the reporter's questions.

In radio, anyone heard on an audio cut is usually identified both before and after the cut. However, identification after the cut should be done in an unobtrusive way that adds information to the story. This is a poor way to reidentify a speaker:

That was arson expert Annette Matsuda.

It is better to write something like this:

And arson expert Matsuda says the fire department is still checking out that mysterious blaze.

Reidentification of a speaker after a cut is not as essential for television as it is for radio—but it is still a good idea.

Radio presents a particularly complex problem if more than one voice is heard in an audio cut. This is one reason that reporters' questions are usually cut out of radio interviews. Before either voice is heard, you must identify both speakers, making it very clear to the audience which voice will be heard first. For example:

Reporter Marc Tyme talked to Governor Fern this morning, and posed some questions about the governor's campaign plans.

Watch How You Lead into Audio Segments

Never lead into an audio segment with essentially the same words that begin the audio material. This is a common failing of student writers. In the example given above, if the first words we will hear from Governor Fern are, "I haven't made up my mind about that yet," then the worst possible lead-in would be, "Governor Fern says he hasn't made up his mind about that yet."

The words that precede an audio or video segment should set the context of the upcoming statement without repeating its contents. For example, the lead-in to Governor Fern's statement might be, "And Governor Fern seems to be closer to a decision on a running mate."

Keep Lead-ins Tight

You should not state the obvious. Don't write, "Reporter Marc Tyme asked the governor about his plans, and the governor said this——." Just write, "Reporter Tyme asked the governor about his plans," and go directly into the interview.

SCRIPTING STORIES WITH INTERVIEWS

Each station has its own way of scripting stories that contain material on film, videotape, or audiotape. The forms we suggest here are probably more detailed than those in use at most stations. We have indicated the kind of information we think should be in such scripts. You will probably find that most stations use shorter forms, which contain less information, but are quicker to prepare. For example, we suggest that each story be accompanied by fill for the audio material. Fill is simply a brief summary of the content of the audio cut that the newscaster can read if—as sometimes happens—the audio is lost because of some technical problem. Most stations today would probably have the newscaster say, "We're sorry. We've lost the audio in that story, but we'll try to have that story for you later in the show." This works reasonably well in long, loosely structured programs. However, in a tight, five-minute show, the chances of getting back to a missed story are not very great. We think students should at least be familiar with the idea of providing fill for stories.

FORMATTING FOR RADIO

We have assumed, for the radio example, that the audio has been recorded on an audio cartridge, or cart. These devices, similar in construction to the eight-track tapes designed for some home and auto music systems, are by far the most common device used for inserting recorded material into radio news programs. However, there are other systems, so the designations given here may differ at some stations.

The particular information given to identify each cart—both in the script and on the label of the cart itself—varies according to the needs of each station. We have provided fairly detailed information here, but some stations may require even more information (*in cues* as well as out cues, for example). Some stations also make a practice of recording more than one cut of a story, or even cuts from different stories, on the same cart. There are some advantages to this, but there is also an increased possibility that the wrong cut on the cart will be cued up. So we have assumed here that each separate audio cut, even in the same story, is on a separate audio cart.

The information we specify in the script here for an audio cart is the cart number, the type of story, the person or sound heard, the running length of the cut, and the out cue. Each cart must be identified. Usually this is done by assigning the cart a number or a combination of letters and numbers. At some stations carts are permanently numbered. There is an advantage to this, since it prevents accidentally assigning the same identification number to two different carts. However, at most stations, the cart number is usually printed onto the label of the cart by the person preparing it for use on the air. Care must be taken that numbers are not repeated. Carts sometimes are used in more than one show, so it is not safe simply to avoid using the same cart identification twice in the same show. The same identification should not be used again for at least a week to be safe.

In news, cart stories are usually either an "ACC" (actuality) or a "VCR" (voicer). A voicer is a story that opens and closes with the voice of the reporter. It usually ends with a standard out cue (SOC) such as, "Reporting from the Pentagon, this is Marc Tyme, KSUL News." The voicer may contain only the voice of the reporter or it may contain other material. When other material is included, some stations use the designation "VCR/W/ACC." And other designations may be found. Anything else is usually designated an actuality.

The running time of the story may be preceded by some word such as "TIME," or an abbreviation such as "TRT" (which stands for "tape running time" or, according to the preference of some, "total running time"). Since running time is unlikely to be confused with any other material in the cart identification, we suggest simply writing the time by itself. For example, ":28."

The out cue of a story is usually the three last words heard on the audio cut. They indicate to everyone involved that the audio portion of the story has ended. The out cue is usually indicated by the abbreviation, "OC." For example, "OC: ' . . . not sure yet.' " If the out cue phrase is used more than once in the story, it must be indicated. Example, "OC ' . . . not sure yet.' (Says 3 times.)"

When a reporter's voice ends the story, there is usually a standard out cue used. This is a phrase used by all reporters of the station when signing off. For example, "At city hall, for KSUL News, this is Paul Pry." When a standard out cue ends a story, the abbreviation "SOC" (for "standard out cue") is usually used in place of the last three words heard on the tape.

Here is an example of a radio script using a brief interview segment:

FERN INTERVIEW—NOON NEWS—7/18/82—JOHNSON   *11 lines*

Governor Larry Fern was in town today, pushing his plan for a cut in

state income taxes. There is strong opposition to that plan in the state

legislature, and the governor admitted that hopes for that tax cut are . . .

not . . . very bright.

> CART 6-1—Fern—ACC—Taxes
> :25—OC: ". . . the Senate leadership."
> FILL Governor Fern said winning the tax cut will be
> difficult because 2 key state senators plan to run
> against him next year.

Despite those glum words, Governor Fern says he has . . . not . . . given

up hope for a tax cut during this session of the legislature.

That script and interview segment follow the rules we have already outlined. And the word "not" was set off between ellipses to make sure the newscaster would not skip over it.

Now, here's a page of a script from station KNAC in Long Beach, California. It's quite a bit different from what we have outlined in this book. However, it provides all the information that the staff of that station needed to get it on the air. The title "MORE DRAFT" indicates that it followed another story about the draft:

MORE DRAFT   *18 lines*

There are those who don't intend to register, however . . . and there are

groups who intend to encourage others not to register.

One of the biggest and most active organizations right now is called the

National Resistance Committee, and Los Angeles spokesman Monte Krel

tells us they have their own plans for next month . . .

(CART   :40   " . . . it involves . . .")

The American Civil Liberties Union also has plans to fight draft

registration once it's signed into law. The A-C-L-U says it'll take it to

court on constitutional grounds because women aren't included in the

program.

FORMATTING FOR TELEVISION

Now, here is a television story, using the format suggested in this book:

FERN INTERVIEW—EARLY NEWS—7/18/82—JOHNSON   *14 lines*

MOC

Governor Larry Fern was in town today,

SI VTR/VO (:08)

pushing hard for that tax cut he wants in the

CG (:04)

state income tax. Opposition to that tax cut

"Governor Larry Fern"

is strong in the state legislature, and the

governor admitted hopes for that tax cut are

not too bright.

SOVTR (:25)

CG

"Governor Larry Fern"

OC: " . . . the Senate leadership."
FILL: Governor Fern says that the opposition
to his tax plan is political, and that winning
the cut will be difficult because 2 key state
senators are planning to run against him in
next year's primary.

MOC

Despite these glum words, Governor Fern

says he has . . . not . . . given up hope for a

tax cut during this session of the legislature.

This television story begins with an on-camera introduction by the newscaster. The newscaster continues speaking as a videotape of the governor appears on the screen. The videotape is silent here, and the governor's name is put on the screen with a character generator.

Then the audience hears the governor speaking for twenty-five seconds. Identification of the governor is given again with the character generator. In the first identification, the cues tell the director to begin identification just after the start of the videotape and to hold the identification on the screen for four seconds. In the second identification, the cues indicate that the director can use the identification at any point that seems appropriate and can keep it on the screen as long as she or he wishes.

Immediately after the out cue, "the Senate leadership," the newscaster returns to complete the story on camera. This *live tag* allows one more verbal identification of the governor.

As you can see, from the writer's standpoint, there are not a lot of words to be written. The videotape carries the story, as it should.

Here's an actual television story from CBS station KNXT in Los Angeles:

ANTIBUSING 5-5 BC --

KR-STL: ANTI-BUSING

Opponents of
forced busing in Los
Angeles admitted today
they haven't got enough
signatures yet to place
an antibusing initiative on the
November ballot . . . but
they say they'll have
more than enough by
the May thirtieth
deadline. The leader
of the initiative drive,
State Senator Alan

VTR: :45 SOT

SOUND UNDER

Robbins, unveiled a
huge stack of signed
petitions today. He
says once the initiative
qualifies, he's going
to try to head off the

ANTI-BUSING--2-2-2-2-2 ---

current L.A.
integration plan,
scheduled to start
this fall.

AT :10 BRING SOUND
UP FULL

SUPER: ALAN ROBBINS
TAPE ENDS AT : 45

Sound Up: " . . . the
first. . . ."

Out cue: " . . . vote on
our initiative."

> Robbins says he
>
> needs one hundred
>
> twenty-thousand more
>
> XXXXXXXXX signatures to
>
> qualify for XX the
>
> ballot.

In this story, a long on-camera lead-in continues over the first part of the videotape, with the natural sound of the tape played faintly under the newscaster's voice. In the on-camera portion, an identifying graphic with the word "anti-busing" was Chromakeyed in the area in back of the newscaster. To save time, the writer has simply crossed out errors as they were typed by using the "X" key on the typewriter; thus the line, "twenty-thousand more XXXXXX signatures to qualify for XX the ballot."

The script indicates that the videotape is to begin running at the first mention of the name "Robbins," that it is to run for forty-five seconds, and that there is sound on the videotape. The sound is heard faintly under the newscaster's voice while the remaining copy is read (about ten seconds), and then the sound for the interview is brought up to normal level so the interview material can be heard. The writer has indicated the first words that are to be heard at normal level on the videotape: "the first." An identifier is to be supered while the sound is running. An on-camera tag after the videotape reidentifies the speaker one more time.

As you can see, the cues used at this station differ somewhat from the cues we have given, but the basic techniques remain the same. You will also notice that the rule against splitting sentences (see Chapter 3) between pages is not observed here. That is because the type of TelePrompTer used for the program presents the script as one continuous strip so the newscaster does not face the problem of not being able to see what is on the next page.

You should spend some time developing your skills as both an interviewer and a writer of interview stories. For if you can prepare interviews well, you have learned to handle one of the most useful types of story in electronic news.

Rules cannot create experts. Some reporters might follow the rules in a hundred interviews yet remain less capable interviewers than others who have never read instructions and have groped their way through only a few interviews. Whatever their lack of preparation and practice, reporters who are personable, adaptable, intelligent, well mannered, and full of curiosity are likely to be better interviewers than those who, however faithfully they may prepare and practice, have none of these qualities. To an indeterminate degree, interviewing is an art. Highly successful interviewers are artists in human relationships. What they know is less important than what they are.

Not that those who doubt their own talent for interviewing should resign themselves to failure. Nor should those who have conducted successful interviews without instruction be satisfied that they have mastered the art. Because interviewing is a craft as well as an art, the ability to interview can be learned. And learning the craft can make anyone a better interviewer.

Exercises
~~~~~~~~~~~~~~~

Exercise 1

You'll find below a summary of Walter Cronkite's career. After reading this summary, list ten questions that you should ask him in order to write a two-minute broadcast story.

> *Walter Cronkite is the former managing editor and television newscaster for CBS from New York City. Born in St. Joseph, Missouri, in 1916, he was a student at the University of Texas from 1933 to 1935. He first joined the Scripps-Howard Newspapers, then worked for ten years for United Press.*

> *Cronkite joined CBS in 1950 and became a Washington news correspondent for four years. He was transferred to CBS in New York as a television news analyst. When the CBS news operation was transformed, Cronkite was made the managing editor. In 1965, CBS became the first of the networks to change the early-evening news program from fifteen minutes to thirty minutes. Throughout Cronkite's tenure as managing editor, the CBS news operation was a leader in reportage.*

Exercise 2

Watch five or more television news programs, paying special attention to interviews. Then write the answers to the following questions:

1. Do the interviewers seem informed about the subjects they cover?

2. Do the interviewers seem antagonistic toward the interviewees—or friendly?

3. Do the interviewers ask questions that interviewees try to evade?

Exercise 3

Practice interviewing by choosing one of your classmates to interview. Ask your fellow student whether the high school curriculum has prepared her or him for college. Let the answer to that question direct your next question and continue the interview until you think you have covered the subject adequately.

Exercise 4

Pick a faculty member on your campus who is a specialist in some area of interest to the public—art, music, sports, politics, energy, or one of a dozen other areas. Arrange to interview the faculty member on some topic within that area. Depending upon the facilities available at your school, you may choose to interview the faculty member on a portable audiotape recorder, a portable videotape recorder, a recorder-connected telephone, or in a radio or television studio.

First, do your research. Check the library and other sources for background material on both the person you are interviewing and the topic that person will discuss. Keep all your research material to turn in with the assignment. Prepare a list of at least ten questions to ask your interviewee and keep two things in mind:

1. The questions you ask are not supposed to show off *your* knowledge of the topic, but should draw out the interviewee's expertise in the area.

2. You should *not* stick slavishly to your list of questions. You may use only one or two of the questions, perhaps none. You should let the natural course of the interview dictate the questions you ask—whether they appear on your list or pop into your mind during the interview.

After you have interviewed the faculty member, edit the interview down to a one-minute story for radio or a two-minute story for television. The specified time lengths should include any introductory or closing material read by you and any lead-in or closing to be read by the newscaster.

Turn in your script and the audio cart, video cassette, or recording device used for the edited interview and include your research material, your list of questions, and the out takes of the interview.

9

Reporting Many Kinds of Stories

A reporter in any medium has to learn to write many different types of stories. The scope of news is as broad as the spectrum of life itself. It would be impossible to describe all the kinds of stories you may be called upon to write during your career as a broadcast journalist. However, we can touch on some of the basic types of reporting.

STRAIGHT NEWS

Straight news is the traditional form of reporting. It has been defined as "the timely account of an event." What you report is delimited by a narrow time span. For electronic news, it is usually what happened "today." We seldom specify times in electronic news, but when they are mentioned, we generally use phrases like "this morning," "early today," or "late this afternoon."

Maintaining Objectivity

Straight news is objective news. Because each report focuses on a specific place at a specific time, the reporter has the chance to do a thorough job on what occurs. However, when you are reporting straight news you must not overlook the fact that what you are reporting is a very small segment of life, taken out of context. The narrow scope of the straight news report makes it easier for a reporter to verify what she or he reports. And because what is reported can be verified, the report can come close to objectivity. Still, that objectivity can sometimes be illusory because the report fails to present the broader context in which the event occurred.

One definition of an objective report is "a report that several unbiased observers would agree is an accurate description of an event." That is your goal in straight reporting. Probably no report of an event has ever been written that would satisfy all those who witnessed the event, but it is possible to write a report that most observers with no axes to grind would say was accurate.

Checking Facts

A major weakness of inexperienced reporters in straight reporting is the failure to check facts. Deadline pressures are constant in electronic news. And most young reporters are too trusting. Indeed, even experienced reporters are sometimes too trusting. In 1979, for example, NBC produced a documentary entitled "College Sports: Big Money on Campus." In that program, reporter Edwin Newman asked Fly Williams, a former basketball player at Austin Peay University, if Williams had been offered a car in return for attending Austin Peay. Said Williams: "Sure. Not only a car, but also a house and everything else I wanted."

Two days after the program aired, Williams announced that his entire statement had been a lie. He told reporters he had made the statements because "a man" had offered him "a couple of hundred dollars" to appear on the show and make those statements. Said Lake Kelly, the coach at Austin Peay while Williams was there: "I do think it was very irresponsible on NBC's part to put it on national television without verifying any of it."[1]

In 1978, an airliner and a private plane collided over San Diego, both crashing into a residential area. It was one of the worst air disasters in history. News stories later went out saying that looters had descended upon the crash area, that seven looters had been arrested, and that one man had been caught trying to steal the dental work from the body of one of the victims. The stories came from a reliable source—the police. But it later turned out the stories were false, or at least could not be substantiated. They were rumors that spread, like all other rumors, from person to person—only in this case, the persons were police officers. The story of the attempt to steal dental work was never substantiated. No one had been arrested for looting. Two persons had been arrested for being drunk, three had been arrested for removing evidence from the scene (taking souvenir pieces of the crashed planes), and thirty-eight persons had been arrested for failure to disperse. The story that seven persons had been arrested for looting evidently resulted from confusion on the part of one of the police officers over the criminal code section under which people had been booked for failure to disperse.[2]

Avoiding Apocryphal Journalism

There are thousands of stories that have made their way into the daily news only to be later proven false. The amazing thing about these stories is that some of them seem to have more lives than a cat. Every few years,

---

[1] "Fly Williams Says He Lied on TV for $200," *Los Angeles Times*, May 2, 1979, III, p. 11.

---

[2] George Frank, "False Looting Stories Haunt San Diego," *Los Angeles Times*, October 5, 1978, II, p. 12.

they crop up again, and they are dutifully reported yet another time. Most of these stories are humorous and do little harm, but they are false. The dangerous thing is that they eventually become accepted as truth. H. L. Mencken once found it necessary to publish an article exposing his own hoax when the bogus history of the American bathtub he had written as a joke began being cited in history books.

James Thurber wrote this account of "reporting" society news from the French Riviera in the 1920s:

> It was then our custom to sit around for half an hour, making up items for the society editor's column. She was too pretty, we thought, to waste the soft southern days tracking down the arrival of prominent persons on the azure coast. So all she had to do was stop in at the Ruhl and the Negresco each day and pick up the list of guests who had just registered. The rest of us invented enough items to fill up the last half of her column. . . .[3]

There is one story that crops up on the news wires every few years—and is always attributed to a supposedly reliable source. In that story, the driver of a stalled car asks a passing driver to give the car a shove to get it started. The driver of the stalled car explains that the car must be pushed at a speed of more than twenty miles an hour. So the good Samaritan backs up and roars down on the rear of the stalled car at twenty miles an hour. It is doubtful this event ever took place. If it did, the actual occurrence must have been at least thirty years ago, because the story has been cropping up in the news for at least that long.

One industrious reporter tried to check up on the history of another such story. The reporter was able to trace it back to about 1940, but the trail ended there. That particular story is a sort of fill-in-the-blanks story that includes slightly different details each time it appears. It goes like this:

> The Lord's Prayer has _____words. The Gettysburg address has _____words, but a government regulation, controlling [the area of your choice], has _____words.

It is no doubt a valid point that government documents are verbose, but in the above story, the alleged document—whatever it is supposed to be—did not exist in any of the various reincarnations of the story. And the stated number of words in the Lord's Prayer and the Gettysburg Address are different in each version of the story. (Of course, a good reporter might start by asking, "Which version of the Lord's Prayer?")

A slightly more sinister kind of false story cropped up during the political unrest of the 1970s. A political activist made the statement that

---

[3] James Thurber, "Memoirs of a Drudge," in *The Thurber Carnival* (New York: Harper and Brothers, 1945), p. 14.

the phrase "law and order" was taken directly from a speech made by Adolf Hitler. The media picked up the story, and hundreds of political figures who weren't fond of the phrase "law and order" used the story. Almost five years passed before anyone took the time to check the story out. So far as any reputable scholar of the subject can determine, Hitler never used the phrase in any of his speeches.

Knowing Where to Check

Although straight reporting requires that you verify your information, time constraints in broadcasting make it necessary for you to develop shortcuts in checking out facts. You need a few good reference books close to your desk. You need a list of phone numbers to call for quick answers on specific issues. (Don't forget the public library. You can often get valuable information by telephoning the library.) Above all, you must have a good store of facts in your own head. Beyond that, you need the sort of sixth sense that reporters develop from experience. There should be an alarm bell somewhere in the back of your mind that goes off when you encounter some item that needs to be checked.

The necessary brevity of broadcast reporting makes straight reporting the kind you will deal with most in radio and television news. Here's a typical straight news story from the evening news on KNXT in Los Angeles:

PARK 5-5 BC --

California's 2 senators were at odds today over whether the Channel Islands should be XXXX included in a new Santa Monica national park.

FUL STL: SANTA MONICA MOUNTAINS

Senator XXX Alan Cranston wants the islands included--but Senator S. I. Hayakawa says there's no need to take them away from the navy and private owners.

The proposed park would include about 80-thousand acres in the Santa Monica

DROP STL

mountains and along the Pacific shoreline.

You can see here that the writer has simply provided the basic facts of the story. There is no attempt at interpretation or providing any particular perspective. We are not told why one faction wants the islands in the park and the other does not, or what the effect of having the islands in the park would be. We know nothing of the uses being made of the islands by the navy and private owners. We know nothing of the value of the islands or what acquiring them would cost. We do not know how the navy and the private owners feel about the property being taken over. The story focuses on the very narrow point that two senators from the same state disagree about including the islands in the park. This is a fairly standard, straight news story for electronic news.

DEPTH REPORTING

Depth reporting is simply the next logical step beyond straight reporting. Because the narrow focus of straight reporting takes information out of context, there is often a need for a kind of reporting that restores perspective by putting the story back in context. Like straight reporting, depth reporting is easier to describe than to do.

We noted in the example of a straight news story that much information was lacking. That is normal in electronic news. We try to keep the number of facts to the minimum. Yet there is also a place in electronic news for stories that provide a context in which the audience can evaluate the information. Television, in particular, can make use of such stories. Radio, with its tighter time limits, provides less of an opportunity, but there is a place in radio, too, for special reports and more detailed coverage of some types of material.

Analyzing a Television Depth Story

Note in the following story from television station KHJ in Los Angeles how the writer has put a problem in terms of its effect on the listener.[4] The story is too short to provide true "depth" in the best sense of the word; but with a two-minute running length, it is fairly long for a television news story and does provide considerable detail:

GAS BILLS

2:00

CK-SLIDE: *energy*
MC *costs*

Here in California, we are in for a tough

winter . . . not so much in terms of the X

weather, but because of skyrocketing

heating bills.

[4] Courtesy KHJ-TV.

SOF AT 23

Those bills are going to go up a staggering 50 percent for gas heat . . . 9 percent for electric heat.

FILM-BG VOICEOVER
AT :02
SUPER: STATE BLDG.

The State Public Utilities Commission felt it was XXXXXX necessary to warn consumers.

After all, this would mean the XXX December heating bill for the average family of 4 in Los Angeles will be almost 27-dollars . . . 9 dollars more than lastX year.

SOF AT 23

P-U-C head John Bryson blamed the XXXXXXXXXXXXXXXXXX high rates X on spiraling oil prices from OPEC, Canada and Mexico.

And he said its important that consumers get X ready.

AT: 23
SOF UP FULL

AT: 25
SUPER: JOHN BRYSON

SOF UP FULL

AT: 47
SUPER: HERMAN MULMAN

AT: 51
AUDIO CUE: . . . FIXED
COSTS, RIGHT.

BG-VOICEOVER

Nevertheless, conservation is the name of the X game. And the Southern California Gas Company suggests ways to do just that.

AT: 1:06
SOF UP FULL

AT: *1:08*
SUPER: BRUCE
MARSHALL

OUTCUE: . . .
CONSCIOUSLY AND
CONSTANTLY

TRT: 1:36

LIVE TAG

SOF UP FULL

About 10 percent of the state's homes are heated with electricity . . . and those bills will come to about 22-dollars this winter. Another spokesman for the Southern California Gas Company said the state's rate predictions are a little short of the mark . . . that heat utility bills may be even higher.

Note how the writer first said that heating bills are going up 50 percent for gas and 9 percent for electricity. Realizing that those figures will mean little to the listener, the writer then explained what the situation will mean in terms of dollars and cents. The story then provides the reasons being given for the increase in rates. It follows this information with some tips the consumer can use to offset the increased costs. A separate section of the story deals with the costs to users of electric heating. Then the story ends with a warning that the figures given may well be low.

Obviously, with more time, a great deal more could have been covered. Were there alternatives to the rate increases? Was there any dispute over the explanations given for them? What would the effect of the increases be on the utilities' profits? Why did the price of electricity—which would seem to be more affected by the cost of oil than is gas—rise less than gas? Was there any indication that gas rates would continue to rise faster than electricity rates, perhaps making it meaningful for the consumer to consider switching to electric heat?

The story shows the usual problem faced in preparing electronic news—too little time. The reporters have had to rely almost exclusively on spokesmen for the utilities to explain the increase. Obviously, such spokesmen know the subject, but they are not unbiased sources. In essence, the story is a lengthy public relations release from the utilities. That does not mean it is necessarily an unfair treatment of the subject, but for real depth reporting, more investigation should have been carried out.

Some broadcast news departments have now faced up to this problem by creating special investigative units. Such a unit can devote many days or weeks, even months, to examining a single problem. Then the unit issues a series of reports on the problem, which are usually presented on successive evenings on the news program.

Unfortunately, only the most affluent stations can afford this type of reporting—or so the station managers seem to think.

Deciding on the Questions

To write an in-depth story, you must begin by asking yourself what questions need to be answered about the issue. Of course, you won't be able to come up with all the questions, but you should be able to compile a fairly lengthy list. As you work on the story, you will undoubtedly add new questions to your list.

Since you won't be able to deal with all the questions, you must assign priorities. Pick the most important questions, then begin compiling a list of sources of information and opinions on the issue. You should do some work on your own. Dig out as many facts as you can without resorting to biased sources. That will help you to know when the people you interview are letting their own bias sneak into the discussion.

Now, do your interviews. Be sure that you get all the information you need. Be persistent.

Illustrating the Story

Next, obtain any other audio or video material you need to illustrate the story and begin the writing and editing. Once you have a rough idea of the length of the story, you will have to consult with the program producer to determine how the material is to be treated. It could be in a documentary, all by itself. It could be a long, single feature story, or it could be a series of short reports. Each treatment requires a different approach. For example, with the series of reports—which is the most common way to approach in-depth reporting in electronic news—you will have to devote some time at the start of each segment to restate the problem and to review the material that has been covered in the previous segments. In the documentary format, you will have to give more thought to the overall structure of the program and to the time blocks created by commercials and other breaks. In a single feature story, you will probably have to edit heavily to get all the key points in.

When the basic format of the report has been determined, the writing and editing begin in earnest. The writing and editing must proceed together. You will need to view or listen to the material you have collected, select key segments, and write copy that will bring those segments into focus. Then it's back to the recorded segments, fitting the copy with the recorded material. There may have to be cuts in copy or cuts in the recorded material. Or you may have to add material here and there.

You must pay careful attention to the balance of the story. Probably by the time you have finished working on the story, you will have reached some conclusion on your own about the issue discussed. But remember that you are not writing an editorial. Your job is to present an unbiased discussion on the problem. That does not mean there must be an exact, second-for-second, line-for-line equality between what is said on each side of the issue, but each side must be given a fair opportunity to make its point.

The final polishing of the story is the same type you would perform on any other story, except you may have more time to work on it. Your job is to arrange all the material and link it with your copy so that the result is a clear and fair description of the problem at hand. Depth reporting is not an excuse for verbosity. Your writing must be just as tight as for any other form of broadcast writing. The difference here is that you can afford more details than in an ordinary story. Those details still must be selected with care, so that each makes an important contribution to the story.

INTERPRETIVE REPORTING

Interpretive reporting, or news analysis, has always had an indeterminate place in broadcasting. Part of the reason is historical. During the depression of the 1930s, American newspapers were hard hit by the decline in their advertising revenues. Part of this decline was attributed—probably correctly—to competition from the new medium of radio. The newspapers put pressure on the wire services, which temporarily suspended service to radio. An agreement was reached that severely limited the amount of news radio stations were allowed to carry. But radio stations and networks quickly found loopholes in the agreement. One such loophole was that news commentary was not counted as news in the agreement. So there suddenly popped up a host of radio "analysts" or "commentators," who read the news, but wound up each show with a brief "commentary." As a result, commentary and analysis on radio came to be almost anything that was not straight news.

Defining "Analysis" and "Commentary"

During World War II, Paul White, the first head of CBS News, gave this definition of news analysis:

> The function of the news analyst is to marshal the facts on any specific subject and, out of his common or special knowledge, to present these facts so as to inform his listeners rather than persuade them. The analyst should attempt to clear up any con-

tradictions within the known record, should fairly present both sides of controversial questions and, in short should give the best available information upon which listeners can make up their own minds. Ideally, in the case of controversial issues, the audience should be left with no impression as to which side the analyst himself actually favors. . . .[5]

At first glance, this seems to be the definition of in-depth reporting as well. It could be. The important distinction is that the emphasis in the in-depth story remains on who, what, when, and where, while the emphasis in interpretive reporting is on why. Very often, the distinction is apparent not so much in the treatment of the story as in the type of material chosen as the topic. An in-depth report might examine "The Crime Rate in the Inner City," whereas an analytical story might examine "Why the Crime Rate is High in the Inner City." (However, a good writer would come up with a snappier title for such a story.)

Admittedly, the line is hard to draw. What one news department defines as "analysis," another might call "in-depth reporting." And at the other extreme, the interpretive report may easily slip into editorializing. Edward R. Murrow was once asked if the analysis he gave at the end of each of his radio shows did not constitute an editorial. Murrow set out some guidelines in his response:

I do not regard the last five or six minutes that I do on radio as an editorial. . . . I do not advocate action; I do not urge a policy. What I attempt to do is to set out a group of developments or circumstances and then to suggest what consequences may flow from them.[6]

The fact that analysis can slip into editorializing—or that it may be perceived to be doing so by the audience—is tacitly acknowledged in the following rule in the *CBS News Standards* manual:

Each item, in a hard news broadcast, which consists entirely or substantially of commentary, will be identified by the use of terms such as "commentary," "background," "perspective," or any similar term which will disclose that a news event is being analyzed.[7]

---

[5] Quoted in *CBS News Standards* (New York: Columbia Broadcasting System, April 14, 1976), p. 3.

[6] Edward R. Murrow, "The Responsibilities of Television," Louis Lyons, moderator (New York: The Fund for the Republic, 1959), p. 16.

[7] *CBS News Standards* (New York: Columbia Broadcasting System, April 14, 1976), p. 4.

Prior to 1974, CBS used the term "analysis" for any generally analytic story. However, CBS now applies the term only to analyses that immediately follow presidential or other speeches. All other material of this type is designated "commentary."[8]

That particular ruling is probably a result of the sharp attack in November of 1969 that then Vice-President Spiro T. Agnew launched against "instant analysis and querulous criticism. . . . by a small band of network commentators and self-appointed analysts. . . ." The vice-president's target was the practice of having network commentators, both regular staff members and special guest commentators, analyze presidential speeches immediately after they are over. Said Agnew:

The President of the United States has a right to communicate directly with the people who elected him, and the people of this country have the right to make up their own minds and form their own opinions about a Presidential address without having a President's words and thoughts characterized through the prejudices of hostile critics before they can even be digested.[9]

(A good editor might ask pointedly whether the vice-president meant that the "President's words and thoughts" or the "hostile critics" should be digested.)

Vice-President Agnew was able to tap a considerable wellspring of hostility against the news media with that and several other attacks. It should be a strong reminder to broadcast newswriters that every effort must be made to keep analysis fair and unbiased. That the vice-president was displeased with the analysis of President Nixon's speech should surprise no one, but the public support that the vice-president was able to muster for his stand gives a strong indication that Americans are suspicious of the objectivity of electronic news.

Problems with the Interpretive Story

There are two reasons why the interpretive story is regarded with suspicion. First, the interpretive story provides clarification, explanation, and analysis. That requires that the reporter weigh and filter facts. The reporter takes a more personal role in the story. Second, there is no set format for an interpretive story. It can take almost any form the writer chooses. That latitude makes it easy for opinions to slip in without the writer being aware they are there. The only solution to that problem is for newswriters to keep their stories like Caesar's wife—above reproach.

In terms of actual writing, there is not a great deal of difference between the preparation of an analytical story and an in-depth story. It is

---

[8] *Ibid.,* p. 3.

---

[9] Speech in Des Moines, Iowa, November 13, 1969.

---

the research that is likely to be somewhat different. It may take you to the library to study up on the philosophies of various thinkers on your topic. Or it may send you to books like the *Statistical Abstract of the United States,* to dig out the necessary data for your story.

Analysis and commentary is more personalized than in-depth reporting. Under most circumstances, most or all of an analysis is written by the person who reads it on the air. According to the style of the program in which it is used, the analysis may use the personal "I" or the editorial "we" as well as the customary third person. The person reading the story is usually identified to the audience as an analyst or commentator. Often it is a staff member who only does analytical stories.

And finally, because analysis or commentary is a more personal type of story than the in-depth report, more of it will come "from your head" and less will be drawn from notes and wire copy. However, never assume that it can all come from your mind. The story must have its basis, like all news, in hard facts.

Writing the Analytical Story

A good way to begin an analytical story is to compile a list of facts about the topic you are discussing. Arrange the facts in order of importance, from the most important to the least important. Then, starting with the first fact on the list, ask "Why?" When you have sketched out some answers, or the sources you hope will provide you with answers, go through the list again and ask, "What will be the result of this?" Usually, this will be all you will have time for in a broadcast story. However, if time permits, there are other questions you can examine such as, "How can this be changed—if it needs to be changed?" You will always have to be on your guard, especially with that last question, against turning commentary into editorial. But it can be done.

Radio, with its tight time limitations, may not seem like a good place for analysis, but here is an example of a short analytical piece prepared by newsman Bill Banks for broadcast on KNAC in Long Beach, California.[10]

RATIONING

Now that the president has had his draft registration proposal approved, he can concentrate attention on another measure he's been trying to push through Congress.

That's his standby gasoline rationing plan.

There are two different ways this system could work—if Congress approves it at all—and economist Allen Goodman has just finished a study on who would benefit from which method.

---

[10]Courtesy Bill Banks, KNAC, Long Beach, California.

Gasoline would be allocated on a coupon basis ... but the coupons could be handed out either to everyone who has a vehicle registered in his name, or everyone who has a driver's license.

Goodman says a ration plan based on vehicle registration would be most beneficial to suburban commuters since they tend to have the most cars per household.

If they were distributed on the basis of driver's licenses, however, the program would mainly benefit the poorest inner-city households.

That's because family members might have a driver's license to get the coupons, but might not have a car to put the gas in.

They could then sell their coupons to those who need them.

Goodman estimates that low-income households would average a 26-gallon a month surplus ... while the wealthier owners of gas guzzlers would need about a hundred gallons worth of extra coupons every month.

Figuring a buck-and-a-half a coupon, Goodman says the poor could boost their income by 40-dollars a month.

INVESTIGATIVE REPORTING

There is a tremendously appealing sound to the words "investigative reporting." Ten years ago, a student entering journalism school was likely to specify that her or his goal was to be a foreign correspondent. In recent years, the goal has shifted more toward investigative reporting. There was a noticeable upsurge of interest in investigative reporting after the Watergate exposés of Bob Woodward and Carl Bernstein contributed to the first resignation of an American president.

To be an investigative reporter is an excellent goal—probably one with better odds for the reporter than foreign correspondent, since there just aren't very many foreign bureau posts for broadcast journalists. There are encouraging signs. "60 Minutes," which specializes in investigative stories, was frequently the top-rated television program during the 1979–1980 season. A 1980 survey by Frank N. Magid Associates, a consulting firm specializing in television news, showed that investigative reporting is now well established in television and is expected to grow. (Ironically, Magid is one of the consulting firms often accused of trivializing news through the types of coverage it recommends.) However, the survey also noted that investigative reporting has not proven itself as a moneymaker. That last revelation could be the kiss of death in a medium as commercially oriented as broadcasting. Moreover, the study found that there was great disparity in what different stations called "investigative reporting." And while some stations reported doing two or three investigative stories a week, others reported only one every two or three months.[11]

In short, if you get to do investigative reporting, it will probably be as a special assignment. Relatively few broadcast journalists are able to make investigative reporting a full-time career. Most broadcast news departments are relatively small, and only the larger stations can afford to have a full-time team of investigative reporters.

Probably the best advice that can be given on writing an exposé is to be careful. A good investigative reporter has a good grasp of the legal concepts of evidence. When you write an exposé, you are also very likely to expose yourself, your news department, and your station to a suit for libel or invasion of privacy. You need to have a clear understanding of the law involving both defamation and privacy. It isn't enough to "know" that what you write is true. You must be able to prove it is true in court—and that can be extremely difficult. Of course, you have more latitude when you deal with public figures, but are you sure you understand what the courts mean by a "public figure"?

Even if you escape a lawsuit, you still have to live with your conscience. Are you certain that what you wrote is correct? Or did the information come from a source you believe, but without any substantiating proof?

Broadcast history is filled with tales of investigative reporting that went awry. NBC, for example, was criticized by the National News Council for a program that accused Shell Oil of diverting oil needed for heating homes to more profitable sales as jet fuel. NBC was accused of failing to make any attempt to get a statement from Shell about the accusations.

Oil companies have been tough customers for investigative reporters. When ABC's "20/20" produced a feature on deregulation of the natural gas industry, Mobil Oil purchased full-page ads in newspapers across the country to attack the program. A similar event had occurred earlier when "60 Minutes" did an investigative report on the Colonial Penn Insurance Group. The insurance company, too, took out full-page ads to present its side.

A most intriguing example of retaliation by a victim of an exposé involved the exposé that the *National Enquirer*, the largest circulation weekly newspaper in the country, did on "60 Minutes" some time after "60 Minutes" had done an exposé on the *Enquirer*. The "60 Minutes" segment had accused the *Enquirer* of publishing material that *Enquirer* editors knew was false or which was supported by only the flimsiest proof. The *Enquirer* took its time, then published an article that detailed stories in which "60 Minutes" had been guilty of equally poor journalism.

---

[11] "Investigative Reporting: Handle with Care," *Radio-Television News Directors Association Communicator,* March, 1980, p. 5.

The Illinois Power Company, another target of a "60 Minutes" exposé, found another means of retaliation. The power company used its own concealed cameras to film the entire interview with the "60 Minutes" crew. When the exposé was broadcast, the power company had its own film ready, showing what it said "60 Minutes" had changed or edited out.

CBS's Dan Rather made a surprising admission to a meeting of the Investigative Reporters and Editors Association in 1980. His remarks should serve as a warning to those intent on working in the field of investigative reporting:

> On "60 Minutes" we make mistakes so often, violating the basics of accuracy, clarity or fairness, that sometimes it shatters me. If, with our budget and our staff and time, we make so many mistakes in exposé material, what's it like under less luxurious circumstances?[12]

Circumstances can be considerably less luxurious. At the end of 1979, the average television news department had 17.6 full-time employees, while the average radio station had only 1.7 full-time news employees.[13] There is little chance at smaller stations for doing investigative reporting because the regular reporting chores leave no time for such luxuries.

There is no simple way to tell you how to write an investigative report. The writing, as we have noted, must be done with care. But what really makes the investigative report is the work that precedes the writing. We are not dedicated to the principle that some news directors espouse—that you can't learn to be a reporter or a writer without working on a newspaper. Broadcasting has developed its own corps of reporters now; and at most stations, you can learn the ropes as a broadcast reporter without ever setting foot in a newspaper office. As for writing, some aspects of newspaper style must be unlearned before you can be a good broadcast newswriter. But in the area of investigative reporting, there is still much to be said for learning your trade at a newspaper. Only at a few stations are there skilled investigative teams from which you could learn investigative reporting. Moreover, the chance of a young, inexperienced reporter being assigned to one of these teams is slight. If you are really set on becoming an investigative reporter, you may do well to take your apprenticeship with a newspaper.

However, that has to be only the beginning. The investigative reporter in broadcasting has problems to solve that the newspaper reporter might

---

[12] *Ibid.*

---

[13] Vernon A. Stone, "Survey Shows TV News Staffs Expanding But Radio Newsrooms Are Little Changed," *Radio-Television News Directors Association Communicator*, February, 1980, pp. 6 and 7.

---

never think of. The investigative reporter often depends on sources who insist on keeping their identities secret from the public. Cameras, lights, and microphones are the last thing such people want to see. Even if the reporter promises not to use any of these important tools of the trade, the source may simply be frightened off by the idea of dealing with the broadcast media. Somehow there is something less "public" about dealing with a newspaper reporter. It has been pointed out that the broadcast media did much to publicize the Watergate scandal, but had little to do with the actual uncovering of the story. Some broadcast journalists have said they believe that key sources such as "Deep Throat" simply would not have risked giving information to reporters from the broadcast media.

Obtaining the pictures and sound that are the key element of broadcast news can be the most challenging part of preparing an investigative story. Young reporters dream of all sorts of gadgets—hidden microphones, hidden cameras, secret recording devices—but the experienced reporter knows that gadgets too often fail to work in real life situations. And there is rarely a chance to do retakes in investigative reporting. So good investigative writing begins with your being able to figure out a good way to get the sound and pictures you need. Sometimes a good engineer is more important than a good writer.

Nevertheless, those who do succeed in making it into the ranks of the investigative reporters have an extremely satisfying job. Good investigative reporting often brings some acclaim to the reporter. But even when it does not, investigative reporting remains one of the most important jobs a writer can perform. It is fulfilling the watchdog role of the media that is so important in our democracy.

To sum up, the four types of writing that we have outlined in this chapter—straight reporting, depth reporting, interpretive reporting, and investigative reporting—all present their unique problems. In all four, the preparations for the story are as important as the writing itself. Do not downgrade straight news simply because it is the most common of the four types. It is straight news that keeps the public informed. In-depth reporting gives you the opportunity to provide your audience with some of those facts that usually have to be edited out of broadcast copy. Interpretive reporting—analysis or commentary—serves to help put important news into perspective. And the investigative report turns the light of publicity on shady activities. You may have the opportunity to practice only one or two of these four basic types of news reporting; but if you study each carefully, you should be able to handle most of the stories you are ever likely to be called upon to write.

Exercises
▓▓▓▓▓▓▓▓▓▓

Exercise 1

You are a reporter for radio station WGVP in New Orleans, Louisiana. The news director has come into the newsroom looking excited. He explains that the city health department has called with news of an encephalitis outbreak. He wants a feature story on the outbreak for your next hourly newscast, which is only forty-five minutes away. He says to keep it under one minute. You go to one of the telephones that is connected to a tape recorder and call the city health department.

You get a lady who identifies herself as Glynda Rennert. You tell her you are calling for WGVP News and that you would like her permission to record the call for later use on the air. She says okay. You start the tape rolling and ask a few trial questions while you set the recording levels. Ms. Rennert says all she will do is read a prepared statement. She reads the following (which has been written out here in regular four-second radio copy lines so you can estimate the lengths of various parts of the statement):

*Some evidence of the presence of the St. Louis strain of
encephalitis has been detected in persons living in our community
using sophisticated testing procedures.*

*The tests were carried out in the city's new public health laboratory
located at 1128 St. Charles Avenue. Five city health department
employees were involved in the testing. As a result of the tests,
we can say that there are eight confirmed cases of the disease in
city residents. The cases have been diagnosed during the last week.
We will not release the names of those having the disease because
of privacy considerations. Three were treated at hospitals in the
city and released. Five persons remain hospitalized. In addition,
there are nine other suspected cases of the disease in the city. So
far, there have been no deaths from the disease this year.*

YOU: Can I ask you some questions?

RENNERT: I can't answer any questions right now. Dr. Jensen should be
           available in two or three hours.

YOU: Who's Dr. Jensen?

RENNERT: Dr. Francine Jensen, director of the city health department.

YOU: Okay. Where is he now?

RENNERT: *She!* She's in a meeting with other city and parish officials.

           (End of recorded interview)

Aided by the news director's memory, the office encyclopedia, and a call to the library, you find out that there was another outbreak of the disease in New Orleans last summer. The totals for that episode were 213 cases, including twelve deaths. Before that, the last outbreak in the city was in 1964. Last summer's cases were reported in mid-July. City health officials declared the threat officially over in early October.

According to the encyclopedia, encephalitis is also known as "sleeping sickness." It is caused by a virus and is defined medically as inflammation of the brain. Symptoms include irritability, drowsiness, headache, fever, stiff neck, and nausea.

The St. Louis strain of the disease is carried to humans by mosquitoes.

You call James Simmons, the director of the city's mosquito control district, and the recorder goes on again.

Simmons says his crews will begin working around the clock, spraying mosquitoes and pools of standing water where mosquitoes breed. He says he will ask the city council for an emergency appropriation of $100,000 for the stepped-up control activities. He says he will also ask the fire department to allow him to use off-duty firefighters to help with the spraying. He says that the best thing folks can do is stay inside after dark and eliminate any sources of standing water around their homes.

Gathering this information has taken you twenty-five minutes. Fortunately, another staff member has prepared the rest of the hourly news, leaving you free to work on this story. He has left a one-minute "hole" in the show for your feature story. You decide not to air any of the recorded audio material, but only to use it as another information source in writing your story.

Write a one-minute radio story based on the facts given. You have twenty minutes to write the story.

Exercise 2

The news director says the story you wrote on the encephalitis epidemic is dull because it has no audio in it. He tells you to rewrite it for the next hourly news program, using at least one audio cut from your interview with Ms. Rennert. He says to be sure that the running length of the story—your opening, the audio cut, and any closing you may wish to use—does not exceed one minute. You also need to work on some other stories for the upcoming program, so you will have to budget your time. It takes you fifteen minutes to edit the audio cut you want and re-record it onto an audio cartridge. You can only afford fifteen minutes to rewrite the rest of the story. Turn to Exercise 1 and indicate which audio material you would use by drawing a circle around it. You must complete this entire assignment in fifteen minutes.

Exercise 3

A difficulty of preparing interpretive or depth pieces for television is that they tend to lack visual interest. At their worst, they consist of nothing but the newsperson talking to the audience. And a mixture of talking-head interviews is not much more exciting.

For this exercise, suppose your city is debating a cut in the city sales tax. The basic points are these:

1. The cut may stimulate the local economy by making goods a bit cheaper.

2. The tax causes extra bookwork for local merchants, who receive no compensation for collecting it.

3. The tax weighs more heavily on the poor because nearly all their income is spent on items that carry the sales tax, while wealthier people bank or invest much of their income and avoid the tax.

4. The tax hurts retired people and others on fixed incomes because it goes up with inflation.

On the other hand:

5. There is no guarantee that local merchants will pass on the savings if the tax is repealed.

6. The local merchants are not completely without compensation for collecting the present tax because they keep the difference between the tax and the amount the purchaser overpays in taxes when the tax is figured to the next highest penny.

7. The merchants also have use of the money, free of interest charges, until it is paid every three months to the city.

8. The tax does hit the rich harder than the poor in some ways because it is collected on expensive luxury goods.

9. It is also fairly certain that the tax can be cut only by reducing city services—although whether these cuts would affect schools, police, fire department, libraries, recreation facilities, or other areas would be for the city council to decide, if the tax cut takes place.

You *could* get most of these points, pro and con, across with a couple of interviews. But what *interesting* visual techniques could you use to present this complex story? Prepare a television script and indicate the visuals you would use.

Exercise 4

One of the toughest jobs for a reporter is to separate facts, opinions, and misstatements of fact for the public without appearing to take sides. Take the following excerpt from an interview with Morton L. Marsupial, who is seeking to unseat incumbent Congressman Cecil R. Wombat. Marsupial is a Republican and Wombat is a Democrat. Each has won his party's nomination for the position. You interview Marsupial, and he makes the following statement.

Cecil Wombat is the worst enemy the farmers of this district ever had. When Congress voted to raise parity prices for corn . . . and that's our major crop here . . . to a price where our farmers could at least break even, Cecil Wombat was the only member of Congress from this state that voted against that increase. I believe that Wombat wants to keep corn prices low so that the grain dealers in his hometown can make a killing.

You get in touch with Wombat's campaign headquarters. His campaign manager says that Wombat has no intention of giving more publicity to the charge by denying it. He says he has heard that Marsupial is trying to make a killing in corn futures by manipulating prices.

You check with the local Farm Bureau Federation. They say that Wombat voted against the increase in parity prices during his first term in Congress, in 1968, and that he has voted in favor of increases in corn parity prices ever since. You can find no evidence that Wombat is working with grain dealers, but his father-in-law is a major grain dealer and several big grain dealers have made large contributions to Wombat's campaign. You also find no evidence that Marsupial is dealing in corn futures, although his son is involved in speculating on corn futures and is rumored to be deeply in debt.

First, decide which elements in the story are facts? Which are opinions? Which statements are conjecture? Which are false?

Next, write a radio script, not more than one minute in length, showing how you would handle the issue.

Then, write a television script, not more than one minute in length, showing how you would handle the issue.

10

Features and Documentaries

It is sometimes difficult to distinguish between the "documentary" and the "feature story." The primary difference today lies in length. The documentary is usually presented by itself as an entire program, while the feature is typically aired as a segment of a longer program. But this distinction has been blurred by the creation of the "mini-documentary," which, like a feature story, is generally shown as a segment of a longer program.

Subject matter, too, may distinguish the documentary from the feature. The documentary deals with serious issues, while the feature tends more toward human interest. But there can be nonserious documentaries and serious feature stories. So again, the distinction is blurred.

One distinction that the writer should be well aware of is structure. A documentary must have dramatic structure; it must set out its purpose, examine the relevant material, and reach some conclusion. The feature, because it is shorter, may lack some of these elements. Also, the documentary, with its greater length, can study a problem in greater depth and provide more details than a feature story.

Both the documentary and the feature story rely heavily upon the editing of recorded material—"actuality material" it is often called. Editing inevitably leaves the writer open to accusations of bias. Because the material in feature stories is briefer, what is used is usually more factual and less subject to interpretations of bias.

Because it ends with a summing up or conclusions, the documentary may be editorial. It need not be, of course. Most journalists would prefer to say that their documentaries present an honest, unbiased picture of a problem. But a documentary can function as propaganda or as an editorial. Moreover, many attempts at unbiased reporting still wind up favoring one side of an issue. It is difficult, after all, for even the most dedicated journalist to do the amount of research needed to produce a documentary without forming some conclusions about the issue at hand. If the writer is not constantly on guard, some of these conclusions may slip into the documentary.

TECHNIQUES OF PREPARATION

To a considerable degree, you can follow the same procedures for preparing either a documentary or a feature story. Obviously, the documentary is the more elaborate, time-consuming, and expensive of the two forms; but the basic procedures are similar.

It all begins with research. You cannot prepare either a documentary or a feature story until you have done your homework. That means digging out all the facts you can about your topic and then preparing a list of knowledgeable people to interview on the topic.

Both forms of writing must grow from the interview material. There are some exceptions, but most documentaries and features rely heavily on interviews. The interviews, of course, grow out of the careful research you did in advance. Inevitably, the interviews will also suggest new lines of research, which you will pursue if time permits.

For the documentary, interviewing must be exhaustive. You must track down all available sources that can contribute to the content. You must strive to answer all the who, what, where, when, why, and how questions. The feature story, on the other hand, often relies upon a single interview—possibly because the interviewee is a unique source of the information sought.

Sometimes, after you have gone over the interview material, you may wish to check back with some of the individuals interviewed and ask for clarifications or additional information. This costs time and money—and sometimes it is not possible—so try to see to it that your initial interviews are as comprehensive as possible. This need for comprehensive interviews is one of the things that makes documentaries and features wasteful. You know you are only going to use a fraction of the material, but at the time of the interview, you are not sure which fraction. If you have done your research well, you can avoid some of this waste by anticipating what type of answers you will get from each of the persons you interview.

For network productions, it is not uncommon to have less than one-thirtieth of the film, videotape, or audiotape you made for the show actually used on the air. We don't recommend such extravagance to students, and neither network nor station management looks kindly upon it; but it is a fact of life that you have to prepare far more material for the show than you will ever use.

THE EDITING PROCESS

When the interviewing is completed, the hard work begins. In elaborate productions, all the material may be sent to a stenographer who transcribes the interviews into typed copy. This step can be helpful, but it is expensive and time-consuming, so you will most likely have to find a way to go through the material and mark the segments you think you will use. It can be very useful for the persons who conducted the interviews to have taken notes on the content of the recorded material.

You begin your selection of material by examining your notes and deciding the key issues to be addressed. The feature will often deal with a single issue. The documentary may examine a single issue, but there will almost certainly be many aspects of that issue to be examined.

You will need to pay careful attention to visual rhetoric if you are preparing material for television. Not every segment that sounds right may work visually. You must be on your guard because visual material may appear to editorialize even when the recorded words and written material do not. Here is what the *CBS News Standards* manual says about editing:

> *The objective of the editing process is to produce a clear and succinct statement which reflects fairly, honestly and without distortion what was seen and heard by our reporters, cameras and microphones. The achievement of this objective requires careful news judgments geared to the individual facts of each situation. These basic standards, developed over the years, should assist you in making those judgments:*
>
> 1. *If the answer to an interview question, as that answer appears in the broadcast, is derived, in part or in whole, from the answers to other questions, the broadcast will so indicate, either in lead-in narration, bridging narration lines during the interview, or appropriate audio lines.*
>
> 2. *If more than one excerpt from a speech or statement is included in a documentary broadcast, the order of their inclusion in the broadcast will be the same as the order of their inclusion in the speech or statement, unless the broadcast specifically indicates otherwise.*[1]

The CBS manual goes on to refer the reader to sections dealing with the use of *reverses*. A reverse is a camera shot taken from the opposite angle of the establishing shot and the majority of shots used. Typically, in news, the reverse is used to show the reporter asking questions or reacting to answers. Since we have cautioned against the reporter showing any positive or negative response to statements made by an interviewee, you may wonder why reverse shots are used at all. The reasons are primarily technical. The reverse shot may be used as a cutaway—that is, a brief shot inserted between two longer shots. Cutaways are often employed in news to avoid putting two shots together that would look odd if one immediately followed the other. The most common use of cutaways is to prevent jump

---

[1] *CBS News Standards* (New York: Columbia Broadcasting System, April 14, 1976), pp. 9–10.

cuts—disturbing cuts between two shots. And reverses can also be used to break up long, boring shots of the interviewee.

If only one camera is available during an interview, the reverses must be shot after the interview has been completed. The camera is set up behind the interviewee, and the reporter repeats the questions asked during the interview. These reverse segments are later edited into the finished interview for the air. At times, the interviewee may not wish to stay for the shooting of the reverses. The camera may be set up in approximately the same location it would be placed if the interviewee had remained; and the cameraperson holds a tight shot on the reporter, who asks the interview questions as if the interviewee were still sitting in front of the camera. On occasion, reporters have even been known to shoot reverses in a different location, such as back at the television studio. A discerning observer may catch the deception, but the audience generally has no way of knowing that the reverses were not taken as part of the regular interview.

The major problem with reverses is that the reporter may not ask the same question or may change the manner in which the question is asked. When such reverses are edited into a finished story, the audience will be led to believe that the interviewee is answering the question posed in the reverse, while the answer shown was, in fact, given to a somewhat different question. The *CBS News Standards* manual specifies that the interviewee must be present when reverses are shot or the procedure must be explained and the approval of the interviewee obtained.

When the basic interview material to be used has been selected, it is carefully timed and the in cues and out cues noted for each segment. The writer can now begin to sketch out the script. The interview material must be organized so that the copy provides a logical structure for the story. In the feature story, the script is likely to include a statement of the issue to be discussed, a presentation of facts and opinions, and a brief summary.

DRAMATIC CONSTRUCTION

The documentary requires more careful plotting than the feature story. And we have drawn that word, "plotting," from dramatic writing deliberately. Of course, the documentary is not fiction, but it should develop in the same manner as a dramatic presentation. First, note the time blocks that you must work with. How much total time have you for the presentation? How much time is there in each segment between commercial breaks? Next, look at the list of the material you wish to include and decide where each item must go.

Probably you will want to open with some sort of *teaser*—a brief segment that illustrates some of the upcoming material in a way that encourages the audience to stay tuned in. Also, documentaries often end with a *tag*—a short segment that sums up the key point of the program.

In addition, your script must provide for such material as opening and closing credits. If the program is being produced for television, you may not have decided what material you will use on the screen while the credits run. That decision is generally made late in the process of preparing the script. But it is important that you allocate time in your script for these items from the start.

When you have decided what material goes into each segment, you can go back and compare the running times for the material you have selected with the times available in the segments of the show. You may decide to move some material to different segments because of time limitations. In most cases, you will then have to begin the painful process of deciding what material you wanted to use will have to be thrown out. However, don't worry about this too much yet. First, get the general outlines of the show.

Now, if you have the manpower available, you can do two things at once: you can decide what additional material you need for the show and then send one crew out to gather this extra material while you begin to write your script. A show should not be all interviews, and it is better if it is not all interviews and narration. For a radio documentary, you can sometimes come up with sounds you may want to mix in with the story—actual sounds from a location to give the story a more authentic feel. On occasion, you may wish to add some music, although this is not done often in contemporary radio documentaries.

For a television documentary, you will want to provide plenty of visual illustrations of what is being talked about. Nothing is duller than just watching someone talk. Think of how you can illustrate the interviews—especially, what material you can run on the screen over the voices of the interviewees so the audience will see what is being discussed instead of just the interviewees' faces. Again, some natural sound from the pictures to run under the voices of the interviewees can be effective.

THE ROUGH DRAFT

While any additional material is being gathered, you begin your rough draft of the script. Outline each segment first, then start writing. Try to make each segment stand as a unit by itself. It is generally a good idea to end each segment with an indication of what will come in the next segment so that the audience will want to stay tuned. The segments should follow logically, one after another, so that the audience will feel that the segment to come will help it to make use of the information presented in whatever segment it is watching.

Unlike fiction writing, you cannot count on being able to provide a dramatic peak for each segment, but you should try to build each segment toward some sort of climax. Save your best material for near the end of the segment, if possible. Start with the least interesting material and progress to more interesting material so that the audience will be drawn into the story.

Try to use writing and illustrative material to give your audience a sense of personal involvement in the story. If you are writing about poverty, try to make the people in your audience feel how it is to be poor. Don't just tell them; give them material that they can identify with. Of course, this can't be done with every subject, but don't feel guilty about seeking to involve your audience emotionally in the material. A dispassionate ticking-off of facts, figures, and opinions rarely holds an audience. As long as you are fair and honest in your treatment of an issue, you should have no qualms about trying to make the audience feel your story emotionally as well as understand it intellectually.

THE FINAL SCRIPT

When you have all the extra videotape, audiotape, or film that you intend to use in your documentary, you can start putting your script in its final form. The process of writing a documentary is one of continually moving back and forth between the typewriter (or word-processing computer) and the editing room. Everything now is cutting and fitting. In most cases, you will have to cut considerably. Now is the time when hard decisions must be made about those various interview segments. You must go over them carefully, looking for places where they can be trimmed to keep them within time limits. Some material will have to be deleted entirely. And, of course, your own incomparable prose must be cut and rewritten and cut and rewritten again.

Periodically, you should refer to your original list of things to be covered in the documentary. In your effort to make everything fit, you may have lost sight of your priorities. Be sure the script says what it was supposed to say. Of course, your priorities may have changed as you worked on the story—but be sure that any changes are deliberate.

Oddly enough, after you have done all this painful cutting, you will probably have to go back and do some padding. Interviews always run in blocks. You can't go through an interview cutting four seconds here and three there. When you cut, it is likely you will have to cut a large chunk of what you had originally selected. The result is that some segments of the program will wind up short, and you will have to write extra material or find other material to fill the time.

POLISHING

The final writing must take place after you have viewed or listened to a *rough cut*—that is, an edited version of the documentary that still requires some final polishing. Now the stopwatch must be used with precision. Everything must check out. It must all make sense. It must sound right. And if it's for television, it must look right, too.

The decisions on the final production are made at this point. The credits must be written, timed, and inserted. Music, if any is to be used, is checked out. The narrator should read through the script to see if there are words or passages that give her or him problems. The timing must be checked again. Still more rewriting may be needed.

Only when the program is in its final version for the air is the writer's job complete. It is a job that requires teamwork and a thorough understanding by the writer of all of the technical aspects of the production.

EXAMINING A DOCUMENTARY

Let's examine the structure of a much publicized documentary entitled "The Selling of the Pentagon." While more than a decade old, this program still offers some unusual insights into the documentary form. Moreover, the passage of time makes it easier for us to examine this controversial program dispassionately.

In structure, the program follows the traditional documentary format we have just outlined in this book. It opens with a short tease that gives the audience an idea of what to expect in the program. It shows a Marine Corps speaker addressing a group of visitors at a Marine Corps maneuver in North Carolina. Within the first minute of the documentary, narrator Roger Mudd sets out the theme and title of the program: "This was a military exercise, but it was also an exercise in salesmanship—the selling of the Pentagon."

There are three breaks for commericals or announcements in the program, dividing this documentary into a tease and three segments. There is no tag at the end, but the last minutes of the program are devoted to a summing up delivered by Mudd on camera. So the program fits a fairly conventional television documentary pattern.

Each segment of the program is an independent unit. In the first segment, Mudd sets out the premise of the program; and then the program concentrates on the military exhibitions put on by the Defense Department around the country. This segment notes that important opinion leaders get invitations to maneuvers such as the one in North Carolina; and it ends with a series of brief statements by several of the guests at those maneuvers, indicating that the guests have been convinced of the correctness of Defense Department policy by what they have seen and heard.

The second segment of the program is devoted entirely to the issue of production and distribution of films by the Defense Department. It focuses on the prominent entertainers and news persons who have participated in the making of these films.

The third segment examines the relation of the news media to the Defense Department public relations people. It shows press briefings by officials at the Pentagon and by military information officers in the field, and it follows the distribution of information about military personnel to hometown news media. This segment discusses the Defense Department's practice of providing speakers for interviews, which members of Congress send back to media in their home districts. And it includes an interview with a former military information officer who says that members of the armed forces interviewed by reporters are carefully selected and coached first by public information officers. The same source claims that some film the Defense Department provided of military action in Vietnam had been staged.

The program ends with Mudd giving the conclusions reached by the people who prepared the documentary. Mudd notes that the president had called on government agencies to reduce their public relations expenditures but that the Defense Department was continuing to provide speakers and public displays of equipment.

As you can see, the structure of this documentary was simple. An issue was suggested in the tease and set out explicitly at the start of the first segment after the tease. Key problems related to the issue were selected and drawn together into logical groups for each segment. The last few minutes of the program were reserved for pulling all the material together and putting it into perspective. It is a format that should function well for almost any documentary you write.

WHY DOCUMENTARIES BECOME CONTROVERSIAL

Why, then, was this program on the Pentagon so controversial? There were several reasons. One reason, obviously, was that it was produced at a time when the United States was involved in the Viet Nam War, and public feelings for and against the war were running high. A criticism of the Defense Department was certain to create a stir.

However, the problem went beyond that. We mentioned earlier that a documentary can be used as an editorial. Except for the fact that this script did not specifically call for action, it was, essentially, an editorial. Investigative reporting—and this was investigative reporting of a sort—always runs the risk of being perceived as editorial. And the reporter who digs into a story is always likely to form opinions. Those opinions have a way of slipping into the copy. In a broader sense, the mere selection of a topic can suggest that the reporter has some opinions on that subject.

THE EDITORIAL STANCE

In this documentary, there was no attempt to conceal that the program was meant to be a criticism of a specific Defense Department policy. It is, of course, the right of journalists in a free society to take such positions. But once a reporter becomes an advocate, the reporter's objectivity is certain to be questioned. The opening statement in this documentary after the first break left little doubt that the approach of the program was to be critical:

> *Nothing is more essential to a democracy than the free flow of information. Misinformation, distortion, propaganda all interrupt that flow. They make it impossible for people to know what their government is doing, which, in a democracy, is crucial. The largest agency in our government is the Department of Defense, and it maintains a public relations division to inform people of its activities. In December, Congress cut the appropriations for this division, but, according to the Pentagon, it will still spend 30 million dollars this year on public affairs, an amount more than ten times what it spent to tell people about itself just 12 years ago. Even this figure may be only the tip of the public relations iceberg. A special, still unpublished report for the prestigious 20th Century Fund estimates the real total at 190 million dollars. The combined news budgets of the three commercial television networks—ABC, CBS and NBC—are 146 million dollars.*
>
> *Whatever the true cost at the Pentagon, there have been recent charges in the press and in Congress that the Department is using these public relations funds not merely to inform but to convince and persuade the public on vital issues of war and peace. Ten months ago, CBS News set out to investigate these charges and to examine the range and variety of the Pentagon's public affairs activities.[2]*

The second paragraph sets out the stated purpose of the program, but more serious charges had already been suggested in the first paragraph—"misinformation, distortion, propaganda." There was ambiguous phrasing about the budget. It could be interpreted as meaning that the Pentagon was spending more on public relations despite the congressional budget cut, but the wording does not say that specifically. And there is an odd switch of terms, from "public relations" to "public affairs." Are they the same? We aren't told. We are told that the Pentagon figure may grossly understate the actual public relations budget. And the source of that information was given added authority by sticking in an adjective—"the prestigious 20th Century Fund." But no attempt was made in the report to establish the correct figure.

In short, a fairly serious indictment was laid out before the stated purpose of the documentary was introduced. The generally hostile tone continued through the documentary—and therein lies a problem. Most

---

[2] Peter Davis, writer and producer, "The Selling of the Pentagon" (New York: Columbia Broadcasting System, 1971). Courtesy Columbia Broadcasting System.

of the segments did precisely what a documentary is supposed to do—they documented the allegations made. But once a documentary has established to the audience that the approach is editorial, the audience is likely to question, first, the objectivity of the reporters and, second, the accuracy of the material presented. And if the audience had any lingering doubts about the attitude of those who prepared this particular documentary, those doubts certainly were dispelled by this stinging summation in the closing of the program:

> On this broadcast we have seen violence made glamorous, expensive weapons advertised as if they were automobiles, biased opinions presented as straight facts. Defending the country not just with arms but also with ideology, Pentagon propaganda insists on America's role as the cop on every beat in the world. Not only the public but the press as well has been beguiled, including at times, ourselves at CBS News. This propaganda barrage is the creation of a runaway bureaucracy that frustrates attempts to control it.[3]

QUESTIONS ABOUT EDITORIAL TECHNIQUES

Such an open condemnation was certain to raise questions about the fairness of the program; and, in the controversy that followed the presentation of "The Selling of the Pentagon," just such criticisms arose. It was pointed out that certain statements by individuals had been presented out of the sequence in which the statements were originally made. There may have been no intent to distort; but because the objectivity of the report was already subject to question, many assumed that the statements had been deliberately twisted out of context. In the wake of the storm that blew up over "The Selling of the Pentagon," CBS News modified its *News Standards* manual to include some of the provisions cited earlier.

Another criticism involved a statement that was used without the audience being told that the person speaking was quoting someone else. It seems likely that the failure to make this clear was simply an editorial slip. Moreover, it does not appear that the quoted material was at odds with the views being expressed by the speaker in his own words. But again, such a slip in an apparently hostile presentation was certain to raise suspicion of a deliberate intent to distort.

In several places, figures used to make a point were stated in a way that was confusing—again raising the question of whether deliberate distortions were intended. For example, the script says, "During the 1960s at least 52 million Americans saw Pentagon motion pictures. . . ." It is not clear if that figure includes military personnel, nor is it clear whether

---

[3] *Ibid.*

it represents 52 million individual Americans or a collective audience of 52 million that could count the same individuals many times. If every member of the armed forces saw two Pentagon films a year from 1960 through 1969, that alone would have provided an audience of 52 million. Again, what was involved here was probably no more than some sloppy writing and, perhaps, some sloppy research, but careless errors become suspect when they turn up in a program that pushes a particular point of view.

Ultimately, the writer's zeal to make a point pressed the conclusions of the program beyond what the evidence provided could support. It may be true that "Pentagon propaganda insists on America's role as the cop on every beat in the world," but such statements are not sustained by the material presented in the program. With the single exception of a reference to Cuba, all Pentagon statements used either concerned the war then going on in Southeast Asia or were generalized references to the threat of communist aggression. Other conclusions were presented on equally shaky bases. In short, the program has many minor faults that may have seemed more serious to viewers because the reporter abandoned the traditional cloak of objectivity.

Quite simply, if you use the documentary to say, "Here's what's wrong, and here's what you should do about it," you should expect that some people will respond, "I don't think that's what's wrong, and I think your solution stinks." That's what freedom of expression is all about. Unfortunately, the only recourse your critic is likely to have is to go buy his own television network. So you have a heavy obligation to be fair. When you do use the documentary to state a position, you must be doubly sure that your approach has been fair, your research scrupulous, and your conclusions well-substantiated. And while polemic may be satisfying, a calm, reasoned approach is more likely to convince more people.

Exercises

Exercise 1

Quotations are extremely hard to work into *written* broadcast copy. They are easily handled, of course, when the speaker is seen or heard in an actuality. But when the quote must be read by the newscaster, it becomes difficult to know when the newscaster is reading regular news copy and when he is reading a direct quote.

The story that follows *might* work on the air—particularly if the medium was television so that the newscaster's facial expressions could assist the way he uses his voice to indicate a quotation. The writer has used a little trick to help distinguish quotes from paraphrases. In paraphrasing, the word "says" or its equivalent almost invariably goes immediately before the paraphrased material. For example: "The governor *says* he's fed up with the lack of action on the plan." In the story below, the writer has inverted the word order, *beginning* each sentence with "says" or "explains." Since much of the meaning of a sentence in English is conveyed by word order, the audience is immediately alerted to the fact that there is something different about the statement coming up. With that clue and the proper vocal inflection, a good newscaster could *probably* make it clear to the audience which statements were direct quotes.

But why take chances? There are safer ways to handle quotations in electronic news. How might the quotations have been better introduced? How might they have been better integrated into the story?

Rewrite this story as a radio news feature running about one and one-half minutes. Reconsider each quotation used in the original version. Is each quotation really necessary? Remember that a quotation is needed only if some essential part of its meaning is lost when it is paraphrased or if the paraphrased version fails to convey something about the nature of the person making the statement. Do all of the quotations in this story qualify under these criteria for selection?

BREAD

Near Rochester, New York, in the community of Piffard, is an unusual bakery.

The bakery serves the general public, but is operated by the abbey of the Genesee, a Cistercian monastery that bakes monk's bread.

The monks form a religious order whose members reside in isolation from society.

The monks have a spokesman . . . Brother Anthony . . . who says they need to remind their distributing company that they do not operate a bakery attached to a monastery, but a monastery with a bakery attached.

The monks bake enough bread during a three-day work week to supply most of their customers and still collect a profit for the abbey.

Says Brother Anthony: "Our rules state that we are not allowed to beg—so we must have some source of income."

The profits are used to finance the monastery . . . and to assist with various charity projects.

Says Brother Anthony: "People are always coming to our door asking for help—and we cannot really turn them away."

The abbey brings ingredients from across the nation and employs modern technology to produce nearly all of the monk's bread on the market. The distributor also has negotiated a special arrangement that allows it to produce additional bread, based on market demands, using the monks' formula.

The bread actually baked at the abbey always says "Made by Trappist monks."

Silence is the rule at the abbey, but the monks have developed an elaborate system of sign language to communicate while working in the bakery.

Explains Brother Anthony: "We have a great respect for another person's right to silence and try to preserve an atmosphere of peace and serenity."

Founded in 1951 on a donated tract of land, the abbey has grown and thrived since then, mainly on the success of its bread.

Comments Brother Anthony: "I am not an objective critic, but I feel that our bread is the best in the area."

Says he: "It is more than simply taking pride in our work—making bread or any work becomes for a monk an act of prayer." He adds: "Our work is an external extension of the devotion we feel for God."

Exercise 2

In the preceding exercise, you rewrote a story as a radio news feature. Now, using the same original copy, turn that same story into a television news feature.

First, think of the story visually. Assume that this story was shot on 16 mm film and that you can have any shots you want, but no sound film equipment was available for the story. In other words, the entire story must be written MOC and SI FILM/VO.

On one sheet of paper, briefly describe each shot you will use in your story in the order it will appear and give its running time. Use standard professional abbreviations to describe the format of each shot: LS (Long Shot), MS (Medium Shot), and CU (Close-Up). A shot should always complete the action taking place in it (unless you cut to a matching action shot of the same activity). However, where no particular action requires completion, four seconds is a fairly average length of time for a shot to run. (But vary the running times a bit to keep the pace of the cutting from becoming monotonous.) Begin your last shot about four seconds before the estimated end of the Voice Over material and end it about three seconds after the estimated end of the Voice Over. That allows leeway for variations in the newscaster's reading speed. Estimated reading time should be one minute.

Now, on another sheet of paper, write a one-minute script to go with the film. Did you find that you handled the quotes for this television story differently than you handled them for radio?

Exercise 3

In some newsrooms, stories are prepared as you prepared the story in the last exercise—the film or videotape is edited first and the copy is matched to the pictures. However, at least as many, and probably more, newsrooms work the other way—the copy is written first, then the film or videotape is edited to match the copy. Understand that, in such cases, writers usually have a chance to see the unedited pictures first, so they know what they have to work with.

For this exercise, list on one sheet of paper all the things that you think a good cameraman would have shot for the story in the preceding exercise. Remember that no sound could be recorded for the story.

On a second sheet of paper, rewrite the story from Exercise 1, keeping in mind the pictures you have to work with. Make the story one minute long, with MOC and SI FILM/VO.

Then, on a third sheet of paper list each shot you would use in the film story and note how long it runs.

Compare the written story from Exercise 2 with the one you have just written. Compare the list of shots for each exercise. What constraints did picking the pictures first in Exercise 2 impose on the writing in that exercise? What constraints did writing the story first impose upon the selection of pictures in this third exercise? Which process did you find easier? Why?

Exercise 4

From the following information, write two leads. Write the first lead for straight news. Make the second one a feature lead. Use radio script format.

Last night local residents reported seeing a bright object flash across the sky. Early this morning, Scott Bailey, a spokesman for the Pentagon in Washington, D.C., said the flash was not a comet but was part of a Soviet rocket launched yesterday. The Pentagon official said the rocket had been tracked by military radar as it descended. The rocket was part of the launch assembly for Cosmos 854. The rocket, which fell in Montana, has not been recovered, Bailey said.

Exercise 5

As you have learned by now, *long* stories are a rarity in broadcasting. A five-minute radio newscast has room for about three and one-half minutes of news. Obviously, in such a newscast, a three-minute story would be out of the question and even a one-minute story would be a luxury. The typical five-minute newscast contains ten to twelve stories, giving an average running time for each story of eighteen to twenty seconds. Television newscasts are generally at least one-half hour long, so there is considerably more time for well-developed feature stories in television.

Still, there are a few places in radio for the longer features. Usually these features are aired as a separate, regularly scheduled program or as a segment within a longer program. This is your chance to put together such a feature story for radio. Make it run three and one-half minutes. For research material, you have two sources. The first source is the transcript of an interview that Morley Safer of CBS's "60 Minutes" conducted with Katharine Hepburn, the winner of three Oscars in the Academy Awards.[4] Your second source is an article based on columnist Terrence O'Flaherty's interview with George Cukor, who directed Hepburn in *The Corn is Green*.[5]

Using both of these transcripts for research material and taking whatever you need from each, write the best radio feature story you can.

Interview with Actress Katharine Hepburn

SAFER: How do you think you're considered by the movie fans?

HEPBURN: They look at me. I'm like some building they pass—one they're fond of, you know. Well, I am. I'm like a building. Don't you get affection for buildings? What would you do if they tore down the Plaza Hotel? Not that I put myself in that class, mind you.

SAFER: What building would you describe yourself as?

---

[4] Courtesy Columbia Broadcasting System.

---

[5] Courtesy Terrence O'Flaherty, *San Francisco Chronicle*.

HEPBURN: I used to say the Flat Iron Building. . . . But that's what has happened. They've gradually got an affection for me. I'm like one of those long-distance runners, a very, very long-distance runner who just keeps a-going and they think, well, she's not bad—been running for a hell of a long time. Now, how did she do that?

SAFER: What of your contemporaries?

HEPBURN: Have all died off. I'm all that's left. I'm in a safe group. I haven't gotten a romantic feeling about age. I think we rot away and it's too God damn bad we do.

A friend of mine called a woman and asked how she felt and there was this long pause and the woman finally said, "Well, I feel fine if you don't ask for details." It's an absolutely divine remark.

I don't believe that acting is all this great. I can't talk about it. If you ask me what I do I haven't the vaguest idea. . . . Mind you, I don't think it's any great art. As Spencer Tracy used to say, "Always remember who killed Lincoln!" And I said, look at Shirley Temple. She was three and she was great. She could laugh and cry and carry on.

SAFER: I think it's fair to say that when Katharine Hepburn agrees to appear in a movie, she does a lot more than play the role. She suggests. . . .

HEPBURN: No, she butts—BUTTS—into everything. When I came to New York I was so shy that I never went into a restaurant. And I don't go into a restaurant now.

SAFER: But you're not shy anymore?

HEPBURN: In a different way. I still don't go to restaurants because they charge $60 a meal. And I can serve you here any time you want to come. You give me the $60 and I'll give you the dinner.

SAFER: Are you just a little bit—how shall I say this?

HEPBURN: Tight?

SAFER: Tight.

HEPBURN: No, I'm not tight. I just don't like injustice. I carry a hard boiled egg to work and a piece of ham. And I take hot water out of the tap and put in some coffee and sugar and carry fruit of some sort and a breakfast tray and it costs me five cents.

SAFER: It's fashionable these days to laugh at the Academy Awards. What do you think?

HEPBURN: Well, I don't know what to think. I once said to my father, "I'm really too shy to go to that party. It would embarrass

Chapter Ten

me." And he said, "Yes, my children are all very shy. They don't dare go to parties unless they're sure to be the bride or the corpse." Well, I've never been to an Academy Award. Why not? Well, it has to be that I'm afraid I'm going to lose, doesn't it?

I don't approve of my attitude—of not going. I think it's cheap of me—second rate—not to go. Film making is a group activity.

You know, I always felt that "they" were out to get me—and that I'd better be good. And I *still* think I'd better be good.

Article about Director George Cukor

"When she started acting, she was a very eager beaver and a little clumsy but always there was something about her that was arresting," said George Cukor here last week.

He was speaking about Katharine Hepburn. He should know a great deal about her after a friendship of nearly 50 years. Last night's The Corn Is Green *was the tenth film they have made together since* A Bill of Divorcement *in 1932, followed by* Little Women.

Has she changed since then?

"Well, she's a more accomplished actress of course," Cukor said. "One never realized that she would have such a distinguished career. No one ever knows about anybody when they start out because then it is difficult to measure the character of a performer."

At 79, Cukor himself is a witty, urbane gentleman, quick to laugh and quick to remember things that amuse him. He is delightful company.

I reminded him of something he told me ten years ago: "I won't do television because I'm too old, too tired, and too rich."

What happened? "I changed my mind," he said.

In assessing his own career, Cukor told me, "It's never good to revisit past films. When I watch them today I say what the hell was I thinking in that particular scene? No, I find it difficult to sentimentalize over the past. But Hepburn does. I remember a dinner party with Ethel Barrymore and Spencer Tracy many years ago during her days of Hollywood affluence when she lived in a house that had once belonged to Charles Boyer. It had a projection room and after dinner she announced that she had a print of the second MGM version of Little Women. *We watched it awhile and finally said, 'Oh, take it off,' and then she said, 'I just happen to have a print of our version,' and at that point Tracy got up and said, 'Goodnight, folks' and left the room."*

Cukor and the two women watched the whole thing.

Cukor recalled the day that a young man visited her when they were filming a country club scene on location.

"Everyone knew that it was Howard Hughes. We couldn't help it. Who else would land his own plane on the golf course? Although she liked him very much, she was never very polite to him. Hepburn was quite a tomboy in those days.

"Today she is ideal for The Corn Is Green. *She admired the character because she was a strong woman. She liked all the others, too, because they weren't self pitying or whining. She thinks there's too much of that today. She believes people should stand up and be counted. It's her rather severe New England ethics. She believes in hard work and in not being too soft. And yet she is extremely generous and kind."*

A reporter asked, "What is your definition of quality?"

"My God, these are eternal questions. You need Socrates to answer them," Cukor replied good naturedly.

He was asked if he had played down the possible sexual implications in the relationship between the spinster and the young coal miner because of the disparity in ages.

"That is a provocative but inaccurate and also irritating question," he replied. "This is the way the play was written. There is nothing romantic in the play, nor any suggestion of it. Nor should there have been."

On the set, he and Hepburn are friends. "Or we are sometimes. She's not as perfect as I am nor as sweet and angelic. On our last picture she was rather waspish and got somewhat crotchety. But, yes, we are good friends. After all, we've really said just about everything to each other by now. . . ."

Exercise 6

In preparing a television feature, you have the luxury of giving yourself more time to cover the subject. Three points are worth noting. First, "more time" still isn't much compared to the time you would spend writing for the print media. A three-minute story for television would take up about thirteen and two-thirds column inches in a newspaper—about two-thirds of a single column on a six-column page, or less than two typed, double-space pages. Second, many television writers do not take full advantage of the extra time they have. Instead of writing more news, they just write more words. And finally, television is sometimes at war with the kind of material that goes into a feature story. Television is a visual medium, while many features tend to be thought pieces—not so much something to *look* at as something to *think* about. There are newscasters who can transcend this limitation, but not many. In most cases, if a story is not visual, the audience will find it dull.

Reread the feature story you wrote for radio in the preceding exercise. What changes would you make in the copy if you were writing it for television? What slides or other visuals would you want to use with the script?

Now, assume that you have access to videotapes of the Hepburn and Cukor interviews in the previous exercise. Assume that you also can use cuts from both the Hepburn and the Bette Davis versions of *The Corn Is Green,* and that you have slides of old black-and-white stills showing Emlyn Williams and Ethel Barrymore in the stage version of that play, as well as slides of Hepburn in *Bill of Divorcement* and *Little Women.*

You need not—and probably should not—use all of these visuals. Write a four-minute feature story, integrating any of the visual material that you wish to use. The slides may be projected in back of the newscaster using Vizmo, or they may be run full screen. All the other material is on videotape. On a separate sheet of paper, describe the visuals you have chosen to go with each section of the script. Clearly identify each cut from each interview that you are using and where you are using it. If you wish, you may intercut between the Cukor and Hepburn interviews to create a "dialogue" between them.

Appendix A

Electronic News Stylebook

I. Format.

A. Paper.

1. Use standard, 8½" × 11" paper.
2. Use soft paper that will not rattle.
3. Use white paper for radio and pastels for television.

B. Typing.

1. Use only one side of a page.
2. Type only one story to a page.
3. Always make a carbon copy. (Television scripts are normally typed on "books" of paper interleaved with carbon sheets. Each page of a "book" is a different color. Scripts are collated according to color, each color designating the recipient of the script. For example, the yellow script goes to the anchor person, the pink goes to the director, and so on.)
4. Set your margins as follows:

    a. For radio, use 10 and 80.
    b. For television, use 40 and 75.

5. Triple space your copy. (Double space if the typewriter has no triple-space setting. Fill material may be single spaced.)
6. Use "down style"—lowercase with normal capitalization.
7. Skip extra lines instead of indenting for paragraphs.
8. Never split a word between two lines.
9. Avoid starting two successive lines with the same word.
10. Indicate the end of a story by triple spacing and typing "#" in the center of the page.

C. Pagination.

1. Do not number the pages of your stories until just before air time.

2. Write the numbers in the upper left-hand corner of each page.

3. Number *stories,* rather than pages. (Make the second page of story number 6, "6-a," and so on.)

D. Preparing scripts for use.

1. Use paper clips to hold a script together—never staple a script.

2. After a script has been used, it can then be stapled for filing.

E. Story Format.

1. Slug each story.

a. The slug is the information at the top of the page that gives the name of the story, the program for which it was written, the date, and the name of the writer.

b. This is the television slug:

FIRE—NOON NEWS—7/12/85—MARTIN

c. The same slug can be used for radio, although some stations prefer that the slug be typed in the upper, left-hand corner of the page.

FIRE
NOON NEWS
MARTIN

(If this second style of slug is used, the page number should go below the slug.)

d. For second-page slugs, see 2-d below.

2. Treat multi-page stories as follows:

a. If a story looks as if it will run on to a second page, find a place to split it after the tenth line.

b. Never split a sentence or a paragraph between two pages.

c. Near the bottom of the first page and in the center of the page, type "MORE"—then circle the word with a pencil and draw an arrow to the right edge of the page.

MORE

d. Begin the second page of a story with the same slug used on the first page, followed by the words "FIRST ADD." Circle the slug and "FIRST ADD" with a pencil. (A third page of a story uses the slug with "SECOND ADD," and so on.)

FIRE—NOON NEWS—7/12/85—MARTIN—FIRST ADD

or

FIRE—FIRST ADD
NOON NEWS
7/12/85
MARTIN

II. Editing.

A. Do not use copyediting symbols.
B. Use a copy pencil to mark out *completely* any words that are to be deleted or corrected.
C. Type or print a correction above material that has been crossed out.
D. Retype any copy that is difficult to read.
E. Circle anything not meant to be read aloud.
F. Underline words to be *emphasized*.
G. Draw a wavy line under any words that may be difficult for the reader, either because of meaning or because of pronunciation.

III. Timing.

A. If time permits, check the running time of each story with a stop-watch.
B. If you cannot time a story with a stopwatch, estimate its running time by counting the number of lines of copy in the story. (Using the margins given in I.B.4., each line of radio copy should take about four seconds to read and each line of television copy about two seconds.)
C. Record the running time of each story in the upper right-hand corner of the story's first page.

   1. The running time of a story includes the running time of any audio or video material in that story. (For example, a television story with a twelve-second introduction followed by forty seconds of videotape has a "52 sec." running time.)
   2. Many news departments prefer to record the story's line count rather than its actual running time in the upper right-hand corner of the first page. (This is usually easier to keep track of. Remember to convert the running time of any audio or video material to line count in this case. For example, a television story with a four-line introduction and twenty seconds of videotape would have "14 lines" written in the upper right corner. A radio story with a ten-line lead-in followed by a twenty-second audio cut would have "15 lines" written in the upper right corner.)
   3. For times greater than fifty-nine seconds, use minutes and

seconds. (Write, for example: "2:08"—not "128 sec." Also, do not write "2:08 min." or "2 min. 8 sec.")

D. Back-time material from the start of commercials, the end of the program, or any other fixed-time program elements. (To back-time a script section, use a red grease pencil to mark the time at which you must begin reading that material to come out on time. Arrange the script when reading it so you can see these marked times and know when to hit them.)

E. Include pad material in every script. (The pad will consist of brief items that can be used to fill in before back-timed material so that the newscaster can start to read the back-timed material at exactly the specified time.)

IV. Transitions between stories.

A. Do not write a transition as part of a story. This makes it too difficult to rearrange stories if you have to. First, arrange script as it is to be used on the air—then, write transitions on separate sheets of paper and insert them in the proper places. A brief transition may be pencilled in at the top of a page, provided material is easy to read.

B. Make each story in a script lead logically to the next story. This minimizes the need for transitions. A carefully arranged script may need no transitions at all.

V. Writing style.

A. A/An.

1. Use "a" or "an" instead of "per" in expressions such as "miles an hour."

2. Do *not* use "a" in expressions such as "a hundred" or "a thousand," where it can be confused with "eight." (Always write "one hundred," and so on.)

B. Abbreviations.

1. The only abbreviations you will use are: "Mr.," "Mrs.," "Ms.," and "Dr." *Write everything else out.* (You may use "Ft." [Fort] and "St." [Saint] when they are commonly used in a place name such as "Ft. Mason" or "St. Louis.")

2. *Very* well known organizations may be referred to by their initials. Use hyphens, not periods, to separate the initials. (For example: "F-B-I." An exception to the rule is "AFL-CIO," which would be confusing if written with hyphens between all letters.)

3. Well-known acronyms should be written without hyphens. (For example: "NATO." But do not use an acronym unless it is known almost universally.)

4. Use a period after initials, when the initial is a regularly used

part of a person's name. (Write: "Senator S. I. Hayakawa," *not* "Senator S-I Hayakawa.")

C. Addresses.

1. Omit addresses except when they are essential to the story.

2. Group numbers in addresses according to normal speech patterns by using hyphens. (For example: "18-0-2 South Main Street.")

3. If the street name in an address is a number, separate it from the house number by a direction or some other written material. (For example: "128 *South* 135th Street," or "number 825 *on* 35th Street.")

4. If it is awkward or impractical to separate the house number and the street number in an address, write out the shorter of the two numbers. (For example: "seventy-five 185th Street," but "12-82 Tenth Street.")

5. Always write out "First Street and "Eleventh Street" because "1st" and "11th" can be confusing to read.

D. Ages.

1. Omit a person's age unless it is essential to your story.

2. If a person's age must be included in a story, do *not* use newspaper style ("Mary Jones, 25"). Instead write: "Mary Jones, who is 25," or "25-year-old Mary Jones.")

3. Ages are customarily used in obituaries and when a person is expected to die soon.

E. Contractions.

1. Use contractions only when they are easy for the reader to say and when there is no chance of misunderstanding them.

2. Never use "n't" contractions except for those few that differ clearly from their positive forms, such as "won't," which cannot be confused with "will." (Do not use a word such as "hasn't," which can easily be misunderstood as "has."

F. Dates.

1. Write all dates as ordinals. (For example: "May 10th, 1938," and "October 2nd, 1987.")

2. Write out "first" and "eleventh."

3. Many writers break the year with a hyphen to indicate the normal way of speaking. (For example: "June first, 19-82.")

4. Because A.D. and B.C. are easily misunderstood, it is preferable to make it "before the birth of Christ" or "after the birth of Christ." (Any date before the birth of Christ must be specified as such. Dates through the year 1000 are usually specified as "after the birth of Christ." Later dates need no such reference except when they are being used in a story that also involves dates before the birth of Christ.)

G. Election returns should be simplified for the listener. (Don't write: "With 53 percent of the precincts reporting, Lubitch has 3,007,593 and Winslow has 3,000,079." Instead, make it: "With more than half the precincts reporting, Lubitch leads Winslow by 75-hundred votes.")

H. License plate numbers are rarely given out in broadcast writing. If needed for a story, give the state of registration and follow it with the numbers and letters separated by hyphens: "California license plate number 4-9-8-R-Z-T." Group long numbers into groups of three, using dots: "Nevada license plate number 8-0 . . . 5-7-5." (If you expect the listeners to remember or write down the number, it should be mentioned at least twice, preferably three times.)

I. Money.
   1. Write out "dollars" and "cents" for all sums of money. (For example: "2 dollars and 28 cents," not "$2.28.")
   2. Round off sums whenever possible. (Make it "almost 2-thousand dollars," not "$1,963.48.")

J. Names.
   1. Never lead a story with an unfamiliar name.
   2. Drop middle initials except when the person is regularly known by the name with the initial included. (For example, write: "Clifford Alexander," *not* "Clifford L. Alexander," but *do* write "George C. Scott."
   3. On occasion, a middle initial may be retained to help distinguish an individual from others with the same first and last names. (For example: "The man arrested was Charles J. Smith, but the warrant had been issued for Charles K. Smith."
   4. Nicknames.
      a. Put nicknames in parentheses to indicate that the reader may either use the nickname or ignore it. (For example: "Ron (the Penguin) Cey.")
      b. Use a nickname without the real name *only* if the nickname is both very well known and unique. (For example, it is safe to say "the Fighting Irish" for the Notre Dame football team, but "the Wildcats" could be one of several teams.)

K. Negatives.
   1. Always stress negatives in broadcast copy.
   2. Underscore a negative, or set it off between ellipses. (For example: "Feldman had not seen the warning" or "Feldman had . . . not . . . seen the warning.")

L. Numbers. (See also: Sports, Statistics, Telephone numbers, and Time.)

1. Avoid using numbers as much as possible.
2. Where they must be used, simplify them and round them off.
3. Try to analogize sums to things the audience is familiar with. (For example, instead of saying a boat was "300 feet long," you could say it is "as long as a football field.")
4. Keep numbers out of the leads to stories and out of the first parts of sentences when possible.
5. If you must use a number as the first word of a sentence, write it out. (For example: "Twenty-eight men arrived," but, "There were 28 men.")
6. Always write out the numbers "one" and "eleven."
7. Treat whole numbers as follows:
   a. Use digits from 2 to 999 (except for eleven).
   b. Combine written numbers and digits for all higher numbers. (For example: "one-thousand-12.")
   c. Write numbers between 1100 and 9900 as hundreds. (For example: "eleven-hundred-2," or "95-hundred-24.")
   d. Write millions and billions like this: "8 (M) million dollars" or "10 (B) billion pounds."
8. Treat fractions as follows:
   a. Write out all fractions. (For example: "one-fifth," not "1/5.")
   b. Write one-place decimals as tenths. (For example: "2-and-three-tenths," not "2.3.")
   c. Convert decimals to regular fraction equivalents, if they have them. (For example: "three-fourths," not ".75.")
   d. Avoid decimals of more than one place—or if they must be used, use digits and write out "point." (For example: "8-point-32 ounces.")
9. Treat percentages as follows:
   a. Write percentages as digits and spell out the word "percent." (For example: "130 percent," or "82-point-35 percent.")
   b. Use "point" with one-place decimals as well as longer ones. (For example: "82-point-6 percent.")

M. Pronouns.
   1. Use pronouns sparingly.
   2. Repeat nouns freely to avoid ambiguity.

N. Pronunciation.
   1. Provide a pronunciation guide for any word that might confuse the reader. Underline the word with a wavy line, and either write the guide in parentheses after the word, like this

"Cholmondeley (CHUM-lee)," or print it above the word, like this: *(AH-vee-lah)*
"Avila."

2. Use the phonetic guide provided here. Do not use diacritical markings such as are used in dictionaries. (For example, write: "Peruzzi (puh-ROOT-see)," not "(pə-'rüt-sē).")

3. Indicate accented syllables with uppercase letters. Wire copy has no lowercase letters, so an accent is shown with an apostrophe at the end of the accented syllable. Some news departments also use this system. Using capitals to show accent, your copy would look like this: "Cordoba (KOHR-doh-bah)." Wire copy would show it "(KOHR' DOH-BAH)."

4. Phonetic spelling.

    a. Use the pronunciation guide for vowels.

    b. Use consonants as they are written, *except* in these cases:

    C: Use *K* for words like "cat," and *S* for words like "center."

    G: Use *G* for words like "go," *J* for words like "genius," and *ZH* for words like "rouge."

    Q: use *KW* for words like "quick," and *K* for words like "croquet."

    T: use *TH* for words like "thin," and *THH* for words like "lather."

    c. Omit silent letters. Do not substitute an apostrophe for the omitted letter, because it may be confused with an accent mark for a stressed syllable.

5. Don't expect to be able to represent the pronunciation of foreign words perfectly. Do your best to approximate them phonetically. Where possible, save your newscaster some work and try to find ways to write the story *without* the tough-to-pronounce words. Remember, too, that many foreign words—especially place names—have been anglicized. Don't try to show off your knowledge of foreign languages by providing pronunciation guides for words that already have accepted English pronunciations. (For example: Paris is "PAYR-iss," *not* "pah-REE.") Give some thought to whether your audience is likely to have seen the word you are using in print. You may need to make some reference to unusually spelled words to avoid confusing your audience. (For example: "Lord Home (HYOOM) . . . that name, by the way, is spelled H-O-M-E, just like the word "home" . . . Lord Home (HYOOM) urged the President to postpone. . . .")

6. The radio wires of both major wire services provide pronunciation guides for most difficult words in their stories. They also run a daily list of names, places, and words in the news with a phonetic guide for pronouncing them. Another good source for pronunciations is the *NBC Handbook of Pronun-*

PRONUNCIATION GUIDE

	A	E	I	O	U	Y
A	apple draught					
AH	arm			opera		
AI*	aisle	eye	I island pi pie sight write paradigm			my
AO				cow bough		
AW	awe paw audition caught			ought		
AY	ale mail mate may	epee eight				
EE		ease seem we	libertine			city
EH		enter				
EW		new		root routine	tune	
I		pretty forfeit	it			
OH		saw tableau		oh so open roe tow		
OO				cook	put	
UH	about	erstwhile		rough thorough	up	
YOO		ewe beauty			unit	

Note: If there is any chance of confusing the reader with this pronunciation guide, use some other method, such as providing a rhyme. For example: "Home (HYOOM, rhymes with room).

*Because AI is easily confused with AY, some writers prefer to use EYE.

ciation, although, at this writing, the last edition is badly out of date. A check with your state capitol or state university library will usually turn up a book that provides pronunciations for names of communities and locations in your state. Any good, up-to-date dictionary will provide you with correct pronunciations of most words you are likely to encounter, and most dictionaries either incorporate in the main section or provide separate sections with pronouncing gazetteers and pronouncing biographical information. A good atlas, gazetteer, and biographical dictionary are three books that should be found in any good newsroom. The telephone is also a quick source of pronunciation information. A call to a consulate or embassy, or to a language department on a nearby campus can often provide the information you need. It is a very good rule to *never guess at a pronunciation. However,* if you have made every effort to find a pronunciation and have failed, make up one that seems likely to be correct. That way there will at least be consistency in the pronunciation used until you can find the correct one.

7. Avoid words like "read," "lead," and "bow," which can be pronounced in more than one way according to meaning.

O. Punctuation.

1. Do *not* use:

a. Semicolons (;)

b. Exclamation points (!)

c. Brackets ([ ])

2. There are three punctuation marks you may use that serve the function typically served by the comma. Each indicates a pause in reading:

a. The comma indicates a short pause. In a few places, it serves more to make reading easier than to indicate a pause, as when it separates a state or country from a city. (For example: "In Phoenix, Arizona, today. . . .") Writers sometimes omit commas where no pause is desired in the reading, as in "Sammy Davis junior," rather than "Sammy Davis, junior."

b. The dash (—) indicates a more complete break in thought, a longer pause in reading, than the comma. Use dashes for parenthetical clauses and wherever they make the reading easier. Be sure you understand the difference between a dash and a hyphen. The hyphen is a single line, with no spacing before or after it, as in "co-operation." On a typewriter, the dash is made by typing two hyphens that are preceded and followed by a space. (For example: "The men — still angry — decided to. . . .") Don't overuse dashes, and never use dashes to string together groups of words that should be a complete sentence.

c.   The ellipsis (. . .) indicates an even longer and more complete break than a dash. (For example: "The contestants were . . . well . . . stark naked.") Use ellipses to draw attention to negative words. (For example: "He did . . . not . . . say.")

3.   Use hyphens freely to make combination words easier to read. (For example: "multi-talented" or "co-operation.") Use them also to link words in multi-word titles like "Attorney-General."

P.   Quotations.

1.   Broadcasters get their quotes on film or tape. Never write a quotation into a script unless it is essential to the story. Paraphrase every statement you can. Quotes that must be read by a newscaster may confuse the listener.

2.   There is no point in using an ellipsis (. . .) to indicate missing words, since this visual cue will not signal a deletion to a listening audience. (For example, if you write, "President Reagan said today, 'We'll get there . . . provided Congress will agree,' " your listeners have no way of knowing that words have been deleted between "there" and "provided.") In the same sense, the listener or viewer may not realize when material has been edited out of a videotape, audiotape, or film. If the deletion is not obvious, you should indicate it to the audience with a phrase like: "Later, the president added."

3.   If you *must* use a quotation, do not rely upon the quotation marks in your copy to clarify things for the audience. Even a reader who is skillful in using vocal inflection to indicate the start and end of a quote can still leave an audience confused. Take this example:

The soon-to-be released prisoner said that, if he gets out tomorrow, he'll go "where I always go."

Hearing that, the listener won't know whether the "I" refers to the prisoner or the newscaster.

4.   Some newscasters begin a quotation with the word "quote," then end it with "unquote." But to make certain that the listeners understand when the quotation begins, you should use one of these introductory phrases:

She said—and we quote her—"That man is a sham."

The governor was, in her words, "a sham."

She praised the conference, calling it "not a boondoggle, the best conference we have ever had."

The best reason to quote this particular speaker directly is her use of "boondoggle" and "sham." Her words are distinctive. If, in the third example above, she had said only, "This is the best conference we have ever had," there would have been nothing distinctive about those words and no reason to quote her directly. In that case, you should paraphrase.

5. When you're quoting someone, keep the quotation short. Always avoid long quotations; the audience may fail to understand when the quotation ends and the newscaster again begins to speak her or his own words.

Q. Sports.

1. Use digits for all scores and sports statistics.

2. Don't write "82–79." It is better to write "82 to 79." However, since "to" may be confused with "2," it is best to separate the two figures carefully and specify each team with its score: "Texas 82 over 79 for Missouri."

3. Don't waste time looking for substitutes for the words "won" and "lost."

R. Statistics.

1. Avoid statistics and other lists of numbers.

2. Where statistics must be used, follow the regular rules for writing numbers.

3. Try to convert statistics into terms the audience can understand. Round off figures whenever possible.

S. Telephone numbers.

1. Telephone numbers should not be used unless they are essential.

2. Type hyphens between the numbers and set off the prefix with dots: "4-9-8 . . . 4-9-8-1."

3. Set the area code in a separate phrase: "The area code is 2-1-3, and the number is 4-9-8 . . . 4-9-8-1."

T. Time.

1. Write time in the regular way: "2 o'clock," or "3:15."

2. Don't write "10 *past*" or "a quarter *of*."

3. Minimize use of the word "today." (The assumption is that electronic news *is* today's news.)

4. Avoid using "A.M." or "P.M." Make it "this morning," "last night," or some similar expression.

5. Specific times are rarely needed. "Early this morning" is usually better than "5:27 this morning."

6. Use present and present perfect tenses as much as possible to reduce need to specify times.

7. Do not write, "This just in," or "We have just learned" unless

the information is less than five minutes old. Don't describe an event as happening "just a few minutes ago," unless it happened less than one-half hour previously.

8. Express time periods greater than fifty-nine minutes in terms of hours. Write, "one and one-half hours," rather than "90 minutes."

U. Titles.

1. Most titles of individuals and names of organizations should be stated in full the first time they are used. Subsequent references can shorten the name or title. (For example: "The Federal Bureau of Investigation is. . . . An F-B-I spokesman said. . . ." Or, "Secretary of Health and Human Services Joseph Johnson has. . . . Secretary Johnson told. . . .")

2. *Very* long titles may be shortened. For example, avoid, "The Joint House-Senate Subcommittee on Tariffs and Import Duties is. . . ." and write, "A congressional committee is. . . ." Then follow it with, "The subcommittee on Tariffs and Import Duties has. . . ." And follow that with, "The joint committee of House and Senate conferees was. . . ." Both versions provide the same information, but the second version offers it in easy-to- follow segments.

3. Avoid combinations titles, such as "House-Senate." Instead, write: "A conference committee of the Senate and House," or "the joint congressional agriculture committee."

4. Don't convert place names into adjectives in titles. Write, "Premier Adoula of the Congo," not "Congolese Premier Adoula." And be particularly careful not to use such adjectives at the start of a story.

5. Use "Mr." for three purposes only:

    a. The president of the United States is customarily referred to either as "President Jones" or "Mr. Jones." (While many stations have taken to just saying "Jones," traditionalists still insist on "Mr.")

    b. The correct title for a male Protestant minister after first mention is "Mr." (However, this rule is widely ignored. It may be useful to check with the minister and see what he wishes to be called.)

    c. Use "Mr." when a story concerns both a husband and wife.

    d. All other references to men with no special title should be "John Jones" on the first reference and simply "Jones" thereafter.

6. Traditionalists refer to women on the first mention as "Mrs.," "Miss," or "Ms." followed by the first name and the last name, then subsequently as simply "Ms. Jones" or "Miss Smith." Today, many stations omit the title and make it "Mary Jones"

at first mention, then "Mrs. Jones." Also, a growing number of stations follow the same rule for both men and women, simply writing "Mary Jones" for the first mention and "Jones" thereafter. It may be necessary, of course, to use Miss, Ms., or Mrs. when more than one person in the story has the same last name.

7. Religious titles are extremely tricky, and your safest bet at all times is to check with the person whose name is being used or with someone who is an official of the religious organization involved. Generally, rabbis should be called "Rabbi John Levin" and subsequently, "Rabbi Levin." Most Christian clergymen and clergywomen should first be referred to with the title "the Reverend," followed by the first and last name. It is not proper to omit "the" or the first name. On subsequent mentions, Roman Catholic, Greek Orthodox, and Anglican clergy are usually referred to as "Father Jones." According to the rule book, Protestant ministers should subsequently be referred to as "Mr. Jones" or "Mrs. Jones." However, usage varies widely, so check to make sure what the correct form is. The title you use when *speaking to* a member of the clergy may differ from the title you use when *speaking of* that person.

8. For most other titles, use the title with the first and last name on first mention. Subsequently, use the last name only or, optionally, the title and the last name. For example, after first reference to "Congressman Chip O'Veal," write either "Congressman O'Veal" or just "O'Veal." Repeat the title if it has any bearing on the story. For foreign titles, check with your interviewee or ask a reliable source, such as an embassy official.

9. A few *very* well-known persons, such as a president or a governor, may be mentioned the first time by title and last name only.

10. Technically, you should use the title "junior" only if there is a "senior" living. However, for news purposes use these two terms whenever there may be confusion about which person is being referred to. Don't bother with them otherwise. Some writers omit the commas around these words because there is no pause in speech where the commas fall.

V. "To" can be a confusing word. It is preferable to say a score was "10 to 6" than to write "10-6," and it is better to write that one candidate beat the other by "32-hundred to 28-hundred," than to write "31,987-28,169." However, because "to" can be confused with "2," it is best to find a way of stating these figures without using either the hyphen *or* "to." Don't go out of your way to find a substitute if there is little danger of the word being misunderstood.

W. Words to watch out for.

1. Strings of sibilants. (For example: "Commissioner Strauss's suggestions.")
2. Alliteration—the repetition of words beginning with similar vowels or consonants. (For example: "In an unenviable spot.")
3. Words that sound alike but have different meanings. (For example: "great" and "grate," "bear" and "bare.") And beware of word combinations that present the same problem. (For example: "a tax on" and "attacks on," or "and effects" and "and defects.")
4. Pronouns—he, she, it, they—may be ambiguous. Check each carefully and repeat a noun wherever possible.
5. Words like "former" and "latter" may confuse your audience.

Appendix B

Glossary of Broadcast Terms

Actuality   The actual record of an event—recorded on film, video-tape, or audiotape—as distinguished from a description by a reporter. Interviews are the most common forms of actuality.

Air Check   A recording, usually used to hear or to see how well a newscaster sounds or looks on the air. May be used for checking other aspects of a program as well.

Air Time   The time at which a program starts.

A Roll   The first of two reels of film (or sometimes videotape) to be run in an A-B roll story. If only one sound track is used, it is normally on the A roll.

Back-timing   The process of marking the stories of a script with the times at which they must begin for the program to end on time.

Back-up Script   Same as fill.

Balop   Short for "Balopticon," trademark of the Bausch and Lomb opaque projector. Often used to designate any projector that shows opaque graphics instead of tran-sparencies. Not as commonly used as it was in earlier days of television.

Beeper   An outdated term for a telephone call recorded for use on the air. It used to be required by law that such recordings have an electronic beep in them at regular intervals.

Billboard   The standard opening of a program, with music and identifying material.

Bloop   To edit out.

B Roll	The second of two rolls of film used simultaneously in a news story. The B roll usually contains silent footage, which is run while the sound from the A roll is heard.
Budget	The list of important news stories of the day.
Carts	Tape cartridges used to record stories. These devices are commonly used to insert recorded material into radio news programs.
CG	Character Generator. General term for electronic titling equipment such as Videfont.
Cold	Done without rehearsal.
Crawl	Credits or other written material moving slowly across the screen. May be used for lists of victims, sports scores, or other information. Some stations limit the term to material moving from right to left across the screen. At other stations, it can also refer to material moving from the top to the bottom or from the bottom to the top of the screen. Where "crawl" refers only to horizontally moving material, another term, "roll," is used for vertically moving material.
Credits	The names of those involved in producing a program.
Cue	The term written on the script to describe the corresponding picture on the screen.
Cushion	Any material that can either be read to fill time or be cut at will. Sometimes called "pad."
Cut	In film or videotape, a direct transition from one shot to another with no overlap, such as would occur in a dissolve. Also a segment of film, videotape, or audiotape, usually one with some particular sound on it (an audio cut). "To cut" means to edit out material, usually to reduce running time.
Cutaway	Any shot that briefly switches attention from the main action to some related activity.
Dateline	The method most newspapers use to identify the location of a story. Few radio or television stations use this style.
Dissolve	A visual technique that causes one picture on the screen to grow dimmer as a second becomes clearer and eventually replaces the first picture. Used to show

a change of scene, a passage of time, or for dramatic effects.

Documentary A radio, television, or film program based on actual facts. By most modern definitions, a documentary should be constructed from "actualities" (material shot or recorded at an actual event) rather than staged in a studio. Early radio "documentaries" often used staged recreations of events or fictionalized stories based on factual material. Today such dramatizations of actual events are usually called "docudramas."

Dolly A camera movement in which the camera moves toward ("dolly in") or away from ("dolly out") the object it is recording. Should be distinguished from "Zoom," which gives similar visual effect, but is accomplished by holding the camera in one location and widening or narrowing the field of view of the lens. Dolly also is used to indicate camera movement to the right or left, although the correct term for this movement is "Truck."

Double System A synchronous separate recording of sound and picture. Time consuming and expensive, but usually produces better results for film. Almost always used for all forms of film production except news.

Dropout A loss of sound or video picture because of defects in tape.

Dub To re-record something or to add recorded material to existing material.

Easel Shot Photographs, drawings, or similar material mounted and shot by a studio camera. Sometimes called a "flip" or a "stand."

Editing Assembling film or videotape for air use. Revising copy.

Establishing Shot A camera shot that sets the relationships between camera and the elements of the scene.

Exclusive A story or interview obtained by a single reporter to the exclusion of competitors.

Fax Short for "facsimile." A system of transmitting pictures or written material via radio or wire transmission.

FCC Federal Communications Commission, the governmental body responsible for regulating broadcasting.

Feed	Material transmitted to a station by the network, by another station, or from a remote.
Fill	Material written to be used only if there are slow moments in some event. In news, fill is written to be read in case there is a loss of audio or picture in a story using recorded material.
Flip Card	Material prepared for an easel or stand shot.
Flub	A minor error by a performer or the act of making such an error. Usually the error is a missed or mis-pronounced word.
Fluff	Same as a "flub." Also refers to light material.
Format	An accepted pattern of arranging material.
Freeze Frame	A visual technique in which one picture remains on the screen with no change for as long as specified.
From the Top	To redo a performance from the beginning.
Full Screen	If no other information is provided, it is assumed the slide will occupy the entire screen. However, since slides may be used in other ways, some stations pre-cede the Slide cue with Full Screen, like this:

FULL SCREEN
SLIDE #N-753-82
Gov. Fern

Glitch	Interference in video.
Glossy Print	The common, shiny type of photographic print. Usu-ally unsuitable for use on television because its surface is too reflective. It can be coated with a dulling spray or some other material to reduce glare. (See "Matte Print.")
Graphics	Any illustrative material.
Green Film	Freshly processed film. May cause problems in use, but often must be employed in news work.
Ground Noise	Sound caused by poor quality recording material.
Hardwall	News programs using Chromakey often keep some picture showing in the Chromakey area at all times. Hardwall is used to indicate that the Chromakey area is to be left blank.
Helical Scan	A system of video recording. Originally used mostly for industrial or home recording purposes. High qual-ity units are now used for commercial television.

High Contrast Film	Film meant to be shown on the air without reprinting. (Film used to print other films is usually low contrast.)
Hiss	Unwanted sound usually caused by poor quality recording equipment.
Hot	Too bright or overexposed.
Insert	A shot, usually a close-up, placed between two shots of the main action. Also, a program item from an outside source included in a program, such as an insert from a remote source into a news program.
Interlock	A system of showing film with synchronized sound track when double-system sound has been used. (See "Double System.")
Item	A news story.
Jump Cut	A sudden shift from one shot to another in which both shots appear identical except for a disturbing change in one object. Often a problem in news film or videotape editing. An example would be a cut between two shots of a speaker in which nothing changes but the position of the speaker's head. Can usually be avoided by the insertion of a cutaway. (See "Cutaway.")
Key	Short for "Chromakey." An image matted into a colored (usually blue) area on the set. The material to be keyed must be specified.
Kicker	A light news story, used for humor. Also, a small spotlight usually mounted on or near the camera and aimed at the head of a performer to make eyes and teeth sparkle. Sometimes called an "eye light."
Kill	To eliminate.
Lead	The first sentence of a news story. Sometimes the first story of a news program.
Lead-in	A line preceding a cued action of some sort, such as a lead-in to an audio cart story in radio news.
Live	Same as MOC. If more than one newscaster is involved both cues—Live and MOC—must be preceded by the name of the newscaster who is reading the story. Also refers to any event that is broadcast as it occurs.
Logo	A symbol used for a program or to designate an organization.

Magnetic Stripe	Magnetically striped film, the type commonly used in television film for single-system recording. (Also called "mag stripe.")
MOC	Stands for "microphone on camera." The newscaster is seen on the screen, reading the story script.
Monitor	Any device used to view or listen to material, usually while the material is being recorded. Also refers to the act of viewing or listening to material. May refer to video material shown on a video screen on a news set.
Montage	Several images superimposed in the same picture, or a rapid series of shots.
Multiplex	To transmit more than one signal using the same radio frequency or wire. Also refers to electronic or mechanical systems of feeding pictures from several sources to a single camera as in a telecine.
Nemo	A remote.
Noise	Any interference in either the audio or the video signal.
OC	Means "Out Cue." That is, the last three or four words heard in a cart segment of a radio story or audio segment of a television story. Also refers to "On Camera," as in "Mary OC" or "Anchor OC."
Optical Recording	Sound for film recorded by a system that prints the sound recording in a strip at the edge of the film. Most film that is to be reproduced in several film copies uses optical sound. Material to be used in its original form, such as newsfilm, is usually mag stripe film. Most optical recording is done double system, beginning with recordings on magnetic tape, which are transferred to optical form later.
Out Take	Material that is edited out and not used in the final version of a program.
Package	The various segments of a story edited together at the station.
Pad	Extra material provided at the end of a script, to be read as needed to make the show come out on time. Also, extra film or videotape at the end of a story, which can be kept on the screen if the newscaster

reads too slowly to complete the story at the proper point.

Paste   To put together a news program by pasting or stapling wire stories in the desired sequence, sometimes including some material prepared by the local news staff.

Playback   To listen to or view recorded material, usually just after it has been recorded.

Polarity   That which determines whether a television picture is seen as a positive or negative image. It is possible to use negative film in some instances in television, and still have the picture be seen by the audience as positive because the engineer has "reversed polarity."

Print-through   Damage to a recording caused by the signal from one layer of tape being transferred to surrounding layers.

Producer   The person responsible for the overall production of a program or a story.

Punch   To emphasize a word or phrase in delivery. Also, to prepare a video or audio source for input on a board or to insert it into a program, as in "punch up camera five."

Radio Wire   A wire service wire written so that the material can be used on the air without rewriting.

Raw Stock   Unexposed film or unrecorded videotape or audiotape.

Reader   A story on television or radio read from start to finish by the newscaster.

Recap   A brief news summary.

Release   A legal form giving permission to use pictures of a person or material produced by that person on the air. Also, a publicity handout.

Reporter Package A complete story presented by a reporter, usually including a lead-in and closing with videotaped or audiotaped material in between.

Reversal Film   The type of film usually used in television news. It is processed to produce a positive image on the original film, obviating the usual steps of making a negative and then making prints from that.

Reverse	A shot from the opposite angle (reverse angle) of the previous shot.
Ride Gain	To manipulate the amplitude of various inputs while on the air, recording, or rerecording material to compensate for material that is too soft or too loud.
Roll	To start film or videotape. Also refers to vertically moving material (usually written) that travels to the top of the screen from the bottom or to the bottom of the screen from the top.
Rough Cut	An edited version of a story that still has polishing to be done on it.
RP	A visual seen on a rear projection screen. The visual must be specified.
RTNA	Radio-Television News Association.
RTNDA	Radio-Television News Directors' Association.
Safe Area (or Safety Area)	The area in a camera viewfinder within which material photographed will be sure to appear uncropped on a television screen. Also called "cutoff."
Single System	Recording sound on the same film that the picture is recorded on, recording both simultaneously. Single system sound is used primarily for television news.
SI FILM	Silent Film.
SI FILM/VO	Same as SI VT/VO, but with film as the visual medium.
SIL	Same as SI.
SI VT	Silent Videotape.
SI VT/VO	Silent Videotape, with the newscaster's voice heard over pictures.
Slide	A 35mm slide seen full screen. The slide must be further identified.
Slug	The top line of the script that gives the name of the story, the date, the program, and the initials of the writer.
Sneak	An audio technique in which the sound is slowly faded in so that its addition to the sound picture is not noticed at first.
SOC	Means "Standard Out Cue." That is, the words spec-

ified by a news department for its reporters to use when signing off a story. For example: "Reporting from the Long Beach City Hall for KLON, this is Alice Wong."

SOF Sound on Film.

SOMT Sound On Magnetic Track. Same as SOF, but used at some stations to specify that film has a magnetic rather than optical sound track.

SOT Same as SOVT.

SOVT Sound On Videotape. Videotape shown with audio from videotape.

SOVTR Same as SOVT.

Split Screen A screen divided to show more than one picture.

Spot Sheet A list of the order of appearance and running time of the shots in a story.

Stand Material that is set on an easel or a stand in the studio to be shot.

Stand-up The opening of a story filmed at the scene and usually in the present tense.

Stripe The magnetic track on the edge of mag stripe film.

Super One picture superimposed over another. The technique is sometimes used for titles.

Tag A short segment at the end of a program that sums up the key points.

Teaser A brief opening that encourages the audience to stay tuned.

Telecine A device for projecting motion pictures on television.

TelePrompTer A commercial device that projects an image of the script over one-way glass in front of the camera lens, allowing newscasters or performers to look directly at the lens while reading the material. Older models put the scripted material just above or below the lens.

Telop See "Balop."

Under Music or some other continuing sound is heard softly along with the main dialog or narrative.

Up A sound that has been heard "under" is raised to normal level.

VCR   Video Cassette Recording. Since most video cassette equipment is not designed for air use, this cue is most likely to be used in classroom projects or in cable news programs.

VF   Videfont. A commercial system of keying letters and numbers onto the screen from a keyboard. The content of the written material and its location on the screen must be specified.

Videodisc   One of several systems for recording television on rotating discs. One form is used for recording "instant replay" shots in sports coverage.

Videotape   A recording medium for television. The standard for commercial television has been the two-inch tape, recorded on a transverse-quad head recorder. Helical scan recorders use tapes in widths of one-fourth, one-half, three-fourths, one, and two inches, with varying head configurations and tape speeds. The one-inch helical scan format is now coming into wide use in commercial television. Various cassette and cartridge systems are used with many forms of videotape.

VIZ   Vizmo. A commercial system for projecting television pictures on a large screen on the news set.

Voice-over   Material read in the studio over a videotape.

VTR   Videotape with sound.

Wild Track   Sound recorded nonsynchronously.

Wipe   A technique in which a picture begins at one edge (usually left) of the television screen and moves across it, replacing the picture on the screen. There are horizontal, diagonal, and vertical wipes.

Wow   Audio distortion caused by inconstant speed in the recording or playback device.

Wrap-up   The closing of a news program.

Zip Pan   A rapid moving blur used to indicate a transition in time, location, or both. Also called "swish pan."

Zoom   A technique in which a camera angle is progressively made smaller ("In") or wider ("Out"). The effect is similar to "dolly," but the camera does not move physically, and movement can be much faster than a dolly.

Appendix C

Radio-Television News Directors Association

The following Code of Broadcast News Ethics for RTNDA was adopted January 2, 1966 and amended October 13, 1973.[1]

The members of the Radio-Television News Directors Association agree that their prime responsibility as journalists—and that of the broadcasting industry as the collective sponsor of news broadcasting—is to provide to the public they serve a news service as accurate, full and prompt as human integrity and devotion can devise. To that end, they declare their acceptance of the standards of practice here set forth, and their solemn intent to honor them to the limits of their ability.

Article One

The primary purpose of broadcast journalists–to inform the public of events of importance and appropriate interest in a manner that is accurate and comprehensive—shall override all other purposes.

Article Two

Broadcast news presentations shall be designed not only to offer timely and accurate information, but also to present it in the light of relevant circumstances that give it meaning and perspective.

This standard means that news reports, when clarity demands it, will be laid against pertinent factual background; that factors such as race, creed, nationality, or prior status will be reported only when they are relevant; that comment or subjective comment will be properly identified; and that errors in fact will be promptly acknowledged and corrected.

Article Three

Broadcast journalists shall seek to select material for newscasts solely on their evaluation of its merits as news.

---

[1] Used by permission.

This standard means that news will be selected on the criteria of significance, community and regional relevance, appropriate human interest, service to defined audiences. It excludes sensationalism or misleading emphasis in any form; subservience to external or "interested" efforts to influence news selection and presentation, whether from within the broadcasting industry or from without. It requires that such terms as "bulletin" and "flash" can be used only when the character of the news justified them; that bombastic or misleading descriptions of newsroom facilities and personnel be rejected, along with undue use of sound and visual effects; and that promotional or publicity material be sharply scrutinized before use and identified by source or otherwise when broadcast.

Article Four
Broadcast journalists shall at all times display humane respect for the dignity, privacy and well-being of persons with whom the news deals.

Article Five
Broadcast journalists shall govern their personal lives and such non-professional associations as may impinge on their professional activities in a manner that will protect them from conflict of interest, real or apparent.

Article Six
Broadcast journalists shall seek actively to present all news, the knowledge of which will serve the public interest, no matter what selfish, uninformed or corrupt efforts attempt to color it, withhold it or prevent its presentation. They shall make constant efforts to open doors closed to the reporting of public proceedings with tools appropirate to broadcasting (including cameras and recorders), consistent with the public interest. They acknowledge the journalist's ethic of protection of confidential information and sources and urge unswerving observation of it except in instances in which it would clearly and unmistakably defy the public interest.

Article Seven
Broadcast journalists recognize the responsibility borne by broadcasting for informed analysis, comment and editorial opinion on public events
and issues. They accept the obligation of broadcasters for the presentation of such matters by individuals whose competence, experience and judgment qualify them for it.

Article Eight
In court, broadcast journalists shall conduct themselves with dignity, whether the court is in or out of session. They shall keep broadcast equip-

ment as unobtrusive and silent as possible. Where court facilities are inadequate, pool broadcasts should be arranged.

Article Nine

In reporting matters that are or may be litigated, the journalist shall avoid practices which would tend to interfere with the right of an individual to a fair trial.

Article Ten

Broadcast journalists shall not misrepresent the source of any broadcast news material.

Article Eleven

Broadcast journalists shall actively censure and seek to prevent violations of these standards, and shall actively encourage their observance by all journalists, whether of the Radio-Television News Directors Association or not.

Index